Copyright for Teachers & Librarians in the 21st Century

D1125519

Rebecca P. Butler

Neal-Schuman Publishers, Inc.
New York   London

Published by Neal-Schuman Publishers, Inc.
100 William St., Suite 2004
New York, NY 10038

Printed and bound in the United States of America.

The paper used in this publication meets the minimum requirements of American National Standard for Information Sciences—Permanence of Paper for Printed Library Materials, ANSI Z39.48-1992.

Library of Congress Cataloging-in-Publication Data

Butler, Rebecca P.
  Copyright for teachers & librarians in the 21st century / Rebecca P. Butler.
    p. cm.
  Includes bibliographical references and index.
  ISBN 978-1-55570-738-5 (alk. paper)
  1. Copyright—United States. 2. Fair use (Copyright)—United States. 3. Teachers—Legal status, laws, etc.—United States. I. Title. II. Title: Copyright for teachers and librarians in the twenty-first century.

KF2995.B885 2011
346.7304'82—dc22
                                                      2011012600

Dedication

To my husband, Tom, my son, Benjamin,
and my parents, Betty and Pete Petersen,
whose support and faith in me
keep me grounded.

Contents

List of Flowcharts xi

Preface xv

Acknowledgments xix

Part I: Essential Concepts of Copyright Law

Chapter 1. Introduction to Copyright Law: What Is Copyright? 3

Introduction 3

Copyright Defined and Explained 4

History of Copyright 7

Why Copyright Law Is Important 8

How to Register Works with the U.S. Copyright Office 8

Conclusion 10

References 11

Chapter 2. Fair Use: When Do You Need to Ask for Permission? 13

Introduction 13

Fair Use Defined and Explained 13

Fair Use Factor 1: Purpose and Character of Use 13

Fair Use Factor 2: Nature of the Work 14

Fair Use Factor 3: Amount to Be Borrowed 14

Fair Use Factor 4: Marketability of the Work 14

Copyright Guidelines for Educational Multimedia 15

Conclusion 17

References 17

Chapter 3. Public Domain: Is There Such a Thing as Free Material? .. 19

Introduction 19

What Is Public Domain? 19

How Long Does It Take a Work to Become Part of the Public Domain? 20

If There Is No Copyright Date on a Work, Does That Mean It Is
   in the Public Domain? 22

What If the Work Is Created as Part of the Terms of Employment? 22

What Works Are in the Public Domain? 23

Are All Federal Government Documents in the Public Domain? 24

Are State and Local Government Documents in the Public Domain? 24

Is Something That Is in the Public Domain in Another Country Also
   in the Public Domain in the United States? 25

Can Something Be Taken Out of the Public Domain and Placed
   under Copyright Protection Again? 25

How Do You Know That an Item Is in the Public Domain? 26

How Do You Make Sure That What You Are Borrowing Is Really
   in the Public Domain? 26

Conclusion 27

References 27

**Chapter 4. Obtaining Permission: How Can You Legally Obtain
Use of Works?** 29

Introduction 29

Obtaining Permission 30

Permission Requests 30

What Is a License? 31

Give Credit Where Credit Is Due 31

Permission Letter 32

Clearinghouses and Other Organizations 33

Conclusion 37

References 38

**Chapter 5. Further Important Copyright Subjects: What Other
Copyright Issues Do You Need to Understand?** 41

Introduction 41

Documentation and Licenses 41

Interlibrary Loan 45

Statutory Exemptions 46

Copying Guidelines 48

State Laws 49

International Copyright Law and U.S. Copyright Law
   with International Provisions 50

Orphan Works 53

Future Copyright Legislation 53

Infringements and Penalties 54

Plagiarism 57

Sample Flowchart 60

Conclusion 60

References 60

Part II: Specific Applications of Copyright Law

**Chapter 6. The Internet and Copyright Law: Everything
on the Web Is Considered Implied Public Access, Right?** 67

Introduction 67

Fair Use 68

Public Domain 71

Documentation and Licenses 72

Permissions 74

You Create It, You Own It 77

Infringements and Penalties 80

International Copyright Law 83

Avoiding Copyright Problems 84

Conclusion 86

References 86

**Chapter 7. DVDs, CDs, Video Streaming and On Demand,
and Copyright Law: Can You Use Such Movie Formats Legally
in Your Classroom?** 89

Introduction 89

Fair Use 89

Public Domain 93

Documentation and Licenses 93

Permissions 96

You Create It, You Own It 99

Infringements and Penalties 106

International Copyright Law 110

Avoiding Copyright Problems 112

Conclusion 114

References 116

Chapter 8. Television and Copyright Law: TV Is Free, Isn't It? 117

Introduction 117

Fair Use 117

Public Domain 120

Documentation and Licenses 120

Permissions 123

You Create It, You Own It 126

Infringements and Penalties 127

International Copyright Law 130

Avoiding Copyright Problems 131

Conclusion 131

References 131

Chapter 9. Computer Software and Copyright Law: Why Is Documentation Important? 133

Introduction 133

Fair Use 133

Public Domain 134

Documentation and Licenses 134

Permissions 140

You Create It, You Own It 143

Infringements and Penalties 143

International Copyright Law 145

Avoiding Copyright Problems 147

Conclusion 149

References 149

Chapter 10. Music/Audio and Copyright Law: Who Will Know If You Copy It? 151

Introduction 151

Fair Use 153

Public Domain 154

Documentation and Licenses 158

Permissions 162

You Create It, You Own It 169

Infringements and Penalties 170

International Copyright Law 173

Avoiding Copyright Problems 175

Conclusion 180

References 180

**Chapter 11. Multimedia and Copyright Law: How Confusing!
Can You Borrow a Variety of Works for Your Production?** 183

Introduction 183

Fair Use 183

Public Domain 184

Documentation and Licenses 187

Permissions 189

You Create It, You Own It 191

Infringements and Penalties 192

International Copyright Law 194

Avoiding Copyright Problems 197

Conclusion 199

References 199

**Chapter 12. Print Works and Copyright Law: Is It Legal to Copy
Print Works for Class at the Last Minute?** 201

Introduction 201

Fair Use 202

Public Domain 205

Documentation and Licenses 206

Permissions 210

You Create It, You Own It 214

Infringements and Penalties 217

International Copyright Law 219

Avoiding Copyright Problems 221

Conclusion 221

References 221

**Chapter 13. Distance Education and Copyright Law: How Is This
Different from Applying Copyright Law in a Face-to-Face Classroom?** . . 223

Introduction 223

Technology, Education, and Copyright Harmonization Act (TEACH Act) . . 223

Conclusion 225

References 227

Chapter 14. Conclusion: What Does All of This Mean
for K–12 Teachers and Librarians? 229

Introduction 229

I'll Never Get Caught 229

Ways to Avoid Copyright Problems 230

How to Deal with Those Who Would Have You Break the Law 230

How and Why to Teach/Train Students, Colleagues, Administration,
and Others about Copyright Law 231

Conclusion 233

References 233

Appendixes

Appendix 1. Selected Sections of the U.S. Copyright Law 239

A. Exclusive Rights in Copyrighted Works 239

B. Limitations on Exclusive Rights: Fair Use 240

C. Limitations on Exclusive Rights: Reproduction by Libraries
and Archives 240

D. Limitations on Exclusive Rights: Exemption of Certain Performances
and Displays 243

E. Limitations on Exclusive Rights: Reproduction for Blind
or Other People with Disabilities 248

F. Ownership of Copyright 249

G. Duration of Copyright: Works Created on or after January 1, 1978 250

H. Remedies for Infringement: Damages and Profits 251

Appendix 2. Definitions for Web Terms in Chapter 6 255

Index 265

About the Author 275

List of Flowcharts

5.1	Sample Flowchart	61
6.1	Web Images	69
6.2	Printing Webpages	70
6.3	Photographs on the Web	71
6.4	How to Decide Whether an Image Is in the Public Domain	72
6.5	Deep Linking	75
6.6	Copying Lists	76
6.7	Borrowing All or Parts of Webpages	77
6.8	Using a Photograph from the Web as a Screen Saver	78
6.9	Copying from the Internet	81
6.10	Attaching an Online Chart to a Wiki	82
6.11	Reading a Book in the Cloud	85
6.12	Is an Electronic Toolbox Legal?	87
7.1	Burning Videos to DVDs	91
7.2	Copying Movie Clips	92
7.3	Public Domain Movies	94
7.4	Using Entertainment DVDs in Class	95
7.5	Using Movies as Rewards	97
7.6	Copying a DVD	98
7.7	Borrowing Movie Clips	100
7.8	Closed-Circuit Systems and DVDs	101
7.9	Using Video On Demand	102
7.10	Statues, Filming, and Copyright	104
7.11	Adding Commercial Film Excerpts to Class-Created DVDs and Videos	105
7.12	Transferring Videos to DVDs	107
7.13	Videotaping Volunteers Reading from a Novel	108
7.14	Showing Student-Owned Works during Recess	109

7.15   Using Personal DVDs on a School Outing 113

7.16   Using Locally Purchased DVDs in Class 114

7.17   Streaming Video and Copyright 115

8.1   Recording from a Major Network 121

8.2   Using Recorded Cable Programs in the Classroom 122

8.3   Recording Television Programs for Instructional Use 124

8.4   Recording Off-Air from Satellite or Cable Transmissions 125

8.5   Digitizing a Television Program 128

8.6   Stringing Commercials Together to Use in Class 129

8.7   Using Place-Shifting Technologies/Video Streaming
        in the School 130

8.8   Recording Foreign Television 131

9.1   Printing from a DVD or CD-ROM 135

9.2   Borrowing from Software 136

9.3   Copying Personal Software to a Classroom Computer 138

9.4   Placing Software on Multiple Computers 139

9.5   Copying Software to Another Format 141

9.6   Making School Software Available for Students 142

9.7   Pirated Software 146

9.8   Using File Conversion Programs 148

10.1   Adding Popular Music to Webpages 155

10.2   Copying Popular Music for Class Use 156

10.3   Copying Sheet Music 159

10.4   Playing Recorded Music in the Library 160

10.5   Posting a Song on a Video-Sharing Website 163

10.6   Performing Popular Music at Public Events 166

10.7   Printing Lyrics from the Internet 167

10.8   Audio-Recording Picture Books 168

10.9   Borrowing Music from One Website for Another 171

10.10   Playing an E-book Aloud for a Class 172

10.11   Using a Foreign Recording for a Public Performance 174

10.12   Free-of-Charge Recording of School Concerts
        for Home Distribution 176

10.13   For-Profit Recording of School Concerts
        for Home Distribution 177

10.14   Playing Popular Music at School Sporting Events 178

10.15 Placing Lip Dub Videos That Feature Popular Songs on a Website 179

11.1 Borrowing a Variety of Works for a Multimedia Production 185

11.2 Using Photographs in Multimedia Projects 186

11.3 Using Student or Commercial Works in Computer-Based Presentations 188

11.4 Using Student Examples in Distance Education 190

11.5 Who Owns Teacher-Created Multimedia? 192

11.6 Using Clip Art in Multimedia Projects 193

11.7 Using Videos in Multimedia Projects 195

11.8 Copying Media to a Server for Curricular Use 196

11.9 Parents Recording a School Variety Show 198

12.1 Photocopying Parts of a Book 203

12.2 Copying Textbooks for Visually Impaired Students 204

12.3 Books in the Public Domain 206

12.4 Magazine Articles in the Public Domain 208

12.5 Performing a Shakespeare Play in Public 210

12.6 Cutting, Pasting, and Photocopying a Teacher's Guide Page 211

12.7 Making Multiple Copies of Articles 212

12.8 Copying Workbook Pages 213

12.9 Digitizing Newspaper Cartoons 215

12.10 Last-Minute Copying 218

12.11 Placing an E-book on a Library Computer 220

13.1 Distance Educator's Flowchart 226

Preface

Over the past 15 years, I have conducted copyright workshops, classes, and presentations for teachers; school, public, academic, medical, and special librarians; technology coordinators; school administrators; college students; and other interested parties. They came to these sessions for much the same reason that you picked up this book: they realized the importance and complexity of copyright issues in the classroom setting—and beyond—and wanted help.

Copyright for Teachers and Librarians in the 21st Century is largely based on the questions and concerns raised by those in my workshops and classes. Thus, *Copyright for Teachers and Librarians in the 21st Century* is, first and foremost, a handbook on copyright law for teachers, librarians, technology coordinators, administrators, public librarians, and others who work with students. As such, I have chosen to use realistic examples with interpretations of the law from copyright experts in the field. Although reading and interpreting the U.S. Copyright Law for oneself would be one approach, teachers and librarians may choose to use the interpretations from copyright experts given in this book so that they don't have to wade through the law on their own. Because copyright law leaves some gray areas, there may be more than one interpretation to any one question. Since that is the case, I have chosen to give the readers the answer I consider most practical and most applicable in a K–12 school setting. For other concerns, or for further information, you may refer to the law itself, at http://www.copyright.gov/title17/.

This book is divided into two practical and necessary parts. Part I introduces the general concepts associated with copyright law. Part II describes the specific applications of copyright law as they affect nine different formats. It is important to use and understand both parts of this book, as they really do speak to each other. Knowing the general concepts will help your understanding and use of the specific applications. In the same way, knowing how copyright applies to your position in education will help you better understand and read the copyright legislation and literature you encounter in your day-to-day work. While you may refer to the chapters of Part II more frequently than Part I, you won't completely understand the information in Part II without having first read Part I.

Through the five chapters of Part I, readers will develop a basic knowledge of the language and provisions of copyright law. Chapter 1, "Introduction to Copyright Law: What Is Copyright?," provides a basic explanation of copyright, a history of legislation, its importance, how it affects media, and the policies and ethics associated with copyrighted materials. Chapter 2, "Fair Use: When Do You Need to Ask for Permission?," introduces readers to the four factors of fair use that will help them make the best decisions for using materials, as well as to other parts of the law specifically of importance to educators: the classroom, handicap, and library exemptions. This chapter also provides some information on state copyright laws and on guidelines for the popular educational multimedia materials teachers and librarians often use. Chapter 3, "Public Domain: Is There Such a Thing as Free Material?," answers questions about one of the most speculated-upon aspects of copyright—public domain materials. This chapter explains public domain, including how something enters the public domain; identifies what media are in the public domain, as well as the relation of government documents to public domain; and discusses how you can identify public domain works. Chapter 4, "Obtaining Permission: How Can You Legally Obtain Use of Works?," gets to the core and function of this book. This chapter outlines permissions (what they are and how they work) and helps you understand their relationship to clearinghouses and licenses. This chapter also explains how to write a permission letter, what goes in it, and an example of an effective letter. Chapter 5, "Further Important Copyright Subjects: What Other Copyright Issues Do You Need to Understand?," explains some of the remaining issues, including international copyright law, plagiarism and citation, open sourcing/Creative Commons, and violations and penalties.

Chapters 6 through 12, in Part II, cover specific applications of copyright law to the Internet, including blogs/vlogs, podcasts, wikis, social networking tools, and more; movies, DVDs, CDs, and television; computer and gaming software; music and audio; multimedia; and print works. Although teachers and librarians are familiar with terms such as *media* and *mediums*, for the purpose of this book, I have chosen to use the word *work* to represent these items, as it is the more common term used with copyright law. Each chapter explains fair use, public domain, documentation and licenses, permissions, creation and ownership, violations and penalties, international copyright law, and avoiding copyright problems as they relate to the specific works. These are chapters that you can consult as the issues arise or read over to become more familiar with the formats you use most often. Chapter 13, "Distance Education and Copyright Law: How Is This Different from Applying Copyright Law in a Face-to-Face Classroom?," discusses the Digital Millennium Copyright Act (DMCA) and TEACH Act and how they relate to the many aspects of distance education. Chapter 14, "Conclusion: What Does All of This Mean for K–12 Teachers and Librarians?," brings it all together and provides some last-minute advice for avoiding problems, how to deal with pressure to break the law, and how and why to teach students and faculty the importance of copyright law.

Much has changed in technology and education since the 2004 publication of my book *Copyright for Teachers and Librarians*. The pages that follow cover technologies that weren't even on our radar screens then. Examples include iPods and other handheld devices (including cell phones that access the Internet); Playaways; blogs/vlogs; wikis; podcasts/vodcasts; RSS feeds; Ning; Second Life and other Internet world environments; social networking: Facebook, LinkedIn, MySpace, Twitter, YouTube, etc.; social/special interest networking: Shelfari, Goodreads, etc.; Moodle, Skype, and similar digital communication tools; social bookmarking; web syndication; video streaming; TiVo and similar systems; computer/video games/gaming; and open sourcing/Creative Commons.

I have approached copyright concerns for these new resources following the same approach used for others. This successor to my earlier book features 82 flowcharts, of which 19 are new to this edition to help readers handle new media.

Copyright law is seldom emphasized in the college and university education of our future teachers and school and public librarians. As such, it is something that you have probably always been aware of but perhaps have never closely examined. The truth is that copyright is an everyday part of your function as a teacher or librarian, and it requires your full attention and knowledge. This guide is meant to be a quick and thorough look into the implications of copyright in K–12 educational environments. I have answered many of the common questions I have encountered in my workshops, while still expanding and fleshing out this source so that it anticipates even the questions that were not asked. In truth, copyright can help advance the education of our youth. Thus, it is necessary to be aware of the various facets of copyright and use them to your own and your students' advantage.

Acknowledgments

I would like to thank the K–12 teachers, school librarians, technology coordinators, school administrators, and other interested individuals whose demand for information on copyright in a "nonlegalese" manner has culminated in this book. In addition, I would like to thank my library information specialist and instructional technology students, other interested master's and doctoral students, graduate assistants, and interested faculty colleagues at Northern Illinois University and East Tennessee State University who have participated in my copyright classes and workshops over the past 16 years and asked insightful questions on the subject. I also wish to express my appreciation for the support of family and friends whose kind words and help—when they were most needed—kept me on track. Last, I especially thank my husband, Tom, and my son, Benjamin, who read over drafts, made comments, and helped create flowcharts. I cannot thank you enough!

PART I

Essential Concepts of Copyright Law

CHAPTER 1

Introduction to Copyright Law: What Is Copyright?

INTRODUCTION

Copyright is a very confusing area of U.S. law—one that can be argued to have an ethical component, since it is possible that the only person who knows whether copyright law is being violated is the individual copying or borrowing the work. Because it is written in a manner that leaves it open to interpretation, copyright law is especially of concern in a K–12 educational setting, where teachers, administrators, school librarians, technology coordinators, students, and others may think, "We're a school. We can copy all we want, because it's for education." If the copyright owner has granted consent for unlimited use of his or her work in this educational setting, then there is no problem. Frequently, however, the dilemma is that the borrower does not have the time or inclination—or is unable—to locate the owner to determine whether the desired use of a work is legal.

Often, those of us in schools think we will not get caught if we borrow without obtaining permission from the work's owner. After all, we do not do it all the time, and who has really heard of copyright police? The opposite approach is just as misguided: for example, when an administrator demands that absolutely no copying occur in his or her school building or district. Here, the misconception is that all copying is illegal. In actuality, the truth lies somewhere in between. As teachers and librarians, we deal with communication technologies in a wide variety of formats, from books to movies and music to the Internet. We are usually busy and often searching for something to use at the last minute. Borrowing a few pages out of a textbook for a math class to take home over the weekend, copying a piece of music for the drum section, or using a popular song for a cheerleading podcast may seem the easiest ways to go. After all, who will know? That the copyright owner may lose money or control over his or her work is not our concern. Following is a list of some of the questions we should ask as we go about our daily responsibilities as educators:

- Can you change a digital image so that using it is not a copyright infringement?
- What can you legally put on a wiki?

- Are there copyright concerns when using a social network—for example, Shelfari—in the classroom?
- Do you need special permission from Internet authors to use their works?
- Can you print anything you want from a CD-ROM?
- Is it okay to record a television program and play it as part of a class unit?
- Is it legal to show a DVD rented from a video store in homeroom?
- Can a teacher lawfully retain students' completed assignments to use in future classes or to show as "best examples" in other settings?
- If you want to make 30 copies of a magazine article for a class reading assignment, is this acceptable under copyright law?

K–12 educators often ask such questions as they develop curricula, prepare lessons, and otherwise go about their daily teaching duties. All of these questions deal with copyright, perhaps the most well-known of our intellectual property rights. These questions and more are covered in the next few chapters, along with other associated copyright topics.

As you use this book, please note that three similar terms are used throughout: U.S. Code, U.S. Copyright Law, and the U.S. Copyright Act. Although they are all related (the U.S. Code contains the U.S. Copyright Law, and the U.S. Copyright Law was built in part on the U.S. Copyright Act), each one is somewhat different from the other two.

The U.S. Code "is the codification by subject matter of the general and permanent laws of the United States. It is divided by broad subjects into 50 titles and published by the Office of the Law Revision Counsel of the U.S. House of Representatives" (U.S. Code, 2009). One part of the U.S. Code is Title 17. Chapters 1 through 8 and 10 through 12 of Title 17 contain the U. S. Copyright Law. This is the U.S. law that is concerned with copyright and, thus, the one we cite in this book when interpreting copyright questions. For example, "Chapters 9 and 13 of title 17 contain statutory design protection that is independent of copyright protection" (Peters, 2010: Preface). The U.S. Copyright Act is part of the U.S. Copyright Law. Passed in 1976, the Copyright Act "provides the basic framework for the current copyright law" (U.S. Copyright Office, 2010b: Preface). In broad terms, this means that the U.S. Copyright Act is a piece of U.S. Copyright Law, which is one part of the U.S. Code, which is the document that contains all of the laws of the United States. For the purposes of this book, we focus on U.S. Copyright Law. Please note that the complete Copyright Law is available in a variety of places, including online at the United States Copyright Office's website (http://www.copyright.gov) and in print from the U.S. Government Bookstore (http://bookstore.gpo.gov) (Peters, 2010).

COPYRIGHT DEFINED AND EXPLAINED

This section presents a brief definition of copyright and an explanation of what it means to those of us in elementary, middle, and secondary schools.

Definition

Copyright law protects for owners "original works of authorship fixed in any tangible medium of expression, now known or later developed, from which they can be perceived, reproduced, or otherwise communicated, either directly or with the aid of a machine or device" (U.S. Code, 2010: 102(a)). Owners of copyrighted works have the exclusive right, by law, to

- reproduce or copy,
- distribute,
- publicly perform,
- publicly display,
- create derivatives, and
- "in the case of sound recordings, to perform the copyrighted work publicly by means of a digital audio transmission." (U.S. Code, 2010: 106(6))

Copyright law violations occur when someone other than the owner attempts to use works in one of the manners described in the previous list (Butler, 2000).

Things That Can Be Copyrighted

Almost anything originally created is copyrightable, i.e., can be or is registered with the U.S. Copyright Office. See the sidebar for examples of works that can be copyrighted.

Concerning the concept of "originality," it is worth mentioning that the perception of an original work is that it "reflects the personality of the maker" (Ploman and Hamilton, 1980: 31). Thus, two different people may write stories about voice classes at the Peking Opera School, and both stories can be copyrighted—assuming that each story is sufficiently unique. Because this can be confusing, sometimes courts must make the determination whether a work is truly an original (Ploman and Hamilton, 1980).

Automatic Copyright

Under current copyright law, almost anything a person creates is automatically copyright-protected,

---

Works That Can Be Copyright-Protected

PRINT
- Articles
- Books
- Letters
- Newsletters
- Newspapers
- Plays and musicals
- Poems
- Sheet music
- Other print works

NONPRINT
- Architecture
- Audio recordings
- CD-ROMs
- Computer software
- DVDs
- Games
- Modern dance and other public performances, including pantomimes and choreography
- Multimedia
- Paintings
- Photographs
- Statues
- Television programs
- Videos
- Other nonprint works

INTERNET
- Blogs/vlogs
- Digitized graphics, movies, and advertisements
- E-mails
- Nings (user-created social networks)
- Podcasts
- Webpages
- Wikis
- Other digitized works available on the World Wide Web

regardless of whether it is officially registered. Thus, every e-mail you send, every paper you write, and every digital picture you take is protected. What this means for K–12 educators is that a high school coach who creates a blog to supplement football practice, a student who writes an original paper on John Brown, and a fifth-grade teacher who films a video of his or her students' artwork have all created copyrightable works. If you like, you may put the symbol for copyright, which is "©," on everything you or your students create. This shows those who view, listen to, or use your work that it is copyright-protected, whether registered with the U.S. Copyright Office or not.

To protect a work, it is best to officially register it with the U.S. Copyright Office; the process for which is discussed later in this chapter. This is an important step because a "copyright owner cannot proceed with a copyright infringement lawsuit unless the work has been registered" (Rich, 1999). In addition, owners of registered works are eligible for statutory damages and attorneys' fees; owners of unregistered works are not. Last, official registration assures the public that the registered work is an original and is owned by the individual or group who recorded said work with the U.S. Copyright Office (Rich, 1999).

Who Owns the Copyrighted Work?

In most instances, the person or group who created a work owns the copyright; for example, a student who burns a CD-ROM of a series of stories that he has written for English class would probably own the rights to his stories. However, it is possible for individuals or companies to own works they did not create. This can occur in one of two ways. The first is when the creator transfers or assigns copyright ownership to a third party. Thus, for example, it is possible for a technology coordinator to create a webpage about care of offspring among penguins on her own time and sell the copyright to an educational Internet company. The second way is "work for hire." This occurs when work is considered the property of the organization that hired the individual or group to do the work (Butler, 2002). For example, a school librarian uses his free period for several weeks to write up a collection-development policy. He was asked to create this policy by the school superintendent; he is doing it on school time; and he uses a school computer. Such a situation may be considered work for hire. Another example might be if a mathematics teacher, working at home, creates a digital math game for an educational software company. If she signs a contract with the company stating that it is work for hire, the teacher does not own what she has created. For her services, the teacher is paid a fee by the company; the company has the right to register the game with the U.S. Copyright Office.

Derivative Works

Derivative works are items created by changing an already existing work. The extent of change to the work can be slight, moderate, or a great deal. Take a graphic of an elephant, for example. A web designer has created a digital image of an elephant for her website. A school student finds the elephant graphic online and borrows it, adding a red hat to its head. The elephant with a red hat is an example of a derivative work. Another example of a derivative work is when a high school cheerleading adviser takes a set of original dance moves borrowed from a musical and changes them slightly to fit a dance number that the cheering squad will perform at a game. When works are changed somewhat but not completely, a derivative work is the result. When derivative works are created from copyrighted works without the proper permissions or licenses, this is an infringement of copyright law.

What Copyright Law Is Not

Copyright is only one of several intellectual property rights addressed generally in the U.S. Constitution: "Exclusive rights to . . . respective writings and discoveries" (1788). Other intellectual property in the United States includes (1) patents, which are issued by the government, for a specific period of time, in order to monopolize an invention; (2) trademarks, including logos, symbols, sounds, etc., which distinguish products from one another; and (3) trade secrets, or company-specific information that makes an item competitive (Silver, 2003; Wherry, 2002).

HISTORY OF COPYRIGHT

Those not interested in history might wonder, "Why is the history of copyright important to my students and me?" Most teachers and librarians have their eyes on the future, on new technologies and how to use them in the classroom. However, as will be explained in the discussion that follows, while the concept of copyright is often seen as a relatively new concern, especially with new technologies, it has, in fact, been around for some time. Understanding how copyright has been treated in the past can help with thinking about where it will go in the future: "One way we have of sensing the future is to look back into the past" (Saltrick, 1995: 44).

Copyright in the United States is greatly influenced by English common law. For example, the Statute of Anne (1710), which is considered the first contemporary copyright law, provided for protecting authors' literary property for a limited number of years (Tryon, 1994). Notions of copyright in the future United States are seen as early as 1672, when bookseller John Usher's petition to the General Court of the Massachusetts Bay Colony resulted in a private copyright for his revised edition of *The General Laws and Liberties of the Massachusetts Colony* (Bettig, 1996; Usher's Printing Privilege, 1672). About 100 years later in the fledging United States, such prominent citizens as Noah Webster and Thomas Paine worked to promote state copyright law. Their efforts were not in vain. In the 1780s, state copyright laws were passed by all 13 original colonies as a result of Noah Webster's work to protect his writings, which was necessary because the Articles of Confederation did not provide federal copyright protection (Bettig, 1996). In 1790, President George Washington signed into law the first federal copyright legislation. U.S. Congress was given the power to "promote the progress of science and useful arts, by securing for limited times to authors and inventors the exclusive right to their respective writings and discoveries" (U.S. Constitution, Art. I, Sec. 8). This law was later expanded and revised in 1831, 1879, 1909, 1976, and 1998. It is the basis of intellectual property rights in our country today and continues to be modified as necessary. At any given point in time, a number of bills dealing in some way with copyright sit in our nation's House of Representatives and Senate awaiting action (Butler, 2003). Many new bills cover digital works, including Internet applications, television broadcasting, DVDs, and more. Indeed, in the 21st century, "one of the primary reasons for copyright law is... the protection of the owners and creators to earn money and recognition for those things that they own or create" (Butler, 2003: 39).

WHY COPYRIGHT LAW IS IMPORTANT

Copyright is important in that it protects creators' and owners' rights to their works. Copyright legislation grants the owner the "exclusive right to reproduce, prepare derivative works, distribute, perform and display the work publicly. Exclusive means only the creator of such work, not anybody who has access to it and decides to grab it" (WhatIsCopyright.org, 2010). However, copyright law also helps the user of the work, in that the owners' rights are limited (see Chapters 2 and 3 for more information on these limitations). As such, this law actually represents both the owners and the users of works.

It is helpful here to look more closely at owners and users of works—usually two distinct groups. Owners are those individuals or groups who either created a work or obtained the copyright for it. Usually, owners are looking for assurance that the rights they own are not being infringed upon. Users of works are those individuals or groups who wish to borrow all or part of a work for their own employ. For example, suppose you are a teacher and you wish to borrow a series of activities from a reading workbook for use with your sixth-grade class. If you plan to photocopy these activities and share them with colleagues, it is likely that you would be violating the rights of those who own the copyright to the reading activities. These two distinct groups are what keep the issue of copyright going, year after year, generation after generation.

HOW TO REGISTER WORKS WITH THE U.S. COPYRIGHT OFFICE

Usually when you think of copyright, you think in terms of how much you can borrow without getting permission from the owner or creator of the book, movie, audio file, webpage, or whatever it is that you want to copy. However, as an educator, it is important to be able to look at this subject from a different point of view: How can you officially register something you have created with the U.S. Copyright Office?

Assume that you are a retired teacher with a hobby in astronomy. As a former middle school instructor, you have decided to try your hand at creating units on astronomy for students, grades six through eight. You have written a number of units, created on your own time, at home, with your own software and computer. These have not been used in the classroom. You compile the units into manuscript form with the idea that perhaps an educational publishing firm would be interested in them. Before you send them out for review, you would like to obtain official copyright registration for your work.

Contacting the Copyright Office

Your first step is to contact the U.S. Copyright Office at the Library of Congress. They can be reached online, by phone, or through the U.S. Postal Service. If you are contacting them by phone or mail, tell them that you want to register your manuscript with their office, and they will send you the materials you need via regular postal mail. Online forms and application instructions, as well as other copyright information, are also available on the Internet at http://www.loc.gov/copyright. (You will need Adobe Acrobat Reader, a free download, to view and print these materials.)

Registering Your Work

Be aware that any kind of work that can be copyright-protected can be registered with the U.S. Copyright Office. While such print forms as TX (literary works), VA (visual arts works), SR (sound recordings), and more are still available via mail from the U.S. Copyright Office, it is easier and cheaper to register a work online. Go to the Electronic Copyright Office at http://www.copyright.gov/eco/ and access the detailed PowerPoint or PDF format tutorial for all online instructions and materials; or download a Form CO, which replaces such forms as the TX, VA, and SR just mentioned. Complete the CO, print it, and send it to the U.S. Copyright Office with your registration fee.

Concerning the previous example, where you are a retired teacher who has created astronomy units in manuscript form for publication: you could file online at any time of the day or night (except Sunday from midnight to 6 a.m. Eastern time) for a $35 fee, download and use the CO for a $50 fee, or receive the TX form by mail for $65 (Electronic Copyright Office, 2010). Other works that can be assigned copyright registration include lyrics, music, plays, movies, scripts, pantomimes, choreography, sound recordings, cartoons, comic strips, photographs, architectural works, games, multimedia works, various digital formats (for example, wikis, podcasts, and so on), and recipes.

Note that there are some works that cannot be registered by the U.S. Copyright Office. Such works include:

- items not fixed in a tangible form of expression, for example an unrecorded, improvised dialogue;
- names, titles, recipe ingredients, short phrases and slogans;
- ideas, concepts, processes; and
- works which have no original authors or that consist of common information, such as calendars, measuring tapes and rulers, etc. (Copyright Basics, 2010: 3)

Information needed by the U.S. Copyright Office in order to register a work includes title, name and address of author, name and address of owner, year of creation, publication date (if applicable), type of authorship, name and address of permission contact person, format of the item, and where the copyright certificate is to be sent (U.S. Copyright Office, 2010a).

When Does Your Work Receive Copyright Registration?

"Whatever time is needed to issue a certificate, the effective date of registration is the day the Copyright Office receives a complete submission in acceptable form. You do not need to wait for a certificate to proceed with publication" (U.S. Copyright Office, 2010c). Therefore, if your work can be registered for copyright protection, it will be protected immediately upon all required information and materials being received by the U.S. Copyright Office.

When Will You Find Out If Your Work Received Copyright Registration?

Normally, the person(s) requesting copyright registration will receive an e-mail notice of receipt of materials from the U.S. Copyright Office, if applying online, with the registration certificate arriving in approximately nine months. If applying with Form CO or paper forms, no receipt will be sent, and the registration certificate, which the work's owner would take delivery of, could be sent up to 22 months after the first contact with the U.S. Copyright Office (U.S. Copyright Office, 2010a).

U.S. Copyright Office Contact Information

U.S. Copyright Office
101 Independence Avenue Southeast
Washington, DC 20559-6000
Phone: (202) 707-3000
Internet: http://www.copyright.gov/

CONCLUSION

Have you ever infringed on someone's copyright while pursuing your teaching activities? Have your colleagues? If you and those with whom you work in the school are completely honest, undoubtedly the answer is yes. Let's take a look at some of the ways that you might infringe on an individual or group/organization/company's copyright in your professional/teaching lives. Have you or a colleague:

- added part of a commercial video which supported a particular curricular unit to an online educational site, such as TeacherTube (http://www1 .teachertube.com)?
- loaded a piece of computer software that a student brought in from home onto more than one classroom computer at the same time (without reading the documentation, which might state that such use is illegal)?
- burned copies of a music CD to several blank CDs so that students could listen to it in small groups while working on group projects?
- "borrowed" liberally from a webpage that you liked to create one of your own?
- showed a personal DVD during recess on a rainy day?
- copied an extra script of a play for the new student director?
- made extra copies of a workbook page because the school didn't purchase enough workbooks for every student in the class?
- used a color copier to copy all of the pages in a picture book, which you then posted on a bulletin board?
- scanned and posted an entire book on the school assignment website?

This list could go on and on; these are possible scenarios that, without obtaining the proper permissions or other exceptions, may be considered copyright infringements. Indeed, abuse of U.S. copyright law probably occurs every day in our schools. Whatever the case, it does not mean that you need to continue along such lines—there is hope! Using this book, it is possible to follow the law rather than rationalize reasons for not doing so. Now, continue on to Chapter 2 for a discussion of fair use, one of the areas of copyright law of most importance to education.

REFERENCES

Bettig, Ronald V. 1996. *Copyrighting Culture: The Political Economy of Intellectual Property.* Boulder, CO: Westview Press.

Butler, Rebecca P. 2000. "Copyright as a Social Responsibility—Don't Shoot the Messenger." *Knowledge Quest* 29, no. 2 (November/December): 48–49.

———. 2002. "Copyright and Electronic Media in K–12 Education." Workshop for Improving Learning for All Students through Technology [grant], San Marcos, CA, February 20.

———. 2003. "Copyright Law in the United States . . . and How It Got That Way." *Knowledge Quest* 31, no. 4 (March/April): 39–40.

Copyright Basics. 2010. "Circular 1: Copyright Basics." Washington, DC: U.S. Copyright Office.

Electronic Copyright Office (eCO). 2010. U.S. Copyright Office, Library of Congress. http://www.copyright.gov/eco/.

Peters, Marybeth. 2010. "Copyright Law of the United States of America and Related Laws Contained in Title 17 of the United States Code, Circular 92: Preface." U.S. Copyright Office, Library of Congress. http://www.copyright.gov/title17/92preface.html.

Ploman, Edward W., and L. Clark Hamilton. 1980. *Copyright: Intellectual Property in the Information Age.* Boston: Routledge and Kegan Paul.

Rich, Lloyd L. 1999. "Advantages of Copyright Registration." Publishing Law Center. http://www.publaw.com/article/advantages-of-copyright-registration/.

Saltrick, Susan. 1995. "The Pearl of Great Price: Copyright and Authorship from the Middle Ages to the Digital Age." *Educom Review* 30, no. 3 (May/June): 44–46.

Silver, Judith A. 2003. "What Is Intellectual Property? Trade Secret Law." FindLaw.com. http://library.findlaw.com/2003/May/15/132743.html.

Tryon, Jonathan S. 1994. *The Librarian's Legal Companion*. New York: G. K. Hall.

U.S. Code. 2009. "Office of the Law Revision Counsel of the U.S. House of Representatives." GPO Access, U.S. Government Printing Office. http://www.gpoaccess.gov/uscode/.

———. 2010. "Circular 92: Copyright Law of the United States of America and Related Laws." U.S. Copyright Office, Library of Congress. http://www.copyright.gov/title17/92chap1.html#101.

U.S. Constitution. 1788. Article I. Section 8.

U.S. Copyright Office, Library of Congress. 2010a. "Copyright" [Home Page]. http://www.copyright.gov/.

———. 2010b. "Copyright Law of the United States of America and Related Laws Contained in Title 17 of the *United States Code*." http://www.copyright.gov/title17/92preface.html.

———. 2010c. "I've Submitted My Application, Fee, and Copy of My Work to the Copyright Office. Now What?" http://www.copyright.gov/help/faq/faq-what.html#certificate.

Usher's Printing Privilege. 1672. In *Primary Sources on Copyright (1450–1900)*, edited by L. Bently and M. Kretschmer. Cambridge, UK: University of Cambridge, Faculty of Law. http://www.copyrighthistory.org.

WhatIsCopyright.org. 2010. "What Is Copyright Protection?" http://www.whatiscopyright.org/.

Wherry, Timothy Lee. 2002. *Intellectual Property in the Digital Age: Copyrights, Patents, and Trademarks*. Chicago: American Library Association.

Chapter 2

Fair Use: When Do You Need to Ask for Permission?

INTRODUCTION

Walk into an elementary, middle, or high school in the United States and ask a teacher, administrator, technology person, or librarian what he or she knows about copyright. In all likelihood, one of the first things that these individuals will mention is the term *fair use*. Now, ask these same people what *fair use* means. After a pause, you will probably get a scattered answer containing half-truths about fair use and how it can be used in an educational setting. This chapter focuses on clarifying the concept of fair use, which is one of the most important areas of copyright for educators.

FAIR USE DEFINED AND EXPLAINED

Probably one of the handiest and yet most easily misinterpreted copyright principles deals with fair use. Fair use "limits copyright holders' exclusive rights" (Butler, 2001a: 35). There are four fair use factors:

> (1) the purpose and character of the use, including whether such use is of a commercial nature or is for nonprofit educational purposes; (2) the nature of the copyrighted work; (3) the amount and substantiality of the portion used in relation to the copyrighted work as a whole; and (4) the effect of the use upon the potential market for or value of the copyrighted work. (U.S. Copyright Law, 1976: 107 (1–4))

These fair use principles, which are found in Section 107 of the U.S. Copyright Act (1976), are explained in the sections that follow.

FAIR USE FACTOR 1: PURPOSE AND CHARACTER OF USE

The first fair use factor, purpose and character of use, looks at how those copying the work are going to use it. Works copied for educational, nonprofit, or personal purposes are much more likely to be considered within fair use than are those items copied for the intention of earning money. Thus, a high school science teacher may be able to copy an article on the 2010 oil spill in the Gulf of Mexico for a class of 27 students studying the environment, but fair use would likely not extend to copying the same article for the purpose of selling it. A good question to ask yourself here is, "What do I want to do with the materials I plan to copy?"

Parodies and other transformative uses, such as commentaries, fit under the first fair use factor. Such use of works is allowed "for purposes such as criticism [or] comment" (U.S. Copyright Law, 1976, Section 107: 16). This means that, for the science class just mentioned, the teacher may assign the students to find a television advertisement that positively portrays the cleanup efforts made by a major oil company in the Gulf states and write a satirical skit that transforms the ad content into a criticism of said oil company.

FAIR USE FACTOR 2: NATURE OF THE WORK

The second fair use factor, the nature of the work, deals with the work's characteristics: Is the work fact or fiction? Is it published or unpublished? Works most usable under this fair use factor are nonfiction published pieces. Therefore, a travel magazine article about the Yanomamo people of Venezuela and Brazil might be reproducible for a social studies class, while a handwritten piece of short fiction about George Washington meeting Squanto—recently found in someone's attic and dated 1799—might not be. Good questions to ask yourself here are, "Is this work fact or fiction? Has this work been published or not?"

FAIR USE FACTOR 3: AMOUNT TO BE BORROWED

The third fair use factor covers the amount of work you plan to borrow. For example, do you want to use an entire hour-long movie or just five minutes of it? Are you interested in copying the Beatles' song "A Hard Day's Night" in its entirety or just a small part of it? With this fair use factor, the smallest amount borrowed is usually the best. This factor is measured two ways: quantitatively and qualitatively: "Quantity considers the amount copied relative to the whole original as well as the amount needed to achieve the objective of the copying. Qualitative measurement is more creative. It involves the concept of substantiality, whereby copying the 'heart' of the work—no matter how small—is too much" (Butler, 2001a: 35). Thus, using five minutes of an hour-long movie about what penguins eat would be appropriate under this factor of fair use—unless that particular five minutes was the heart of the video, i.e., showing what the penguin actually eats. Good questions to ask yourself here are, "How much do I need to borrow? Is this the heart of the work?"

FAIR USE FACTOR 4: MARKETABILITY OF THE WORK

The fourth fair use factor features the marketability of the work. In essence, this means that if this work were to be copied and sold, either as part of a newly created item or by itself, would such a sale affect the amount of money that the owner or creator of the original work could earn from it? For instance, if copying an extra script of a high school play means that the publisher who owns the rights to that play does not get royalties, then such copying is in violation of the law.

Another example is that dealing with sheet music. Perhaps the school's band director finds that there is one student too many in the clarinet section for the available music. That student needs his or her own copy of the second clarinet part for the concert coming up in three weeks. The band director decides to make one copy of the sheet music—after all, the selection was purchased for the use of the whole band! Unfortunately, unless there is no other way to get the clarinet part before the concert, such copying may be in violation. In addition, if the concert is imminent and a copy is made, that copy needs to be destroyed right after the concert, unless the copyright holder granted proper permission. A good question to ask here is, "Will my copying this item mean that the copyright holder will earn less money?"

Since the mid-1990s, the licensing of works is now also being considered in evaluating this factor with "for-profit organizations," which could include some private educational institutions. This is a result of *American Geophysical Union et al. v. Texaco Inc.* (1992), in which several Texaco scientists were found to have violated copyright law by copying a number of scientific journal articles without paying royalties to the publishers. There are exceptions to almost every rule, and these fair use factors are not exempt. For example, copying, in excess of the four fair use factors, is allowed at times for disabled users, depending on the disability and how the reproduction is made and used. Such exemptions are addressed in depth in later chapters. Two Internet sites that support fair use determination are the Copyright Clearance Center's (2008) Fair Use Check List and the Copyright Website LLC's (2010) fair use flowchart.

COPYRIGHT GUIDELINES FOR EDUCATIONAL MULTIMEDIA

The four fair use factors just discussed are very important to K–12 teachers and librarians as they work with new and old technologies, with students and colleagues. However, these four factors were purposefully written so they are vague (Rose, 1993) to permit flexibility in their use—which makes many educators uncomfortable when they are trying to use all or part of a copyrighted work. Thus, users of works may want to have an exact amount in mind when considering how much they can and cannot copy without permission. This is where directives such as the "Fair Use Guidelines for Educational Multimedia" come into play.

Guidelines are far more rigid than the fair use factors just discussed, are not binding under the law, and represent minimum amounts rather than maximums. Basically, when used by the borrower of a work, it means that he or she is trying to act in good faith. Because of this, many copyright experts do not encourage their use. They are covered here because, while they do not have the power of law, "they give the courts a sense of how... fair use [is] to be interpreted" (Butler, 2001b: 34). The "Copyright and Fair Use Guidelines for Teachers" table (Davidson, 2002) is an example of copyright guidelines for school materials.

One set of copyright guidelines, the "Fair Use Guidelines for Educational Multimedia," was originally developed by the Consortium of College and University Media Centers (CCUMC) in 2002, when this organization participated in the Conference on Fair Use (CONFU). These guidelines, recently updated (UW©opyright Connection, 2011), solely apply to the creation and use of educational multimedia; thus, when creating a multimedia presentation for a class with excerpts from a video, CD, digitized music, televised cartoon, book, etc., the limits stated in the sidebar can be applied. Moreover, two copies, one for viewing and one for reserve, in addition to one for each of the creators of the multimedia presentation, may be made and kept for two years. If you want to keep using the project after that time period, you must obtain permissions from the owners of the original works borrowed. These permissions will have to be obtained from everyone from whom you borrowed, whether the borrowing originally fit under the fair use guidelines or not. However, the multimedia project can be kept intact after the two years without obtaining permissions if used by the creator(s) for a portfolio, unpaid workshop, or presentation for peers (Lehman, 1996).

Quantities of Media Recommended for Borrowing under the Fair Use Guidelines for Educational Multimedia

Motion media	10 percent or three minutes
Text	10 percent or 1,000 words
Poems of less than 250 words:	3 lines
Poems of more than 250 words	Up to 250 words; 3 excerpts by a poet; 5 excerpts by different poets in same collection
Music, lyrics, music videos	Up to 10 percent or 30 seconds
Illustrations and photographs	5 by the same artist or photographer; 10 percent or 15 images from one published work
Numerical data sets	10 percent or 2,500 fields or cells

(UW©opyright Connection, 2011)

Be aware that CONFU, discussed previously, first convened in 1994. It was composed of a number of individuals representing such user organizations as the American Library Association and the National Education Association and such owner groups as the Motion Picture Association of America and the Software Publishers Association (now the Software & Information Industry Association).

The purpose of CONFU was to talk about fair use and develop guidelines for librarians and educators to use when working with copyrighted works. The CONFU concept was that such guidelines would be agreeable to both users and owners (Lehman, 1996: 2). As one might have expected, representatives of the two groups found it difficult to agree on copyright guidelines; while user groups tended to feel that the suggested guidelines were too stringent, owner groups felt that the same guidelines were not strict enough.

CONCLUSION

If copyright law were a color, it would be seen in shades of gray. Oftentimes, there is no one answer to a copyright question. Instead, there are any numbers of points that a borrower must consider when using a work owned by someone else. This also means that those interpreting the four fair use factors may not always agree on interpretations. For some illustrative examples of variances within understandings of fair use, refer to discussions found in current copyright books, professional periodical articles, and websites (Aufderheide, Jaszi, and Hobbs, 2007; Center for Digital Research and Scholarship, 2009; Greenhow et al., 2007; and Hobbs, 2010).

Because such lack of agreement is often the case, it is important to remember that all four of the fair use factors need to be followed—that "none in theory is given more weight than another, as fair use is an equitable concept" (Lipinski, 2005: 156). Another good point to keep in mind is that, whether using copyright law or guidelines, when borrowing without permission from copyrighted works, always use the smallest quantity that you can.

REFERENCES

American Geophysical Union et al. v. Texaco Inc. 1992. 802 F. (S.D.N.Y.).

Aufderheide, Patricia, Peter Jaszi, and Renee Hobbs. 2007. "Media Literacy Educators Need Clarity about Copyright and Fair Use." *Journal of Media Literacy* 54, no. 2–3: 41–44.

Butler, Rebecca P. 2001a. "Copyright as a Social Responsibility—Fair Use: I Need It Now!" *Knowledge Quest* 29, no. 3 (January/February): 35–36.

———. 2001b. "Fair Use Guidelines for Educational Multimedia." *Knowledge Quest* 29, no. 4 (March/April): 34–35.

Center for Digital Research and Scholarship. 2009. "Revamped Copyright Website from Columbia University." Columbia University Libraries, Center for Digital Research and Scholarship. http://cdrs.columbia.edu/cdrsmain/?p=732.

Copyright Clearance Center. 2008. "Copyright Basics: Fair Use: Fair Use Check List." The Campus Guide to Copyright Compliance for Academic Institutions. http://www.copyright.com/Services/copyrightoncampus/basics/fairuse_list.html.

Copyright Website LLC. 2010. "The Law: Fair Use." http://www.benedict.com/Info/FairUse/FairUse.aspx.

Davidson, Hall. 2002. "The Educator's Guide to Copyright and Fair Use." http://www.halldavidson.net/downloads.html#anchor928768/copyrightTEACH-1.pdf.

Greenhow, Christine, J.D. Walker, Dan Donnelly, and Brad Cohen. 2007. "Fair Use Education for the Twenty-First Century: A Comparative Study of Students' Use of an Interactive Tool to Guide Decision Making." *Innovate* 4 no. 2. http://www.innovateonline.info/index.php?view=article&id=443.

Hobbs, Renee. 2010. *Copyright Clarity: How Fair Use Supports Digital Learning*. Thousand Oaks, CA: Corwin.

Lehman, Bruce A. 1996. *The Conference on Fair Use: An Interim Report to the Commissioner*. Washington, DC: U.S. Patent and Trademark Office.

Lipinski, Tomas A. 2005. *Copyright Law and the Distance Education Classroom*. Lanham, MD: The Scarecrow Press.

Rose, Mark. 1993. *Authors and Owners: The Invention of Copyright*. Cambridge, MA: Harvard University Press.

U.S. Copyright Law. 1976. Public Law 94-553, sec. 107: Limitations on Exclusive Rights: Fair Use. http://www.copyright.gov/title17/92chap1.html#107.

UW©opyright Connection. 2011. "Fair Use Guidelines for Educational Multimedia." University of Washington. http://depts.washington.edu/uwcopy/Using_Copyright/Guidelines/Fair.php#1.

CHAPTER 3

Public Domain: Is There Such a Thing as Free Material?

INTRODUCTION

As the amount of information on the Internet increases, digital overload is a common complaint; masses of material are available at our fingertips. It is easy to assume, since the information is "right in front of us," that it is also free for us to use in any way we want. In actuality, anything found on the web, like any other medium, may or may not be copyright-protected, depending on the whims of the owners of the works. In addition, many K–12 educators use any number of rationalizations for borrowing all sorts of material without permission, including variations on the following: (1) We are a nonprofit educational institution, so it's okay; (2) no one will know anyway; and (3) it's for the kids; they need it; and we can't afford to purchase it. Such arguments are often in direct contrast to copyright law. However, a great deal of free material does exist on the web and in other formats—specifically, material that is in the public domain.

WHAT IS PUBLIC DOMAIN?

Essentially, works in the public domain are free to use any way that you want. For example, Grimm's fairy tales, including the stories of "Cinderella" and "Snow White," are in the public domain. This means that you can create a wiki where your students rewrite these stories into new ones based on modern times, print out the new stories for all students in your school, and even sell copies of these stories at a school fair. Thus, public domain also encourages creation of new works. What is not in the public domain is a revised fairy tale, which is a version of the classic story that someone else has already changed. Thus, while "Cinderella" is in the public domain, the Disney version of it, whether book or movie, is not. This is because derivatives of the original piece are protected under copyright law. Consequently, while "Cinderella" remains in the public domain, a cartoon version or any other revision of the story is likely copyright-protected.

When using public domain materials, you can borrow all or part of a work—print or nonprint, fiction or nonfiction—and not worry about copyright infringement. The idea behind public domain is that the copyright owner has given up, to the public at large, all of his or her original rights to the work (see Chapter 1 for the list of original rights).

HOW LONG DOES IT TAKE A WORK TO BECOME PART OF THE PUBLIC DOMAIN?

It used to be that public domain followed copyright law as it existed at the time of the creation or publication of the work. The Copyright Term Extension Act (CTEA) was passed in October 1998, and there are now exceptions to this rule. CTEA changes U.S. copyright law by extending the term of copyright protection for works created January 1, 1978, or after from the life of the author plus 50 years, to the international criterion of life plus 70 years, and works for hire to 95 years from publication or 120 years after creation (Torrans, 2003; U.S. Copyright Office, 2010b). In addition, the CTEA applies retrospectively as well as prospectively to all works still under copyright on the bill's effective date, October 27, 1998. This is very confusing and is a result of U.S. Copyright Law being amended many times since its inception. Because of this, "No simple statement can be made to the effect that 'the term of protection for Y types of works is X years.' Rather, works of the same type but produced at different times will often have different terms of protection" (Karjala, 2002). Still, some rules (Gasaway, 2003; Hirtle, 2011; U.S. Copyright Office, 2010a) apply:

1. Works published before 1923 are in the public domain.
2. Works published between 1923 and 1963, when a copyright notice is attached, can have their copyright renewed for a total of 67 years beyond the date of publication. (However, if the copyright is not renewed or if the work originally had no official copyright notice, then the work is already in public domain.)
3. For works published from 1964 to 1977 with an official copyright notice attached, copyright is automatically renewed for a total of 95 years.
4. Works created but not published before January 1, 1978, which is the effective date of the 1976 Copyright Act (Butler, 2001), are legally copyrighted for the life of the owner plus 70 years.
5. All works published on or after January 1, 1978, are copyrighted for the lifetime of the creator/owner plus 70 years (Butler, 2001: 47–48; Karjala, 2002). If there is more than one creator/owner, the 70-year rule applies based on the lifetime of the longest living copyright holder. If they have a corporate author or are work for hire, then works published on or after January 1, 1978, are copyrighted for 120 years after the date of creation or 95 years from publication, the lesser amount being the one that applies (Torrans, 2003). The 70-year rule is a direct result of the Sonny Bono

Copyright Term Extension Act of 1998 (Public Law Number 105-298) mentioned previously in this chapter. The purpose of this act was to bring the U.S. copyright term of ownership in line with the same conditions as that of many European nations, thus giving U.S. owners of works the same protection as that afforded European owners (Sinofsky, 2000). Because the Sonny Bono Act is retroactive, the result is that the earliest any work copyrighted after 1978 can enter the public domain is December 31, 2047.

How Do We Know If a Copyright Has Been Renewed or Not?

Concerning rule #2 in the previous list, how would one know whether a copyright had been renewed? Generally, if renewed, the new copyright date would be listed on the verso page of a newer version of a book in the area where copyright information is listed. However, this would not answer the question for older works, which would contain only the original copyright date. For such older works, it is possible to obtain public domain information by contacting the U.S. Copyright Office. While the Copyright Office does not compile or maintain lists of public domain materials, it can conduct a search to find the answer—for a fee of $165 per hour with a two-hour minimum—or you may search their records online yourself for free (U.S. Copyright Office, Library of Congress, 2009). Other ways to find out if an item has been renewed include accessing the Catalog of Copyright Entries (U.S. Copyright Office, Library of Congress, 1960), the Copyright Renewal Database (Board of Trustees, Leland Stanford Junior University, 2006), or the University of Pennsylvania's "Online Books Page" (Ockerbloom, 2010).

Are There Any Simple Strategies for Knowing What Is Definitely in Public Domain at the Present?

While the terms *simple strategies* and *public domain* appear to be polar opposites, following is a list of some guidelines that apply. Works that are definitely in the public domain include those published:

1. before 1923,
2. between 1923 and 1963 with a copyright notice but no renewal of copyright,
3. between 1923 and 1977 with no copyright notice,
4. between 1978 and March 1, 1989, with no copyright notice and no registration, or
5. to which the author/owner has given up all rights. (Gasaway, 2003; Hirtle, 2011)

Two online resources are also helpful in determining whether something is in the public domain. The first is the "Digital Copyright Slider" published by Michael Brewer and the American Library Association's Office for Information Technology Policy (2007). With this digital slider, select the work's copyright date. The slider will then let you know the copyright status of the particular item and whether permission is needed to use it. Be aware that the result for many of the dates on the slider is "Maybe." This is because only works published before 1923 are always in the public domain. In addition, because the slider "is licensed under a Creative Commons Attribution-NonCommercial-Share Alike license," it is possible to use this item in your school, as long as you follow the conditions of the license. The second item is a flowchart developed by the Sunstein Copyright Practice Group (Sunstein Kann Murphy and Timbers LLP, 2002). This flowchart takes the viewer from works published before 1923 on into the present.

IF THERE IS NO COPYRIGHT DATE ON A WORK, DOES THAT MEAN IT IS IN THE PUBLIC DOMAIN?

Sometimes a work seems to have no copyright notice posted anywhere on it. While this is especially true of many webpages, it is also the case for various older works. Can we assume if there is no copyright notice that the work is in the public domain? As usual, the answer to this question depends—in this case, on when the item in question was first published. For example, works published between 1923 and 1963 with no official copyright notice are already in public domain. However, in our 21st century world—since 1989, in fact (Bruwelheide, 1995)—all works are automatically copyright-protected, whether or not the authors and owners put a copyright notice on their creations. Thus, it is good to remember that most works in the public domain are there because the copyright term has expired.

WHAT IF THE WORK IS CREATED AS PART OF THE TERMS OF EMPLOYMENT?

What is work for hire?

> Section 101 of the copyright law defines a "work made for hire" as . . . a work prepared by an employee within the scope of his or her employment or a work specially ordered or commissioned for use as a contribution to a collective work, as a part of a motion picture or other audiovisual work, as a translation, as a supplementary work, as a compilation, as an instructional text, as a test, as answer material for a test, or as an atlas, if the parties expressly agree in a written instrument signed by them that the work shall be considered a work made for hire. (U.S. Copyright Office, Library of Congress, 2010c: 1)

Thus, when the high school mechanics teacher creates a vlog (video blog) of his students repairing a car engine during second period for the online school newsletter, it may be considered part of his job and thus a work for hire. If he is hired by an educational design company to construct a unit on car repair at home, during his time off from school (evenings, weekends, and school vacations), that could also be considered work for hire.

If a work is created as part of an employee's job description or is work for hire, then the organization that employs the creator owns the copyright for either the publication date plus 95 years or 120 years from the time of creation—

with the term that expires first applying. After that period, the work will be in public domain. For example, this means that if you created a webpage for your school's library media center using school time, computers, and software, that the school would own your work for 95 to 120 years. For those works published between 1923 and 1978, the term of copyright varies, based on what the copyright law stated at the time of publication (Gasaway, 2003). A general rule is to assume that whatever you want to use is still under copyright unless a statement on or near the item clearly indicates that it is in the public domain. This includes the Internet. It is a misconception that the Internet, because it is so accessible, is not copyrighted (Simpson, 2001). Because the Internet is a relatively new phenomenon, the only way a website can be in the public domain is if the author/owner of the website's content chooses to place it there.

WHAT WORKS ARE IN THE PUBLIC DOMAIN?

Works in the public domain include:

- most federal documents (see the section in this chapter titled Are All Federal Government Documents in the Public Domain? for discussion on which federal documents are in the public domain and which are not);
- phone books;
- works with expired copyrights;
- works for which creators/owners have chosen to give up their copyrights;
- freeware;
- some open-source documents;
- works registered with Creative Commons and similar organizations;
- things that cannot be copyrighted, for example, names, short phrases, titles, ideas, and facts,
- some clip art (Internet and print);
- works published in 1923 or before; and
- some works published between 1923 and 1963 (Gasaway, 2003).

Do You Have to Purchase Public Domain Material or Is It Free?

Because educators are often on tight budgets and trying to avoid unnecessary spending, this question can be critical to the classroom teacher, school librarian, and other school faculty and staff. Therefore, it is important to note that public domain materials, just like other works, may be free, as in the cases of an Internet site that states it is in the public domain or free downloadable software found on the web. Public domain materials may also be sold, although the cost is usually not as much as works that carry copyright notices. For example, someone could take the U.S. Constitution, Bill of Rights, and Declaration of Independence and print them up in booklet form for purchase. While these three pieces of U.S. history are in the public domain, a printed booklet containing them might be sold for replication costs and whatever the printer thinks could be earned over and above that. No royalty expenses need be figured into the cost.

Please note that it is also possible to copyright reprinted public domain materials if there are any changes to the works. For example, a new publication includes public domain materials not originally printed together in one volume; a public domain collection is given a new title; there is a graphic added to the collection that was not available with the originals. But be aware that only the revised sections of the public domain work will be copyrighted; that which remains original is still in the public domain.

ARE ALL FEDERAL GOVERNMENT DOCUMENTS IN THE PUBLIC DOMAIN?

Federal government documents, created as work for hire, are not normally copyright-protected. As such, they are in the public domain. Examples of such documents are U.S. House of Representatives and U.S. Senate legislation, texts of federal court decisions, agency circulars, and federal reports. However, if the federal government hires outside contractors to produce works, such works may or may not be copyrighted—depending on the contract between the government and the contracted individuals or company.

Say, for example, that the federal government hires a historian to write a definitive history of the House of Representatives. If the contract between the government and the historian states that copyright ownership is the historian's or does not state who will own the copyright, then ownership stays with the historian. However, if the contract states that the work is for hire, then the government owns the copyright. In addition, the federal government can own the copyrights to works transferred to it. This means that if you transfer the copyright to an educational website on Alaskan king crabs—one you created as a classroom unit—to the U.S. Department of Education (DOE), then the DOE will own whatever copyrights came with your gift. For legal reasons, it is best to retain a print copy of the records of all copyright transfers you make.

Another instance in which federal government documents are not public domain material occurs when an individual or organization takes a federal government document that is in the public domain and adds original elements, such as critiques, indexing criteria, conclusions, summaries, or other original elements to it. In such a case, the individual or group creating the document derivative can claim copyright to the derivative parts. Since there is no specific rule to federal government documents and public domain, if you are unsure, it is best to contact the document author or issuing agency or department and inquire as to its copyright status.

ARE STATE AND LOCAL GOVERNMENT DOCUMENTS IN THE PUBLIC DOMAIN?

The answer to this question depends on the state or local government. For the purposes of copyright law, these agencies—considered owners of works in much the same way as are individuals or companies—may choose the works for which they want to own the copyright and the works they want to place in the public domain. State and local government documents include state legislative materials, texts of state and local court cases, minutes of city council meetings, birth and death records, tax files, real estate transactions, county board proceedings, and more public records of this kind. Again, there is no one rule, guideline, or principle. Therefore, check with each particular agency or state for information about what is in the public domain and what is not. Such information may be accessible from:

1. state offices, such as the state attorney's office in your county seat,
2. the city manager's secretary, or
3. other state, county, and community offices.

Information may be just an e-mail or phone call away.

IS SOMETHING THAT IS IN THE PUBLIC DOMAIN IN ANOTHER COUNTRY ALSO IN THE PUBLIC DOMAIN IN THE UNITED STATES?

The United States is a member of a number of international treaties that cover or are concerned with copyright law. Generally, when a work is disseminated in the United States, U.S. law applies, and when an item is distributed overseas, the laws of the particular countries receiving the item apply. Therefore, it is possible for a work to be in the public domain in one country and copyright-protected in another.

CAN SOMETHING BE TAKEN OUT OF THE PUBLIC DOMAIN AND PLACED UNDER COPYRIGHT PROTECTION AGAIN?

Copyright law, as written by our forebearers and current lawmakers, is a very gray issue. Public domain is no exception. For example, the Uruguay Round Agreements Act (URAA) of 1994 implemented the General Agreement on Tariffs and Trade (GATT). One result of GATT is that as of January 1, 1996, a number of foreign works, at that time in the public domain in the United States, were placed back under copyright protection. These works were from a number of countries, including Japan, Germany, and several Spanish-speaking countries, and titles varied from *Hipokuratesu-tachi* to *Echo der Heimat* to *Aguiluchos Mexicanos* (U.S. Copyright Office, Library of Congress, 1998). This change was made because these works were still under copyright in their own countries (Sinofsky, 2000). What this means for us as educators is that how much of an artwork we can copy, put on a website, blow up for bulletin boards, or include in a multimedia art project may depend on whether we are using a U.S. edition or another country's edition of the work. For more information on international copyright protection, see Chapter 5.

HOW DO YOU KNOW THAT AN ITEM IS
IN THE PUBLIC DOMAIN?

To determine whether an item is in the public domain, it is best to start by finding out when the item was first copyrighted—or in the case of new material being added to a later edition of a work, the publication date of the new material—and then figure it out based on copyright law. The easiest way to determine the first copyright date is to look for the oldest of the copyright dates listed on the work in question. Remember that copyright can be registered either from the date of publication or the date of creation. An easier approach is to look for a statement on the item in question or use the "Digital Copyright Slider" or a public domain flowchart (see previous examples in this chapter). If an item says that it is public domain material, it probably is. Nonetheless, be aware that *probably* is the operative word here since, hypothetically, it is possible to label a work in the public domain when it is still under copyright. For example, a clip-art website owner may have a statement at the beginning or end of his or her webpage stating that it is in the public domain. This means that you should be able to borrow any of the clip art from this site and use it in any manner that you wish. However, a site owner or administrator could feasibly take art from a copyrighted site and put it on his or her site without your knowledge. Thus, you could, in good faith, borrow a piece of copyrighted art from a site that supposedly was in the public domain. The best advice in cases like this is to make sure that the clip art you use is from a professional and legitimate site, for instance, a well-known and reputable software company.

HOW DO YOU MAKE SURE THAT WHAT
YOU ARE BORROWING IS REALLY
IN THE PUBLIC DOMAIN?

Since users or borrowers of works must often rely on media documentation that an item is in public domain, the best solution is to choose public domain material from reputable sites (Internet), publishing companies (books, articles, recordings, software, etc.), and vendors.

While public domain material cannot be "recopyrighted," except for certain foreign works as noted previously, it is possible to alter a public domain piece and create a derivative work. When this happens, as was discussed in this chapter, the pieces of the public domain work that were changed can be placed back under copyright protection. A work by Shakespeare can serve as an example. Shakespeare's works are in the public domain. However, an artist may illustrate a copy of *Hamlet* by sketching scenes from the play in the margins or drawing beautiful curlicue letters to begin each act. If this artist wishes, she or he can then sell this newly illustrated copy of *Hamlet,* copy it, or display it in public. In other words, since original work has been added to alter *Hamlet,* the artist now owns this particular version of the play and the copyright to it.

CONCLUSION

We are currently in an economic environment where education often does not have the money to support its many needs. At such times, teachers, librarians, and others who work with them become creative at getting more for less. In such cases, public domain materials may help, for with such materials educators may copy, create derivatives, and, in essence, use these works any way they want as they strive to teach their students and better support their curriculums. Last, a quick piece of advice: If a work does not state it is in the public domain, assume it has a copyright, unless it was published before 1923 or you have been able to find out otherwise from the owners of the work.

REFERENCES

Board of Trustees, Leland Stanford Junior University. 2006. "Copyright Renewal Database." Stanford University Libraries and Academic Information Resources. http://collections .stanford.edu/copyrightrenewals/bin/page?forward=home.

Brewer, Michael, and American Library Association Office for Information Technology Policy. 2007. "Digital Copyright Slider." American Library Association. http://www .librarycopyright.net/digitalslider/.

Bruwelheide, Janis H. 1995. *The Copyright Primer for Librarians and Educators.* 2nd ed. Chicago: American Library Association.

Butler, Rebecca P. 2001. "Public Domain: What It Is and How It Works." *Knowledge Quest* 29, no. 5 (May/June): 47–48.

Gasaway, Lolly. 2003. "When U.S. Works Pass into the Public Domain." Updated November 4. http://www.unc.edu/~unclng/public-d.htm.

Hirtle, Peter B. 2011. "Copyright Term and the Public Domain in the United States." Cornell University, Copyright Information Center. Updated January 3.http://www.copyright .cornell.edu/resources/publicdomain.cfm#Footnote_1.

Karjala, Dennis S. 2002. "Chart Showing Changes Made and the Degree of Harmonization Achieved and Disharmonization Exacerbated by the Sonny Bono Copyright Term Extension Act (CETA)." Teaching and Research Faculty Homepages, Arizona State University Sandra Day O'Connor College of Law. May 15. http://homepages.law.asu .edu/%7Edkarjala/OpposingCopyrightExtension/legmats/HarmonizationChart DSK.html.

Ockerbloom, John Mark. 2010. "The Online Books Page: Information About the Catalog of Copyright Entries." University of Pennsylvania Libraries. Accessed December 5. http://onlinebooks.library.upenn.edu/cce/.

Simpson, Carol. 2001. *Copyright for Schools: A Practical Guide.* 3rd ed. Worthington, OH: Linworth Publishing.

Sinofsky, Esther R. 2000. "The Privatization of Public Domain?" *TechTrends* 44, no. 2 (March): 11–13.

Sunstein Kann Murphy and Timbers LLP. 2002. "Flowchart for Determining When U.S. Copyrights in Fixed Works Expire." Sunstein: Winning Intellectual Property. http://www .sunsteinlaw.com/practices/copyright-portfolio-development/flowchart.htm.

Torrans, Lee Ann. 2003. *Law for K–12 Libraries and Librarians.* Westport, CT: Libraries Unlimited.

U.S. Copyright Office, Library of Congress. 1960. "21. The Catalog of Copyright Entries." U.S. Government Printing Office. http://www.copyright.gov/history/studies/study21 .pdf.

———. 1998. "List Identifying Copyrights Restored Under the Uruguay Round Agreements Acts for Which Notices of Intent to Enforce Restored Copyrights Were Files in the Copyright Office." Federal Register 63, no. 157 (August 14): 43830–32. Docket No. 97-3E. http://www.copyright.gov/fedreg/1998/63fr43830.html.

———. 2009. "Services of the Copyright Office." Revised August 5. http://www.copyright .gov/help/faq/faq-services.html#whoowns.

———. 2010a. "Copyright Law of the United States of America and Related Laws Contained in Title 17 of the *United States Code*, Circular 92, Chapter 3, Duration of Copyright."Library of Congress. http://www.copyright.gov/title17/92chap3.html.

———. 2010b. "Frequently Asked Questions about Copyright." Library of Congress. Revised September 21. http://www.copyright.gov/help/faq/.

———. 2010c. "Works Made for Hire Under the 1976 Copyright Act." Circular 9. Library of Congress. April. http://www.copyright.gov/circs/circ09.pdf.

CHAPTER 4

Obtaining Permission: How Can You Legally Obtain Use of Works?

INTRODUCTION

It has been a difficult day, and on top of that you are not feeling well. A physical education teacher who does not want to move may seem an oxymoron, but you are so tired. You hit upon the idea of using a popular music video game, *Dance Dance Revolution* (*DDR*) in class. The students love it because it is a video game with lots of sound and action, and you can stand back and let them compete with each other. You are not teaching them; you are letting them entertain themselves. Is it legal to use this game in such a manner?

Now, let's imagine that you, as the physical education teacher, have purchased a DVD of a popular entertainment movie that you would like to show to all classes in the school the afternoon before winter vacation. This is to be the students' reward for a semester of hard work on a Junior Olympics project. The principal has agreed to assemble the students in the auditorium for the showing of this movie, if you are able to obtain permission to use it in such a manner. The first thing you do is go to your school librarian, who tells you, since the movie is for entertainment rather than an instructional purpose, that you need to obtain the right to perform it in public before it can be shown in the auditorium.

Movies and Copyright

Movie owners' copyrights are limited in that movies (DVDs, CDs, videos, and digital formats) used for instructional purposes in nonprofit educational institutions can be displayed without infringement (U.S. Copyright Office, Library of Congress, 2010). This means that whether you purchased the movie from a discount store or an educational company, whether it is marked "For Home Use Only" or not, if it is for use in a teaching situation, you may use it without obtaining the permission of the movie's copyright holder. However, if you are using it for entertainment or reward, permission is needed. For more information on movies and copyright, see Chapter 7.

In both of these cases, you may need permission to use the item in the manner described. A question to ask is: Did you obtain such rights when you purchased or borrowed the item? This chapter will look at how to obtain permission from the author or owner of a work, which is the ideal way of making sure that you are following the law.

OBTAINING PERMISSION

Sometimes the owner of a work will state up front in the work that permission is being given to a user for certain rights. One example of this is from the Digital Copyright Slider created by Michael Brewer and the American Library Association Office for Information Technology Policy (2007). The main page of this Internet site sends the would-be user to a Creative Commons (2011) license called Attribution-NonCommercial-ShareAlike 3.0 Unported, which informs you exactly what rights you have to the Digital Copyright Slider. In this case, the user is given the rights "to copy, distribute and transmit the work . . . to adapt the work . . . Under the following conditions: Attribution—You must attribute the work in the manner specified by the author or licensor (but not in any way that suggests that they endorse you or your use of the work). Noncommercial— You may not use this work for commercial purposes . Share Alike—If you alter, transform, or build upon this work, you may distribute the resulting work only under the same or similar license to this one" (Creative Commons, 2011). Another example can be found in Kembrew McLeod's book, *Freedom of Expression.* McLeod, the author and copyright holder, states, "I thoroughly approve if you copy this book for noncommercial uses" (2005: 10). A third case in point is "The Code of Best Practices in Fair Use for Media Literacy Education": "Feel free to reproduce this work in its entirety. For excerpts and quotations, depend upon fair use" (Center for Social Media, 2011).

In such cases as these three, the would-be user simply follows the copyright owner's specifications. But what happens when the owner has not placed any usage agreements, other than a copyright notice, on the product? In those situations, you would ask for the rights that you need from the owner or purchase a license to use or copy the work. (How to find copyright owners and clearinghouses for copyrighted works will be addressed later in this chapter.) Remember that the copyright owner has the right to give, sell, or refuse your request to use the work.

PERMISSION REQUESTS

It is always best to put requests in writing so that you have a record of the permission criteria, should any disagreements occur between you and the copyright owner or clearinghouse. If that is not possible, then take notes on your conversation with the copyright owner or clearinghouse and keep these on file for future reference. Once you have found the owner of the work, information that should be included in the permission request is as follows:

1. Identify what it is that you want permission to use by author, title, format, and other identifiers.
2. Determine what kind of permission you need; that is, how, where, how many times, and how long are you going to use this item. (For example, given your movie question, you need permission to show the DVD one time, in an auditorium, for the entire school population.)

Remember to request permission as early as possible. There is no time limit to replies, and just because you do not hear from an owner does not mean that she or he has tacitly agreed that you may use the works. Thus, you may find that you need to follow up on permission requests or contact another source if you discover that the organization you originally contacted is not the owner. In addition, if the owner's reply is refusal of permission, you now have some time to find a substitute item.

WHAT IS A LICENSE?

A license provides the user with the rights of the work that have been obtained from the owner or an organization representing the owner. For example, the American Society of Composers, Authors, and Publishers (ASCAP), which functions as a clearinghouse representing a large number of those who compose, write, and publish music, "licenses the right to perform songs and musical works created and owned by the songwriters, composers, lyricists and music publishers who are ASCAP members and also those members of foreign performing rights organizations who are represented by ASCAP in the United States" (ASCAP, 2010b). To get back to the movie question from the beginning of this chapter, a group that might help you resolve your DVD use question would be the Motion Picture Licensing Corporation (MPLC) at http://www.mplc.com/, which can provide the user with "a reasonably priced facility-based license which allows any organization to publicly perform Videos produced by MPLC's Member Licensors" (MPLC, 2010). This means the MPLC might be able to offer you the ability to use a movie you have rented from a local video store or purchased from a commercial establishment in a public performance, such as for your Junior Olympics reward day.

GIVE CREDIT WHERE CREDIT IS DUE

Payment is not necessarily required for permission. The owner or author may want nothing more than to be recognized for his or her work. Thus, always give credit to the copyright owner(s) in a reference or citation section at either the beginning or end of the use or presentation of the work and follow any stipulations for the format of the citation. Remember, however, that such citing does not replace the need to acquire permission. Also, you should be aware that while technically payment is not required for permission, it is possible that the work's owners will request that you pay a fee or purchase a license before you are allowed to use the work.

PERMISSION LETTER

For the purposes of this exercise, assume you are requesting clearance to use a DVD for a public showing. Formats other than movies may require different criteria and are discussed later in this chapter. It's important to be sure your criteria match the format and type of request that you are using or need. Sample general information includes the following:

- Author, title, format
- Type of permission you are asking for (how often you will use the work, length of time of use, number of copies needed, intended audience, and whether you will be charging your audience for use of the work)
- Your name, address, phone and fax numbers, e-mail
- Your signature
- A place for the copyright holder's signature

The following format information should also be included in a letter requesting appropriate permission.

Print
   ○ Volume number
   ○ Edition
   ○ ISBN (book) or ISSN (magazine) number
   ○ Editor, compiler, or translator
   ○ Publisher
   ○ Place of publication
   ○ Copyright date
   ○ Page, figure, table, or illustration identifiers
   ○ A copy of what you want to borrow
Nonprint
   ○ How the borrowed item will be used (multimedia project, online class, etc.)
   ○ Distributor
   ○ Where you plan to use or market your creation
   ○ Expected date of publication or use (if appropriate)
   ○ Copyright date
   ○ URL, site manager, name of site (if part or all of a website)
   ○ Footage amount (if a video, DVD, or television program)

You may also add a date by which you would like to hear back from the copyright owners. While they do not need to comply with your request, it may be an incentive to their granting permission information more quickly. In addition, you may wish to ask them to provide you with the correct copyright owner, if you have sent your permission request to the wrong place. It is also important to thank those from whom you are requesting permission for their time and effort in providing you with the use of their copyrighted item(s).

Remember that the more complete the information is that you include in your request, the quicker the response time may be (Crews, 2006). Send the request-for-permission letter to the copyright owner, clearance center, distributor, or publisher of the work(s). Including a self-addressed stamped envelope (SASE) may speed up response time.

Make sure that the permission is both sent and received either in a letter, fax, or e-mail form. It is imperative that you have a written record of all copyright permissions granted. This way no one can come back at a later date and say "I did not say that" or "That's not what I meant."

The Sample Request for Permission sidebar shows an example of a letter that you might use for the DVD/movie question previously discussed.

Sample Request for Permission

Your name and address [letterhead]

Date

Name and address of copyright owner or publisher

Dear [_____],

I would like to request permission to show the DVD [citation: including such things as title, copyright date, distributor, publisher] to the students of [_____ High School] on [date] in the high school auditorium. This will be a one-time showing. The purpose of this showing is to reward the students of my school for their participation in our Junior Olympics program. If you are willing to grant this permission, would you please sign this letter below and return to me by [date] or as soon as possible? Also, if I should be contacting someone other than you for this request, could you provide me with the name and address of the party to contact? I have included a SASE for your use. Thank you for considering my request.

Sincerely,
[Your name]

PERMISSION GIVEN FOR [_____] TO USE MY DVD, [title], ON [date specified above].

DATE: _____

SIGNATURE: _____

(Bellingham Public Schools, 2003; Crews, 2006)

CLEARINGHOUSES AND OTHER ORGANIZATIONS

If you are unable to find the owners or authors, where do you send your request for permission to use or copy their works? You can approach the publisher of the work for contact information. You can also go to an organization such as an agency or royalty house, company, or clearinghouse that specializes in helping users obtain copyright clearance. Such a group, usually for a fee, will work with you to obtain the proper clearance or license that is needed. The type of work that you need permission to use or copy determines where you go to find permission or further information. Note that clearinghouse fees typically depend on the nature of the use the borrower requests. The following sections discuss some of the organizations that may be able to grant permissions.

Cartoons, Columns, and Editorial Features

Featured in this section are two organizations illustrative of those that provide permission, in the form of contracts and licenses, for the use of such works as editorial and political cartoons, featured columns, and other editorial features.

- United Media: http://unitedfeatures.com
  For those users who want to place a published cartoon or editorial feature on a webpage, in a multimedia production, etc., United Media can provide permission and fee information.
- Universal Uclick: http://universaluclick.com
  This organization operates in a similar manner as United Media, allowing users to select and purchase lifestyle and opinion columns for inclusion in new creations/productions.

DVDs, CDs, and Video

Yes, there are times when you *can* use motion pictures legally in the school! Either follow the copyright law for classroom works, which is covered in Section 110 (1) of U.S. Copyright Law, or look to a movie clearinghouse for permission.

- Motion Picture Licensing Corporation (MPLC): http://www.mplc.org/page/umbrella-license-andreg
  "...who has the time or the budget to track down the copyright owner of each title, and report the dates and times for each exhibition? The MPLC has solved this problem with the Umbrella License®" (MPLC, 2010).
- Movie Licensing USA: K–12 Schools: http://www.movlic.com/k12/license.html
  With this company's Public Performance Site License, you can legally show entertainment films in your school for reward, recess, holidays, assemblies, activities, because you need a break from the students—whatever!

Images

An online search will result in a variety of image clearinghouses, many specializing in a particular kind of imagery, such as wildlife, space shuttle imagery/aerial photography, history, and more. The two sites listed in this section are good examples of such image use.

- Illinois Historical Aerial Photography 1938–1941: http://www.isgs.uiuc.edu/nsdihome/webdocs/ilhap/

Aerial photographs of Illinois from 1938–1941, many of them digitized, are available free of charge from this website, which is part of the Illinois Natural Resources Geospatial Data Clearinghouse (2007).

- Mira: http://www.mira.com

  Through Mira, online users may view stock photographs/images from a photographers' cooperative called the Creative Eye and obtain permission to use/publish them.

Music

For the purposes of this chapter, various music clearinghouses are grouped together. According to DigiLaw Publishing, which is a part of WeblawResources.com:

> There are three aspects of musical works that must be separately considered under the copyright laws. The first aspect is the sound recording itself. The sound recording embodies the actual sound of the music. The second is the visual transcription of the words and music involved in the musical work (the lyrics and sheet music). The third aspect is musical sound that is part of a motion picture or audiovisual work. (DigiLaw Publishing, 2008)

Therefore, there is a lot to consider when looking at music, such as:

1. the format on which the music is recorded (CD, other audio files, digitized materials for use with electronic devices such as iPods and MP3 players, etc.);
2. the originally written sheet music and lyrics; and
3. the musical performance or broadcasts.

With these three aspects of musical works come a variety of licensing rights, among them:

1. mechanical rights, or the "permissions granted to mechanically reproduce music onto some type of media (e.g., cassette tape, CD, etc.) for public distribution";
2. "print rights...based on sales of printed sheet music";
3. "performance rights, which "allows music to be performed live or broadcast"; and
4. "synchronization rights...needed for a song to be reproduced onto a television program, film, video, commercial, radio, or even an 800 number phone message. This type is so named because you are 'synchronizing' the composition, as it is performed on the audio recording, to a film, TV commercial, or spoken voice-over" (HowStuffWorks, 2010).

Chapter 5, "Further Important Copyright Subjects: What Other Copyright Issues Do You Need to Understand?," and Chapter 10, "Music/Audio and Copyright Law: Who Will Know If You Copy It?," offer more discussion on licensing.

The following list provides information about several music clearinghouses:

- American Society of Composers, Authors, and Publishers (ASCAP): http://www.ascap.com

"ASCAP protects the rights of its members by licensing and distributing royalties for the non-dramatic public performances of their copyrighted works. ASCAP's licensees encompass all who want to perform copyrighted music publicly. ASCAP makes giving and obtaining permission to perform music simple for both creators and users of music" (American Society of Composers, Authors, and Publishers, 2010a).

- Broadcast Music, Inc. (BMI): http://bmi.com/index.php
  BMI represents over 400,000 songwriters, composers, and music publishers and over 6.5 million works in all styles of music. "BMI issues licenses to various users of music, including television and radio stations and networks; new media, including Internet services and websites" (Broadcast Music, Inc., 2010).
- Harry Fox Agency (HFA): http://www.harryfox.com/index.jsp
  "HFA licenses the largest percentage of the mechanical and digital uses of music in the United States on CDs, digital services, records, tapes and imported phonorecords" (Harry Fox Agency, 2010).
- SESAC, Inc.: http://www.sesac.com/
  SESAC is a "performing rights organization ... designed to represent songwriters and publishers and their right to be compensated for having their music performed in public" (SESAC, 2010). SESAC is similar to ASCAP and BMI.

Print

Publishing companies often serve as a sort of clearinghouse for print materials. That said, the following agencies also address this issue:

- Authors' Licensing and Collecting Society (ALCS): http://www.alcs.co.uk/
  This British group's Copyright Licensing Agency (CLA) "licenses organisations to copy from magazines, books, journals and digital publications on behalf of authors, publishers and visual creators" in order to "permit the photocopying, scanning and digital copying of limited parts from these publications without having to seek permission from the copyright owner each time" (ALCS, 2010).
- Publications Rights Clearinghouse (PRC): https://nwu.org/publications-rights-clearinghouse
  Part of the National Writers Union, the PRC "is a collective licensing agency for writers. It collects royalties on behalf of writers from publishers with whom it has agreements for distributing such royalties.... Writers give the PRC permission to act as their agent in licensing secondary rights to their previously published articles" (National Writers Union, 2010).

Religious Media

Remember that even religious groups can infringe on copyright ownership. Thus, using a religious clearinghouse can be important.

- Christian Copyright Licensing International (CCLI): http://www.ccli.com
Christian Copyright Licensing International (2010) is an example of an organization that provides religious groups with licenses for congregational music and videos used in church services and worship-related settings.

Theatrical Performances

Please note that school play clearinghouses may charge licensing fees based on such factors as the planned number of performances, the performance dates, the number of script copies needed, and sometimes even the number of rehearsals. Two examples of such clearinghouses follow:

- Musical Theatre International (MTI): http://www.mtishows.com/
MTI offers online applications to obtain licenses for many musicals, including those for both professional and amateur performances.
- Theatrefolk: School Plays Now: http://www.theatrefolk.com/
This Canadian company provides schools—including elementary, middle, and high schools—with original plays created by the company's owners. In addition, this organization features a Script Bank, which is touted as "a revolutionary new concept in play licensing... An inexpensive license giving unlimited access to one-act plays. The license fee **includes scripts and royalties**" (Theatrefolk: School Plays Now, 2010; boldface in the original).

Other Types of Media

There are clearinghouses for many media formats. If you cannot find what you are looking for, it may be time to pursue help from a more general clearinghouse.

- Copyright Clearance Center (CCC): http://www.copyright.com
This well-known copyright clearinghouse provides licensing agreements for a wide variety of both print and nonprint and electronic (digital and analog) works. The CCC can also help users locate hard-to-find or unregistered copyright holders. While the CCC maintains information and materials that may be of interest to those in the K–12 schools, it focuses on serving such groups as higher education, the business world, as well as authors and publishers (CCC, 2010).
- U.S. Copyright Office: http://www.copyright.gov/forms/search_estimate.html
"For a fee of $165 per hour or fraction thereof (2 hour minimum)" the U.S. Copyright Office will search its records to find permission information/ whether or not "a work is under copyright protection" (U.S. Copyright Office, Library of Congress, 2009).

CONCLUSION

When requesting permission for a work, obtain your license or user/borrower agreement in writing, and be sure to follow all stipulations of the agreement. In addition, keep in mind that you can always ask your school librarian for help.

Please note that much of Chapter 4 is based on the content of six published articles by Rebecca P. Butler (2001, 2002a, 2002b, 2006, 2007a, 2007b) that deal with obtaining copyright permissions.

REFERENCES

American Society of Composers, Authors, and Publishers (ASCAP). 2010a. "About ASCAP." http://www.ascap.com/about/.

———. 2010b. "Customer Licensees." http://www.ascap.com/licensing/.

Authors' Licensing and Collecting Society (ALCS). 2010. "Copyright Licensing Agency." Accessed June 8. http://www.alcs.co.uk/About-us/Who-we-work-with/Copyright-Licensing-Agency-(1).aspx.

Bellingham Public Schools. 2003. "Copyright Permission Letter." Bellingham Public Schools. http://bellinghamschools.org/sites/default/files/COPYPERM.HTM.

Brewer, Michael, and the American Library Association Office for Information Technology Policy. 2007. "Digital Copyright Slider." American Library Association. http://www.librarycopyright.net/digitalslider/.

Broadcast Music, Inc. (BMI). 2010. "About BMI." http://bmi.com/about/entry/538061.

Butler, Rebecca P. 2001. "Obtaining Permission to Copy or Perform a Work, Part I." *Knowledge Quest* 30, no. 2 (November/December): 43–44.

———. 2002a. "Obtaining Permission to Copy or Perform a Work, Part II." *Knowledge Quest* 30, no. 3 (January/February): 32–33.

———. 2002b. "Obtaining Permission to Copy or Perform a Work, Part III." *Knowledge Quest* 30, no. 4 (March/April): 45–46.

———. 2006. "Obtaining Permission to Copy or Perform a Work, Part I, Revised 2006." *Knowledge Quest* 35, no. 2 (November/December): 56–58.

———. 2007a. "Obtaining Permission to Copy or Perform a Work, Part II, Revised 2006." *Knowledge Quest* 35, no. 3 (January/February): 48–49.

———. 2007b. "Obtaining Permission to Copy or Perform a Work, Part III, Revised 2006." *Knowledge Quest* 35, no. 5 (May/June): 62–64.

Center for Social Media. 2011. "The Code of Best Practices in Fair Use for Media Literacy Education." Center for Social Media, American University. http://www.centerforsocialmedia.org/fair-use/related-materials/codes/code-best-practices-fair-use-media-literacy-education.

Christian Copyright Licensing International (CCLI). 2010. "What We Offer: Our Licenses and Services." http://www.ccli.com/WhatWeOffer/.

Copyright Clearance Center (CCC). 2010. Homepage. http://www.copyright.com.

Creative Commons. 2011. "Attribution-NonCommercial-ShareAlike 3.0 Unported (CC BY-NC-SA 3.0)." Accessed March 3. http://creativecommons.org/licenses/by-nc-sa/3.0/.

Crews, Kenneth D. 2006. *Copyright Law for Librarians and Educators: Creative Strategies and Practical Solutions.* Chicago: American Library Association.

DigiLaw Publishing. 2008. "Copyrighting Music." WeblawResources.com. http://www.weblawresources.com/Copyright/copyrighting_music.htm.

Harry Fox Agency (HFA). 2010. "About HFA." http://www.harryfox.com/public/AboutHFA.jsp.

HowStuffWorks. 2010. "How Music Royalties Work." Discovery Communications. http://entertainment.howstuffworks.com/music-royalties4.htm.

Illinois Natural Resources Geospatial Data Clearinghouse. 2007. "Illinois Historical Aerial Photography 1938–1941." University of Illinois at Urbana-Champaign. http://www .isgs.uiuc.edu/nsdihome/webdocs/ilhap/.

McLeod, Kembrew. 2005. *Freedom of Expression: Overzealous Copyright Bozos and Other Enemies of Creativity.* New York: Doubleday.

Mira. 2010. "About Mira Images." Creative Eye: An Artists' Cooperative. Accessed June 8. http://library.mira.com/c/miraimages/about.

Motion Picture Licensing Corporation. 2010. "Umbrella License." Motion Picture Licensing Corporation. http://www.mplc.org/page/umbrella-license-andreg.

Movie Licensing USA: K–12 Schools. 2010. "Annual Site License." Movie Licensing USA. Accessed June 8. http://www.movlic.com/k12/license.html.

National Writers Union. 2010. "Publications Rights Clearinghouse." National Writers Union. Accessed June 8. https://nwu.org/publications-rights-clearinghouse.

SESAC. 2010. "About SESAC." SESAC. Accessed June 8. http://www.sesac.com/About/ About.aspx.

Theatrefolk: School Plays Now. 2010. "Welcome to the Script Bank." Theatrefolk: Original Playscripts. http://www.theatrefolk.com/scriptbank.

United Media. 2009. "United Media: United Feature Syndicate/Newspaper Enterprise Association." United Feature Syndicate. http://unitedfeatures.com.

Universal Uclick. 2010. "Welcome to the New Universal Uclick Website." Universal Uclick, an Andrews McMeel Universal Company. http://universaluclick.com.

U.S. Copyright Office, Library of Congress. 2009. "Search Request Estimate." U.S. Copyright Office. http://www.copyright.gov/forms/search_estimate.html.

———. 2010. U.S. Copyright Law, Section 110(1). U.S. Copyright Office. Accessed December 5. http://www.copyright.gov/title17/92chap1.html#110.

CHAPTER 5

Further Important Copyright Subjects: What Other Copyright Issues Do You Need to Understand?

INTRODUCTION

This chapter identifies a number of topics concerning or related to copyright, and defines and discusses them in a general manner. These subjects include licensing, interlibrary loan, selected areas of U.S. and state law, international treaties and organizations, future legislation, infringements and penalties, and plagiarism. Some of these subjects are also covered in subsequent chapters. Other topics are covered only in this chapter, where they are discussed in order to provide a greater context in which to place the copyright conversation.

DOCUMENTATION AND LICENSES

Documentation

The term *documentation* is used here to mean those informational and identifying records that each work possesses. As such, the documentation is, at least partially, that information usually found in the reference section of a work. The examples used here are a print item, a web item, and a piece of computer software. First, look at a book or a print item. The documentation for a book includes the author, title, copyright date, place of publication, publisher, and any special permissions that the copyright owner is willing to give the book owner or reader. Second, take a look at the Internet. Documentation for a website can vary somewhat from that for a print piece. It may also include the author, title, copyright date, place of publication, and publisher. In addition, it may include an e-mail link to the webmaster or moderator of the site, the point of access to the site (URL), the date the site was last reorganized, agreements with which site users must abide, etc. The third example is computer software. Software documentation also includes such basic things as author/creator, title, copyright date, publisher, and place of publication. It usually also includes a copy of the contractual agreement (license—see below) between the purchaser of the software and the software seller. It is always best to read the documentation of any work from which you plan to borrow before doing any copying.

Licenses

"A license is a physical or virtual document between two or more parties that allows an intellectual resource owned by one party (the licensor), to be used by another or multiple other parties (the licensees) for a fixed duration of time" (Rupp-Serrano, 2005: 178). Licenses, which are legally binding contracts, are very important in the world of copyright. For users, they define the ways that a protected (copyrighted) work can be used. The owner of the copyright uses the license to delineate which exclusive rights in a work are granted to others for their use. Keep in mind that the rights granted to the user are limited and nonexclusive, and they extend to use of the work for specified purposes only. Normally licenses for works are automatically purchased with computer software, sheet music, and theater scripts; as part of database documentation; in the rental of DVDs; etc. One example would be computer software, where there are three common types of licenses: shrink-wrap, click-wrap, and browse-wrap. Shrink-wrap licenses are called such because they are located in the packaging along with the software. Upon opening the plastic wrapping, the consumer is assumed to have agreed to the license—whether or not he or she has read it. With click-wrap licensing, the consumer has a chance to read the license online before installation and before agreeing or not agreeing (through a mouse click) to the license. The third type of computer license, browse-wrap, is similar to the click-wrap license in that both are found online. However, with the browse-wrap license, the user must go to a site identified online in order to obtain and read the license (Chilling Effects Clearinghouse, 2010). The browse-wrap license itself is not found "on the screen and the user is not compelled to accept or reject the terms as a condition of proceeding with further computer operations. Instead, a browsewrap agreement appears only as a hyperlink that is accessed by clicking on the link. It is optional, not required" (Kunkel, 2002). Thus, a user quickly moving through a site might not even realize that he or she has agreed to a contract via the browse-wrap license.

Essentially, licenses are a part of the package that buyers purchase in conjunction with most works. Licensing information is most often located near the front or beginning of a work's documentation. It is usually in fine print, and often online it can be something that the user can quickly click through. Be sure to read this fine print before you click through or accept. You may be signing away rights that you need—or it is also possible that the license provides rights that you would like to use, of which you would be unaware if the license goes unread.

Suppose, for example, that your school purchases the license to place electronic publishing software on the computers in the English lab. The license is for 30 computers. If there are 31 computers in the lab, then legally either one computer may not have the software on its hard drive or no more than 30 computers at a time may use the software, even if it is loaded on all 31 computers. Such actions depend on the contract between the purchaser and the seller.

Take a further example: You, a biology teacher, bring the class to the library for research on a genetics unit. The librarian informs you that the school has purchased two database licenses from companies dealing in high school science. One database focuses on plant and animal genetics. With that particular license, your students may search the database and print as many copies as they want of full-text articles on genetics. The second database also covers works focusing on plant and animal genetics. However, that license allows users to print only one copy of any full-text article, without permission from the publisher. In each case, you need to follow the license directions. Even though the databases may be similar in format and subject areas, their licenses are not necessarily the same.

As still another example, let's suppose that you would like to use a particular movie in your biology class. You feel that it will illustrate, in an understandable manner, some of the influences of genetics research. When you sign the form at the video rental store, you have essentially signed a license, or contract, and must abide by it. The form may be as simple as saying when the video must be returned. It could also include penalties for destroying or losing the video, returning it late, etc.

Remember, a license is contract law, not copyright law. If you are dealing with both a license and copyrighted material, follow the licensing or contractual requirements. This works because when you obtain a license—a contract—to use a copyrighted work, you are essentially contracting to use certain copyrights afforded that work.

In addition to contracts/contract law, the past few years have found creators of works with another choice—that of creating their own software licenses, which is addressed in the next three sections.

Open-Source Software Licenses

Open sourcing means that the software in question is free to be used and modified in any number of ways. This means that derivative works may be made without asking for permission from the copyright owner. Open sourcing, as a consequence, is more like a contract than part of copyright law. Thus, concerning the licensing of open-source software:

1. distribution is free (no royalties or other fees);
2. the software source code must be available or accessible via the Internet in a form usable by computer programmers;
3. the license must allow derivatives and modifications to the software as well as distribution of the modified work(s) under the same license as that of the original work;
4. the license can, at times, restrict source code modification, if "patch files" are acquired at build time;
5. the license cannot discriminate against any person or group;

6. the license cannot restrict the use of the software in a particular field;
7. program rights must apply to all who wish to use the software;
8. the license cannot be specific to a particular artifact;
9. no restrictions can be placed on other software that is distributed with the open-sourced software; and
10. the open-source license must be technology-neutral (Open Source Initiative, 2010).

Creative Commons

Creative Commons is a nonprofit organization that has developed a number of standardized copyright licenses that works' owners may use when licensing their creations. These copyright licenses have been written in such ways as to allow the works' owners to determine how others may use the works. As *The Chicago Manual of Style*, 16th Edition, states, a "Creative Commons license throws any work subject to it open to public use of all kinds" (University of Chicago Press, 2010: 178). While this sounds confusing, it means that a public library consortium which develops a handbook on teen literacy may assign a Creative Commons license stating that K–12 schools can take said handbook and modify it to fit their own particular needs. (Under U.S. Copyright Law, such a modification could be a derivative work and a copyright infringement.) As Creative Commons states, their licenses define "the spectrum of possibilities between full copyright and the public domain. From all rights reserved to no rights reserved. Our licenses help you keep your copyright while allowing certain uses of your work—a 'some rights reserved' copyright" (Creative Commons, 2010).

An example of a book published in pdf format that has been released under a Creative Commons license is Marcus Boon's *In Praise of Copying* (Doctorow, 2010), a publication of Harvard University Press.

GNU

The Free Software Foundation feels that all software should be free to use and modify, with free licenses. With this in mind, the organization often uses the GNU General Public License (GPL), which states the following:

Nobody should be restricted by the software they use. There are four freedoms that every user should have:

- the freedom to use the software for any purpose,
- the freedom to change the software to suit your needs,
- the freedom to share the software with your friends and neighbors, and
- the freedom to share the changes you make.

When a program offers users all of these freedoms, we call it free software. Developers who write software can release it under the terms of the GNU GPL. When they do, it will be free software and stay free software, no matter who changes or distributes the program. We call this copyleft: the software is copyrighted, but instead of using those rights to restrict users like proprietary software does, we use them to ensure that every user has freedom. (Smith, 2007)

Using GNU, this means that the third-grade teacher who develops a computer program on volcanoes on her own time and using her own computer and software, can choose to assign the newly developed program—instead of following copyright law—a GNU General Public License. Such a license would thereby guarantee future users the ability to use the volcano software any way they wanted, change it, and share the software and changes with others.

For the curious, "The name 'GNU' is a recursive acronym for 'GNU's Not Unix!';—it is pronounced g-noo, as one syllable with no vowel sound between the g and the n" (Free Software Foundation, 2010).

INTERLIBRARY LOAN

Like much of copyright law, those parts of the law that deal with interlibrary loan (ILL) can be very confusing. ILL, the borrowing of an item for use by another library, school, system, or individual who does not own that item, is a common occurrence in public and academic libraries. For K–12 school environments, ILL is an important way to obtain information not easily acquired by purchase. Usually ILL materials are those that a particular school cannot afford or does not often need. If ILL is not available in your school, you can usually go to your local public library and request this service.

In our swiftly evolving technological world, ILL has hit a new high—no longer do libraries need to send original items to their requestors via snail mail or paper copy. Now—with the help of scanners and the Internet—a copy of a requested material can be sent digitally. In its original purpose ILL was about distributing material, not copying it. Digital ILL is concerned with both. Herein lies the rub. Using the Internet, you obtain speed, easy access, and . . . possibly more copies than copyright law allows: the original paper copy (at the owner's library); the scanned copy (on the hard drive of a computer in the owner's library); the copy on the receiving library's hard drive; the digitized copy, which the requestor receives via the Internet; the copy that the requestor prints out for ease of use; and possibly more. Now, instead of two copies, there is a minimum of four or five. When a library purchases an item, it usually purchases only that item, not the ability to make unlimited copies. Thus, while it is possible for the library to lend out its own copy, the creation of other copies may violate the agreement of the original item's purchase.

How do you get around this thorny issue and still have access to information and materials in a quick and easy manner? Take an article out of an obscure sports magazine as an example. Instead of borrowing the item via ILL, you could purchase the magazine issue in which the article is found, get a subscription to that magazine, or pay a fee to the copyright owner to have it copied. However, ILL is still a viable alternative. If you only want to borrow a copy, perhaps the lending library can send you the original. If borrowing it in a digital format is the best option available, you can encourage the lending library to immediately erase the scanned copy from its computer hard drive once the article has been sent. Upon receipt of the item, immediately print out a copy—or send it electronically to your requesting patron along with a statement that only he or she can use the item and must not share it with others—and erase the digitally received version from your hard drive. Libraries may also have licenses to post articles on the web or use specific databases. Sometimes, ILL can occur by accessing these sites through URLs.

It is important to mention the National Commission on New Technological Uses of Copyright Works (CONTU) Guidelines at this point, given the sports article example. Under Section 108(g)(2) of the U.S. Copyright Law of 1976, which is the part of the law covering "reproduction by libraries and archives," the lender is not allowed to send more than one copy of one article from a periodical issue. If more are sent, then the borrower must pay copyright fees. The CONTU Guidelines interpret Section 108(g)(2) and help librarians, copyright owners, and other interested parties in "understanding the amount of photocopying for use in interlibrary loan arrangements permitted under the copyright law" (CONTU, 1978). If a library chooses to adhere to the CONTU Guidelines, borrowers may not receive more than five copies in one year from a single journal title published within the last five years. While the guidelines do not address nonjournal publications or material that is older than five years, they do give both the lenders (libraries and archives) and the borrowers some direction. An intended purpose of these guidelines is to discourage the use of ILL as a substitute for magazine subscriptions. In addition, when material is requested from a digital medium, licensing (see the previous Licenses section in this chapter) may be involved (Copyright Clearance Center, 2005).

Probably your easiest way to obtain an item via ILL is to go to your school librarian and ask for help. She or he has usually been trained in such areas of intellectual property access and can help you obtain what you need, in a timely manner, with a minimum of copyright fuss.

STATUTORY EXEMPTIONS

There are many statutory exemptions in U.S. Copyright Law. Located in Sections 107 through 122 of Title 17 of the U.S. Code (2010), not all of them directly affect teachers, librarians, and other school personnel. Nonetheless, there are some very important exemptions that do affect those directly and indirectly involved in K–12 education. First, though, it is helpful to define exactly what a statutory exemption is.

Definition

Statutory exemptions are written into the copyright law to provide some ways to use others' works without infringing on an owner's copyright and without needing to obtain permission to use a work. For example, fair use (see Chapter 2) is a very important exemption, one that educators should definitely apply. Basically, with fair use, U.S. Congress tells us that there are certain ways that copyright-protected works can be used for educational or research purposes while still protecting the owner's rights. There are other exemptions as well that are important to those in the K–12 environment, for example, exemption of certain performances and displays and reproduction by libraries and archives.

The Classroom Exemption: Limitations on Exclusive Rights: Exemption of Certain Performances and Displays

In addition to fair use, another example of a statutory exemption of importance to teachers and librarians is the classroom exemption. According to U.S. Copyright Law Section 110 (1 and 2) of the 1976 U.S. Code, "Limitations on Exclusive Rights: Exemption of Certain Performances and Displays," covers exemptions in educational classroom settings and provides for the use of lawfully obtained copyrighted works in face-to-face instruction as well as in transmissions (distance education), under certain parameters. Use of the copyrighted works (all points below apply) must be:

- in a nonprofit educational institution;
- in a classroom or similar place of instruction;
- a performance or display that is a regular part of systematic instruction;
- a performance or display directly related to the teaching content; and/or
- for persons who are disabled or in special circumstances which otherwise prevent them from attending class. (U.S. Copyright Law, 1976: Sect. 110)

The TEACH Act of 2002 amends Section 110(2) by adding films and other dramatic works to the exemption, and also by redefining the terms of use by nonprofit educational institutions of copyrighted materials in distance education, including web courses (Crews, 2006). However, you and your school must abide by all of the TEACH Act's requirements in order to use this additional exemption. (See more on the TEACH Act in Chapter 13, "Distance Education and Copyright Law.")

Thus, under this exemption, a science teacher may play a recording of bird songs to his class (face to face or via a distance-education format) before the class goes on a field trip to a prairie restoration area so that the students can recognize sounds of birds of the prairie.

The Handicap Exemption

The handicap exemption is actually part of "The Classroom Exemption: Limitations on Exclusive Rights: Exemption of Certain Performances and Displays."

The Library Exemption: Limitations on Exclusive Rights: Reproduction by Libraries and Archives

Another important statutory exemption for K–12 educators is found in Section 108 of the 1976 copyright law. Section 108 talks about exemptions that are afforded libraries (for our purposes, school libraries and media centers) to copy works without violating copyright law. Section 108 provides that libraries may, within certain limits, make copies for preservation purposes, for private study, and for ILL. In order to do so, however, they must meet several requirements (all apply). These include:

- being open to the public or outside researchers,
- making copies that have no direct or indirect commercial advantage, and
- including a copyright notice on each copy made (or a statement that the work may be copyright-protected, if there is no copyright notice on the original). In most cases, the library can make only single copies. However, up to three copies can be made for purposes of:
  - preservation and security;
  - replacement of a lost, stolen, deteriorating, or damaged item; and
  - changing the format of an obsolete work to one that can be used in the library (including if the machine on which the format is played is obsolete) or an "unused replacement" is unavailable at a fair price. (U.S. Copyright Law, 1976)

In addition, there are some limits under this exemption as to what libraries may and may not copy. While almost anything may be copied for preservation purposes, for purposes of ILL, or a researcher's needs, libraries may not copy the following types of works: audiovisual works, including motion pictures; musical works; and works such as pictures, graphs, and sculptures (U.S. Copyright Law, 1976: Sec. 108). This means that libraries may copy for researchers or ILL "other types of works that are not specifically excluded [from previous list] ... audiovisual works 'dealing with news' ... pictures and graphics 'published as illustrations, diagrams, or similar adjuncts' to works that may otherwise be copied. In other words, if you can copy the article, you can also copy the picture or chart that is in the article" (Crews, 2006: 76). These statutory exemptions are discussed in more detail in other parts of this book, where they affect copyright use of a certain work.

In March 2008, a group of copyright experts who called themselves the Section 108 Study Group first convened to address issues concerning the library exemption and possible amendments in light of digital works and other technological advancements. While the outcome of this group is a 212-page report, as of yet no governmental action has been taken. The study group "entrusts to the Copyright Office the task of proposing draft legislation" (U.S. Copyright Office and the National Digital Information Infrastructure and Preservation Program of the Library of Congress, 2008). Because action in this arena is possible, please be aware that the library exemption may be amended at some point in time.

COPYING GUIDELINES

Many guidelines are available for educators who need information on copyright. Usually created by various interest groups, these guidelines are not legal precedent, but they can be helpful when trying to abide by copyright law. Classroom guidelines include those for:

- books and periodicals,
- music,
- off-air recordings,
- digital imaging,
- distance learning, and
- multimedia (see Chapter 2).

Classroom guidelines are flexible; they provide a conservative definition for the use of works, not the maximum that the law permits. You actually could, in good faith, use more of a work than those moderate amounts suggest without infringing on the owners' copyright. Unfortunately, the maximum use is not clearly defined in copyright law. Therefore, be aware, the further beyond the guidelines that you borrow from a work, the greater your chance of copyright infringement. If teachers and librarians follow the guidelines, they are considered to have acted in good faith (Guidelines—Copyright and Fair Use, 2010).

Schools often will choose to place a set or sets of classroom guidelines in their schools' copyright and ethics policies, because they are more understandable and definite than the law itself. Confusion arises when teachers, school librarians, technology coordinators, administrators, students, and others in the school understand the guidelines as if they were the maximum amounts allowable, rather than representing the more conservative approach. While using minimal amounts of works will guarantee that there will be no copyright infringements, it is also limiting to those who use, borrow, or copy materials for instructional purposes. Keep this in mind when the guidelines are referred to, for example, the "Copyright Guidelines for Educational Multimedia" (Chapter 2), the "Guidelines for Classroom Copying" (Chapter 12), and Appendix 1.

Once again, please note that guidelines *do not have the force of law*; instead they are directives that, if followed, will probably never result in litigation or anger by copyright owners, since guidelines are much more stringent than most interpretations of copyright law.

STATE LAWS

Mention of copyright may exist within state codes, but "States cannot enact their own laws to protect the same rights as the rights provided by the Copyright Act.... State 'copyright' laws... are limited to works that cannot be protected under federal copyright law" (Radcliffe and Brinson, 2010: 1). In addition, the term *copyright* can be found within state laws that focus on related subjects. One example would be Section 27-13.3 of the Illinois School Code, which states that "Each school may adopt an age-appropriate curriculum for Internet safety instruction of students in grades kindergarten through 12 . . . [including] copyright laws on written materials, photographs, music, and video" (Illinois Compiled Statutes 105 ILCS 5 School Code, 2010: 1). Thus, the place to look for copyright laws, acts, and bills would be with the federal government.

INTERNATIONAL COPYRIGHT LAW AND U.S. COPYRIGHT LAW WITH INTERNATIONAL PROVISIONS

> There is no such thing as an "international copyright" that will automatically protect an author's writings throughout the world. (U.S. Copyright Office, Library of Congress, 2009: 1)

As if U.S. copyright law is not complicated enough, there is also international copyright law to consider. While every country has its own laws in this area, which may or may not conform to U.S. federal laws, there are some organizations to which we—and many other countries—belong. These organizations' treaties principally state that we will abide by the copyright laws of the other countries that have signed each treaty, and they will abide by ours. Several treaties, organizations, and acts that exist in this area, and of which the United States is a part, are discussed in this section. Two pieces of U.S. copyright law—the Digital Millennium Copyright Act (DMCA) and the Sonny Bono Copyright Term Extension Act (CTEA)—and database protection, another area of interest to educators, are also covered. The following treaties and agreements are arranged by international, then U.S. law, and in order of importance, as determined by this author.

Berne Convention for the Protection of Literary and Artistic Works
International

U.S. membership in the Berne Convention dates from March 1, 1989 (Besenjak, 1997). This international copyright treaty, signed by 96 countries, is the benchmark of all copyright agreements worldwide. "This convention posits the notion that member nations will treat works from another country as they do those published in their own country, except if the protection term in the country of origin has run out. Then that particular work is also no longer protected in the member countries regardless of their particular copyright laws. . . . Berne member countries . . . do not need to have a copyright notice attached to be protected by law" (Butler, 2007: 74). Other international agreements that focus on intellectual properties include the General Agreement on Tariffs and Trade (GATT) and the Trade-Related Aspects of Intellectual Property Rights (TRIPS) agreement.

A K–12 example of the use of this convention might be when a band director, wishing to use a musical score that he purchased in Sweden, discovered that he did not have enough clarinet parts for all the clarinetists in his band. If the score were found to be in the public domain in Sweden, then the U.S. band director might copy extra clarinet parts without the need for obtaining permission or a license to do so from the Swedish copyright holder of the work.

Universal Copyright Convention (UCC)

International

Along with the Berne Convention, this remains one of the two most pivotal copyright organizations to which the U.S. belongs (U.S. Copyright Office, Library of Congress, 2010). The United States joined the Universal Copyright Convention (UCC) on September 16, 1955. This group does not enforce copyright. Instead, it relies on its member nations to enforce its agreements (Besenjak, 1997). This convention was created to ensure that international copyright protection is available to countries that might not be members of the Berne Convention. A premise of the UCC is that its members must offer works from other participating countries the same copyright protection as those works created in their own country.

An example of a case of use of the UCC in a U.S. elementary public school could be when a student brought in a DVD that she had purchased in New Zealand. Without knowledge of New Zealand copyright laws, the teacher could apply U.S. copyright law to the use of that particular DVD in the classroom.

World Intellectual Property Organization (WIPO)

International

The World Intellectual Property Organization (WIPO) is a United Nations agency that "is dedicated to developing a balanced and accessible international intellectual property (IP) system, which rewards creativity, stimulates innovation and contributes to economic development while safeguarding the public interest" (World Intellectual Property Organization, 2010b).One area of its IP focus is "on the development of international norms and standards in the area of copyright and related rights" (WIPO, 2010a). For example, this organization ruled that Time Warner would have sole ownership to Harry Potter–related Internet domain names (Neal, 2002; Torrans, 2003).

Trade-Related Aspects of Intellectual Property Rights (TRIPS)

International

Part of the WIPO, TRIPS focuses on copyright protection of such items as computer codes and programs, international broadcasting, and sound recordings (Butler, 2007).

A case in point for the necessity of TRIPS might be if K–12 district technology coordinators turned to this international intellectual property treaty when considering the copyright implications of computer code that they had purchased online from a non-U.S. site.

European Union Database Directive

International

This directive speaks to both the creation and content of databases and has possible sway with research worldwide in that "the potential is that public domain databases could by virtue of having their content copyrighted come back under copyright protection in particular countries" (Butler, 2007: 75). With this in mind, many compilations currently in the public domain in the United States would become protected under copyright law. This issue is of special interest to educators and scientists. The way students and researchers access information could be affected if they were at some point required to obtain permission to use, or pay for the use, of databases that until now have been in the public domain. Research could become more difficult—information harder to obtain and more expensive. Database protection is an area of interest to educators that bears watching in the future.

Digital Millennium Copyright Act (DMCA)

United States

The DMCA, signed into law in October 1998 by President Clinton, made changes to U.S. copyright law in a number of areas, including online service provider liability, distance education, exemptions for libraries and archives, computer maintenance and copying of software, and digital performances of sound recordings. In addition, the DMCA implements the World Intellectual Property Organization treaties, thus bringing U.S. copyright law into compliance with the WIPO. In actuality, while the DMCA implements the WIPO treaties, it also "creates two new prohibitions in Title 17 of the U.S. Code (1976 Copyright Law)—one on circumvention of technological measures used by copyright owners to protect their works and one on tampering with copyright management information—and adds civil remedies and criminal penalties for violating the prohibitions" (U.S. Copyright Office, Library of Congress, 1998: 2). This means, for example, that an industrial arts education teacher could not legally create a way to unlock a piece of software for a computer-aided drafting class.

Sonny Bono Copyright Term Extension Act (CTEA)

United States

In an effort to maintain consistency between the United States and the other members of the Berne Convention, in 1998 U.S. Congress passed the Sonny Bono Copyright Term Extension Act (CTEA). So named because Congressman Bono was working on this at the time of his death, CTEA extends the duration of copyright in the United States retroactively from the life of the author plus 50 years to the life of the author plus 70 years and, in the case of works for hire, to 120 years (Butler, 2007). With this act in mind, unless permission were granted by the owner(s) or a license obtained, the school librarian would not be able to legally copy material from a website on childhood obesity for a science class that had been personally created by a dietician until 70 years after the dietician's death.

The purpose here is not to discuss these issues in depth. Instead, it is to give an impression of selected items of importance occurring in this area. More specific information related to international copyright law, national legislation, and various works is covered in Chapters 6 through 14. For additional information on which countries are members of various conventions and treaties with the United States, see Circular 38A: International Copyright Relations of the United States (U.S. Copyright Office, Library of Congress, 2009).

ORPHAN WORKS

Orphan works are works where finding the owner(s) is problematic or next to impossible. When educators wish to borrow or copy from such a work, they have difficult choices to make. Should they:

1. continue searching for an owner in order to obtain permission to use the work?
2. use only that part of the work which might fit under fair use or another copyright exemption?
3. "give up" and use something else?
4. argue, after searching for a "reasonable amount of time," that in good faith they have tried to obtain permission with no success and risk using the work anyway?

With orphan works, like many copyright issues, there is no one answer. For several years, library organizations, publishers, the U.S. Copyright Office, and other users with a vested interest in orphan works, have pushed to have federal legislation passed that would simplify borrowing from orphan works. Other suggested solutions have included creating online databases to locate missing owners, placing all works considered orphan in the public domain, revising tax and bankruptcy laws (which might reduce the number of works becoming orphans), and establishing a capped fee that could be paid an owner, if he or she were found (Public Knowledge, 2009; Sigall, 2006). As of 2010, there are no definite solutions on the horizon; thus the educator with such a dilemma might choose, for example, to find another work to use or document what he or she considers a "reasonable amount of time" for a search, and then use as little of the work as possible. At this point in time, the choice of use of an orphaned work is a decision of the borrower.

FUTURE COPYRIGHT LEGISLATION

At any one point in time, there may be bills and acts dealing with copyright issues somewhere in the U.S. House of Representatives or Senate. One recent example, from the June 2010 Copyright Update of the American Library Association (ALA)

Office of Government Relations (OGR), is the Fair Copyright in Research Works Act (H.R. 801). According to the OGR, this bill "negates or reverses the National Institutes of Health (NIH) Public Access Policy currently in place, rolling back hard-fought progress on public access to taxpayer-funded NIH research on the Internet.... Library advocates should continue to...strongly oppose H.R. 801" (ALA, OGR, 2010). In addition, various groups and organizations representing users and/or owners of works may propose possible legislation. A case in point is the Copyright Reform Act of 2010, drafted by Public Knowledge, a public interest group. It proposes five general topics for copyright change:

> 1) strengthen fair use, including reforming outrageously high statutory damages, which deter innovation and creativity; 2) reform the DMCA (Digital Millennium Copyright Act) to permit circumvention of digital locks for lawful purposes; 3) update the limitations and exceptions to copyright protection to better conform with how digital technologies work; 4) provide recourse for people and companies who are recklessly accused of copyright infringement and who are recklessly sent improper DMCA take-down notices; and 5) streamline arcane music licensing laws to encourage new and better business models for selling music. (Hart, 2010: 1)

From reading these two brief summaries, it is clear that the first proposed change favors the owners of works, while the second tips toward users and their needs. Whether either will eventually become law depends on the U.S. federal legislative bodies. For the purposes of those of us who work in K–12 schools, it is best to note that future legislation may change copyright law, including how it is interpreted and enforced. Thus we need to remain up to date in this area through current print, nonprint, and Internet sources; attendance at professional presentations; attending workshops and classes in copyright law and related issues; and pursuing as many other opportunities as possible to become more familiar with this subject area.

INFRINGEMENTS AND PENALTIES

Imagine that at a teacher's meeting after school, your principal asks you and your colleagues to stand if you think you have violated copyright law. If the group is truthful—and even somewhat knowledgeable about copyright—it is likely that the whole room will stand. At this point, it is a common occurrence that at least one teacher will declare, "I copy all the time, and I've never been caught." Then a conversation will ensue about how schools and school districts don't have enough money and that borrowing from sample textbooks, copying that extra workbook unit, using music from a popular CD for a multimedia presentation for the PTA, showing a rented DVD during a rainy recess, and so on, are okay because, "We're educators; we aren't going to earn any money from what we copy anyway." At this point, the school librarian and technology coordinator may also speak up, asking, "Are we in trouble if we provide the equipment and software by which our teachers copy?" Several misconceptions are going on here that are worth examining.

"Everyone in the Room Has Violated Copyright Law"

Because of the ambiguity in U.S. copyright law, with its duality of representing both borrowers and owners of works, infringing on copyright law is easy to do. It may be a conscious or unconscious act.

Imagine that you are a computer teacher in an elementary school. You find a great piece of software that you are just positive will make learning keyboarding a quick and easy activity. However, the technology coordinator does not have enough money to purchase a license for it. You copy it to all the computers in your lab anyway—even though you know that the documentation on the software says that this cannot be done without a license. Are you in violation of copyright law? Most definitely! (You are probably also in violation of contract law—see the Documentation and Licenses section in this chapter.) This is an example of a conscious violation.

Assume that you are the middle school art teacher. Because of the popularity of the Harry Potter series, you decide that you will teach a unit on knitting, building on the idea of knitting hats for house elves that Hermione does in *Harry Potter and the Order of the Phoenix* (Rowling, 2003). You make copies of a pamphlet about knitting hats that you bought in a craft shop and hand it out to all of the students in your middle school classes. In your excitement to create this new assignment, you totally forget that such copying may be in violation of copyright law: the pamphlet is not in the public domain. It fits under only two of the four fair use factors (purpose and character of use and nature of the copyrighted work), and permission has not been granted. Have you violated copyright law? Perhaps. This may be an example of an unconscious act of violation.

"I'll Never Get Caught"

You are an exhausted kindergarten teacher. The kids have been running amok all week. It is now Friday afternoon, and all you want to do is get through the rest of the day. You can't take the students out for recess because it is raining. So you grab a Disney DVD from your bag—one you had rented to show your own children that night—and pop it into the DVD player, then sit back for a little badly needed rest. If you are coherent enough at this point to recognize that you are violating copyright law—showing a video in public performance for entertainment purposes, without proper licenses or permissions, is an infringement—you rationalize that the students are too young to realize that fact. Chances are that you are right. You will have a couple of hours of relative quiet and no one will be the wiser.

But now assume that one of your students, Ashley, has a father who works for the Disney Corporation. She goes home and proceeds to tell her family at the dinner table all about the movie that her class saw in school that day, instead of going outside for recess. Will you get caught? If Ashley's father decides to pursue the matter, you definitely could be found to have infringed on Disney's copyright. (More on copyright and videos is found in Chapter 7. More on how to deal with those who violate, how and why to respect copyright law, and related topics is found in Chapter 14.)

"We Don't Have Enough Money to Buy Everything That We Need, So It's Okay to Copy; After All, We're in Education"

Some educators feel that they should be able to copy or borrow from sources indiscriminately. Because schools often do not have a lot of money for those extras, educators then feel they must purchase the items themselves. For instance, a teacher may find a sample workbook in a commercial teachers' store with an exercise that is perfect for a specific learning module. The teacher purchases the workbook with full knowledge that each page of the book states that the material therein cannot be copied for classroom use. (One could ask then why such a workbook exists at all, but that is another discussion altogether.) The teacher, however, feels that since this is for an educational purpose, it is okay to copy the exercise for every student in the class. Unfortunately, the workbook's creator feels that every student in the class should own a workbook instead. The creator has the right, under copyright law, to specify how the work is used. There are ways to obtain use of an owner's works by means of fair use, public domain, and permissions and licenses (see Chapters 2 through 4), or possibly by statutory exceptions or the "Guidelines for Classroom Copying." Therefore, the teacher is infringing, unless the copying falls under one of the exceptions noted. Just being an educator or working with students in an educational setting does not mean that you can legally disregard copyright law.

"I Don't Violate Copyright Law; I Am in Charge of Equipment and Software That Others Use to Make Copies"

Assume that you are the school librarian. It is a small school, so you function as the technology specialist as well. All equipment, such as computers, DVD players, televisions, audio recorders, and the like, is under your jurisdiction. The same holds true for all software. A sixth-grade teacher comes in and sits down to use one of the lab computers. You pay no attention to him; he knows what he is doing, and you are busy with other things. Only later do you realize that he was burning a mix of songs from purchased CDs and Internet sources onto a CD for personal use. You recognize it is highly likely that this is a copyright infringement. Should the teacher be caught for this act, would you also be held in violation for providing the instruments used for the copying? Unfortunately, you could be. This is an example of contributory or indirect infringement. "Anyone who knows or should have known that he or she is assisting, inducing or materially contributing to infringement of any of the exclusive rights by another person is liable for contributory infringement" (Simpson and Weiser, 2008: 87). Be aware that you can protect yourself from contributory or indirect infringement by posting notices about the illegality of copyright infringement on equipment that can be used for copying purposes in your library, computer lab, or classroom. This is covered under Section 108(f)(1) of the U.S. Code (U.S. Code, 2010).

In fact, there are three kinds of copyright infringement: (1) direct, in which a user violates the rights of the owner or author by making illegal copies or derivatives of copyrighted works, distributing these copies/derivations, or publicly performing or displaying the works; (2) contributory, in which an individual or group is aware that what they are doing assists another in copyright infringement; and (3) vicarious, where those with authority over an infringer gain benefits from the infringement (Simpson and Weiser, 2008).

Penalties

Penalties for copyright infringements vary from fines to prison sentences. Two examples of penalties involving money and schools follow:

- A Chicago suburban school was required to pay a settlement of $50,000 to a computer association after it was discovered that a school employee had illegally downloaded software programs onto several school computers ("School District Pays Copyright Penalty," 2001).
- A California school district paid a fine of $300,000 and replaced illegal software totaling $5 million after being sued for making and installing on school computers over 1,000 illegal copies of Microsoft and Adobe software (Bissonette, 2009).

As a deterrent to potential violators, copyright warnings are posted on DVDs, videos, audio recordings, print materials, and more. For example, the DVD warning for *Harry Potter and the Half-Blood Prince* reads as follows:

> The unauthorized reproduction or distribution of this copyrighted work is illegal. Criminal copyright infringement, including infringement without monetary gain, is investigated by the FBI and punishable by up to 5 years in federal prison and a fine of $250,000. (Heyman and Barron, 2009)

In reality, I am unaware of any cases in which teachers have been imprisoned for copyright violation, although fines and loss of employment have occurred (Bissonette, 2009; "School District Pays Copyright Penalty," 2001). Penalties for illegal commercial use of works do exist in the U.S. Code (Title 17, sec. 506(a); Title 18, sec. 2319), however. Why? The Copyright Law of the United States of America affords damages. As a consequence, there are ramifications for infringing on copyright law. Given some individuals' propensity toward using works indiscriminately, this is an issue to examine carefully.

Also remember that at any given time, while there are a number of bills and acts in the federal legislature concerned with copyright, many of them are focused on increasing the fines or other penalties for disobeying the law.

PLAGIARISM

Plagiarism occurs when you borrow from another source without crediting the source or person from whom it was borrowed. Some examples of plagiarism include buying a term paper from an online paper mill, borrowing part of a paper from another student and turning it in as your own, and copying or paraphrasing from an original work without citing the source. Plagiarism can be intentional or unintentional. Intentional plagiarism is when someone purposely steals from another. For example, if you are an English teacher and one of your students knowingly copies a poem from a poetry anthology and submits it to you as an original work, that student has intentionally plagiarized. Unintentional plagiarism occurs when someone does not cite (or does not properly cite) his or her sources. One instance of this might be if you, as a teacher, write an article for a professional journal. Because of sloppy note taking, you forget to cite one of the book chapters from which you obtained some of your information. The simplest ways to avoid plagiarizing are to not borrow indiscriminately and to cite your sources (Office of Graduate Studies, 2010). In addition, a National Bureau of Economic Research study shows that being educated in what plagiarism is and learning how to follow the rules can reduce plagiarism in students (Jaschik, 2010).

There are a number of online plagiarism detection sites (which range from charging per paper to free use) where a teacher or student can plug in a written assignment and find out what parts, if any, are plagiarized. Included in this list of sources are such services as Turnitin (http://turnitin.com), SafeAssign (http://safeassign.com; part of the Blackboard online course package), and DupliChecker (http://www.duplichecker.com). In addition, a number of middle and high school teachers have informed me that it is possible to check phrases and sentences for plagiarism just by plugging them into the search box in Google (http://www.google .com). Moreover, to obtain information on how "not to plagiarize," there are a wide variety of Internet articles on this subject as well as print periodical articles and books. A quick browse through two books on avoiding plagiarism suggests such activities as making sure that students do their own work, using their own words, and citing all sources correctly; making sure students know not to mix different quotations together; teaching students how to narrow online search options; and encouraging students to create original bibliographies (Gilmore, 2009; Menager and Paulos, 2009).

How to Cite

It is better to cite something that you have borrowed rather than risk plagiarizing. How to cite what you borrow is another issue—one that is not within the scope of this book. However, there are any number of citation styles available for K–12 students. Some of the most common and popular include those based on conventions standardized by the American Psychological Association (APA), the *Chicago Manual of Style* (*CMS*), and the Modern Language Association (MLA). Webpages, including blogs and wikis, as well as other items posted online, are especially confusing to cite and may vary from style manual to style manual. Below are citation style examples used by APA, *CMS*, and MLA to cite an Internet site/article from an online periodical.

- American Psychological Association (2010):
  Last Name, A. A., & Last Name, B. B. (Year of publication, month if available). Title of article. *Title of Online Periodical,* volume number (issue number if available). Retrieved from www.someaddress.com/ full/url/.
- *Chicago Manual of Style* (University of Chicago Press, 2010):
  Last Name, First Name. "Title of Article." *Title of Online Periodical* Volume Number, Issue No. (Publication Date): Page Range if Available. URL.
- Modern Language Association (2008):
  Last Name, First Name. "Article Title." *Title of Online Periodical* Volume. Issue (Year of Publication): n. pag. Web. Access Date. URL.

Manuals of style can be found in a number of places: online on college and university sites, some K–12 school sites, other websites, and for sale in commercial bookstores. There are also other websites that provide information on citation, such as NoodleTools, an Internet site that "provides innovative software that teaches students and supports teachers and librarians throughout the entire research process" (NoodleTools, 2010) and EasyBib.com, "The Free Automatic Bibliography and Citation Maker" (ImagineEasy Solutions, 2010).

Thus, while correctly citing material borrowed is an important skill to have when authoring any intellectual work, its relationship to copyright is only peripheral.

Plagiarism and Copyright

Copyright is not directly related to plagiarism. However, the two are often associated with each other. For example, courts may recognize cases of plagiarism as copyright infringement (LawBrain, 2010). Perhaps this is because both involve copying materials. Historically, copyright and plagiarism are also linked. In England, the 18th century is noted for the first copyright statutes as well as a strong concern about plagiarism (Mallon, 1989). In addition, it may be possible to both break copyright law and plagiarize. A case in point would be if Mr. Brown, a computer teacher, decides to take a chapter from a book detailing presentation software and claim it as his own on a personal website. Assuming that the book is not in the public domain, if he does not ask for permission to use the chapter and borrows more than fair use allows, he violates copyright law. Putting his name on something he did not write is an example of plagiarism. Thus, Mr. Brown manages to both violate copyright law and plagiarize. Plagiarism might be avoided simply by citing where the software information came from; however, such citing would not mean that it is permissible to violate copyright law.

In 2008, Turnitin, one of the Internet plagiarism detection services discussed earlier in this chapter, won a court case it had been battling involving the use of student papers. Several high school students had sued Turnitin, saying that copyright ownership to their papers was violated, since the company stored "digital copies of their essays to check future submissions for academic dishonesty"

(Oleck, 2008). The court found in favor of Turnitin, stating "fair use was not violated because under federal law, the unauthorized use of copyrighted work for purposes such as teaching, scholarship, and research 'is not an infringement of copyright.' Fair use allows limited use of copyrighted material without requiring permission from the rights holders" (Oleck, 2008). In this particular case, at least, copyright and plagiarism parted ways.

SAMPLE FLOWCHART

Flowchart 5.1 is an example of the flowcharts that are used in Part II of this book to respond to copyright questions that have more than one answer. Read through each diagram in Chapters 6 through 14 from top to bottom to obtain the answers to the questions posted above all flowcharts. Remember that when you use the flowcharts in this book, you are trying to find any criterion under which you may borrow a work. Therefore, you need only to follow each flowchart until you come to that point where you satisfy one of the criteria. Once you reach that point, there is no need to go further.

CONCLUSION

This chapter looks at a number of copyright-related items, including documentation and licenses, interlibrary loan, statutory exemptions for educators and librarians, and classroom copying guidelines. It also addresses international copyright law and ways the United States has chosen to add to its own laws in order to comply with international copyright treaties, orphan works, copyright infringements in K–12 schools, educators' attitudes toward such infringements, and the penalties for copyright violations. All of these are topics of which you need to be aware. Although not directly related to copyright law, plagiarism and correct citing styles are also part of this chapter because many educators associate these topics with copyright.

Now that you have an idea about a variety of issues that come into play when you are applying copyright law to works in a variety of formats, it is time to turn to the practical application of copyright in the K–12 school setting.

REFERENCES

American Library Association (ALA), Office of Government Relations (OGR). 2010. "H.R. 801 'The Fair Copyright in Research Works Act.'" American Library Association. http://www.ala.org/ala/issuesadvocacy/copyright/activelegislation/hr801/index.cfm.
American Psychological Association (APA). 2010. *Publication Manual of the American Psychological Association*. 6th ed. Washington, DC: APA.
Besenjak, Cheryl. 1997. *Copyright Plain & Simple*. Franklin Lakes, NJ: Career Press.
Bissonette, Aimée M. 2009. *Cyber Law: Maximizing Safety and Minimizing Risk in Classrooms*. Thousand Oaks, CA: Corwin.

Flowchart 5.1. Sample Flowchart

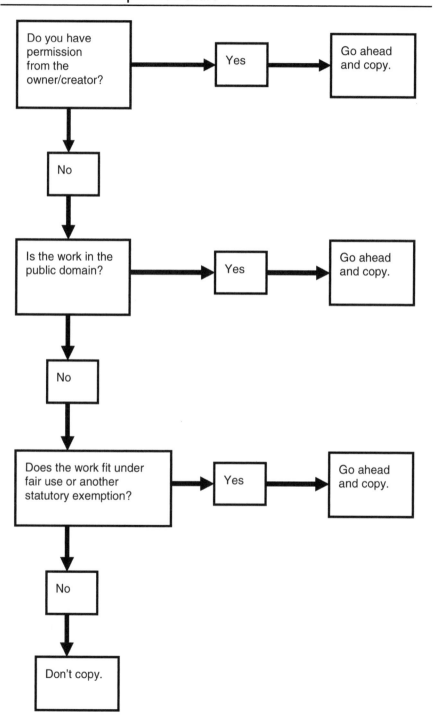

Butler, Rebecca P. 2007. "Borrowing Media from Around the World: School Libraries and Copyright Law." *School Libraries Worldwide* 13, no. 2 (July): 73-81.

Chilling Effects Clearinghouse. 2010. "Question: What Are Shrink-Wrap, Click-Wrap, and Browse-Wrap Licenses?" Chilling Effects. Accessed June 29. http://www.chillingeffects.org/question.cgi?QuestionID=207.

Copyright Clearance Center. 2005. "Using Content: ILL: The CONTU Guidelines." http://www.copyright.com/Services/copyrightoncampus/content/ ill_contu.html.

Creative Commons. 2010. "About." Accessed June 7. http://creativecommons.org/about.

Crews, Kenneth D. 2006. *Copyright Law for Librarians and Educators: Creative Strategies and Practical Solutions.* Chicago: American Library Association.

Doctorow, Cory. 2010. "*In Praise of Copying*, CC-Licensed Book from Harvard Uni Press." Boing Boing. October 23. http://www.boingboing.net/2010/10/23/in-praise-of-copying.html.

Free Software Foundation (FSF). 2010. "GNU Operating System." http://www.gnu.org.

Gilmore, Barry. 2009. *Plagiarism: A How-Not-To Guide for Students.* Porstmouth, NH: Heinemann.

"Guidelines_Copyright & Fair Use." 2010. Devereaux Library, South Dakota School of Mines and Technology. Accessed June 29. http://library.sdsmt.edu/copy/Copyright Guidelines.htm.

Hart, Kim. 2010. "Public Knowledge Proposes Copyright Reform Bill." The Hill. http://thehill.com/blogs/hillicon-valley/technology/81117-public-knowledge-proposes-copyright-reform-bill.

Heyman, David, and David Barron, prods. 2009. *Harry Potter and the Half-Blood Prince.* Directed by David Yates. Warner Bros. Pictures. DVD. 153 min.

Illinois Compiled Statutes 105 ILCS 5 School Code. 2010. "Section 27-13.3." onecle. http://law.onecle.com/illinois/105ilcs5/27-13.3.html.

ImagineEasy Solutions. 2010. "The Free Automatic Bibliography and Citation Maker." EasyBib. http://www.easybib.com/.

Jaschik, Scott. 2010. "Plagiarism Prevention Without Fear." Inside Higher Ed. January 26. http://www.insidehighered.com/news/ 2010/01/26/plagiarize.

Kunkel, Richard G. 2002. "Recent Developments in Shrinkwrap, Clickwrap, and Browsewrap Licenses in the United States." *Murdoch University Electronic Journal of Law.* September. http://www.murdoch.edu.au/elaw/issues/v9n3/kunkel93.html.

LawBrain. 2010. "Plagiarism." Updated March 18. http://lawbrain.com/wiki/Plagiarism.

Mallon, Thomas. 1989. *Stolen Words: The Classic Book on Plagiarism.* New York: Harcourt.

Menager, Rosemarie, and Lyn Paulos. 2009. *Quick Coach Guide to Avoiding Plagiarism.* Boston: Wadsworth.

Modern Language Association (MLA). 2008. *MLA Style Manual and Guide to Scholarly Publishing.* 3rd ed. New York: MLA.

National Commission on New Technological Uses of Copyright Works (CONTU). 1978. Final Report of the National Commission on New Technological Uses of Copyrighted Works. "CONTU Guidelines on Photocopying under Interlibrary Loan Arrangements." Coalition for Networked Information. Updated July 3, 2002. http://www.cni.org/docs/infopols/CONTU.html.

Neal, James G. 2002. "Copyright is Dead . . . Long Live Copyright." *American Libraries* 33, no. 11 (December): 48–51.

NoodleTools. 2010. Accessed June 30. http://www.noodletools.com.

Office of Graduate Studies. 2010. "Plagiarism: What It Is and How to Avoid It." University of Nebraska-Lincoln. http://www.unl.edu/gradstudies/current/ plagiarism.shtml.

Oleck, Joan. 2008. "Judge Rules That Turnitin Does Not Violate Students' Copyrights." *School Library Journal*. March 31. http://www.schoollibraryjournal.com/article/ CA6546427.html.

Open Source Initiative. 2010. "The Open Source Definition: Introduction." Accessed June 8. http://www.opensource.org/docs/osd.

Public Knowledge. 2009. "Orphan Works." http://www.publicknowledge.org/issues/ow.

Radcliffe, Mark F., and Brinson, Diane. 2010. "Copyright Law." FindLaw. http://library .findlaw.com/1999/Jan/1/241476.html.

Rowling, J. K. 2003. *Harry Potter and the Order of the Phoenix*. New York: Scholastic Press.

Rupp-Serrano, Karen, ed. 2005. *Licensing in Libraries: Practical and Ethical Aspects*. Binghamton, NY: The Haworth Information Press.

"School District Pays Copyright Penalty." 2001. *Chicago Tribune*, October 12, sec. 2, 3.

Sigall, Jule L. 2006. "Statement of Jule L. Sigall, Associate Register for Policy and International Affairs before the Subcommittee on Courts, the Internet, and Intellectual Property, Committee on the Judiciary." Washington, DC: United States House of Representatives, 109th Congress, 2nd Session. March. http://www.copyright.gov/docs/ regstst030806.html.

Simpson, Carol, and Weiser, Christine. 2008. *Copyright for Administrators*. Columbus, OH: Linworth.

Smith, Brett. 2007. "GNU Operating System: A Quick Guide to GPLv3." Free Software Foundation. http://www.gnu.org/licenses/quick-guide-gplv3.html.

Torrans, Lee Ann. 2003. *Law for K–12 Libraries and Librarians*. Westport, CT: Libraries Unlimited.

United States Code. 2010. "Title 17: Copyright Law of the United States of America and Related Laws." Washington, DC: U.S. Copyright Office. Accessed December 5. http:// www.copyright.gov/title17/92chap1.html.

University of Chicago Press. 2010. *The Chicago Manual of Style*. 16th ed. Chicago: The University of Chicago Press.

U.S. Constitution. 1787. http://www.usconstitution.net/ const.html.

U.S. Copyright Law. 1976. Public Law 94-553, sec. 108, 110.

———. 1998. The Digital Millennium Copyright Act of 1998: U.S. Copyright Office Summary. Washington, DC: U.S. Copyright Office.

———. 2009. "Circular 38A: International Copyright Relations of the United States." Washington, DC: U.S. Copyright Office.

U.S. Copyright Office, Library of Congress. 2010. Washington, DC: U.S. Copyright Office.

U.S. Copyright Office and the National Digital Information Infrastructure and Preservation Program of the Library of Congress. 2008. "The Section 108 Study Group Report." http://www.section108.gov/.

World Intellectual Property Organization (WIPO). 2010a. "Copyright and Related Rights." Accessed June 30. http://www.wipo.int/copyright/en/.

———. 2010b. "What is WIPO?" Accessed June 30. http://www.wipo.int/about-wipo/ en/what_is_wipo.html.

PART II

Specific Applications of Copyright Law

CHAPTER 6

The Internet and Copyright Law: Everything on the Web Is Considered Implied Public Access, Right?

INTRODUCTION

According to the *Chicago Tribune* (Rubin, 2010), teens and tweens spend almost 53 hours a week accessing/using media. The items in the sidebar represent some of the media choices available to today's students: social networking tools; objects that can access the web, including cell phones; online software; websites that sell music, e-books, and online applications; access points for information; and more. Items such as these open up the possibility of violating copyright law through the ease of borrowing, copying, and sharing of online resources. Because the Internet is a relatively new phenomenon in terms of copyright—and early copyright law was interpreted solely in terms of print ownership (Bettig, 1996)—how to protect yourself and your students in terms of copyright law and media can pose a conundrum.

> **Web Items**
>
> wikis, blogs, podcasts, video streaming, Second Life, Facebook, Shelfari, Flickr, cloud computing, wordles, Moodle, iPads, BrainPOP, myYearbook, Free Online Games, Mousebreaker, Chatroulette, Ning, MP3 players, iPods, Playaway, Animoto, eReaders, Kindles, Nooks, MySpace, Twitter, Goodreads, Skype, Delicious and other social bookmarking sites, web syndication (example: RSS feeds), Google Wave, ScreenToaster, Prezi, Slideshare, file sharing, electronic toolboxes, hyperlinks, Adobe Connect, Box.net, video streaming, computational knowledge engines, LimeWire, VoiceThread, social media, YouTube, TeacherTube, Web 2.0, iTunes, Pageflakes, Netvibes, Excite MIX, Protopage, social gaming networks, LinkedIn, Scribd, concept-mapping tools, Plurk, DRM, Xanga, web feeds, content aggregators, online video games
>
> *For definitions of all terms above, please see Appendix 2.*

This chapter addresses questions that cover the Internet and a wide variety of copyright issues. Questions with more than one answer are presented in flow-chart form. Remember that when you use the flowcharts in this chapter, you are trying to find any criterion under which you may borrow a work. Therefore, you need only follow each flowchart until you come to that point where you satisfy one of the criteria. Once you reach that point, there is no need to go any further. In addition, for more information on each area discussed, please refer to the chapter (Chapters 1 through 5) that covers that particular subject, as well as Appendix 2, which defines the terms located in the sidebar. Also, refer to the Index and Table of Contents for more material on the topics that interest you.

FAIR USE

Question: Is there fair use on the Internet?

Answer: While U.S. copyright laws are still catching up when it comes to Internet usage, it is best to apply fair use to all websites, e-mails, and other electronic communications.

Question: Can school library media specialists use images (book covers, photos, etc.) from online booksellers or other vendor sources to promote books and other media on their own library websites?

Answer: Since vendors are in the business of making money, it is likely they will not mind their images existing on your site to promote those things that they sell. However, since images on vendor sites can be copyrighted, please consult Flowchart 6.1 when considering borrowing images for your website.

Question: Can I print a webpage and make a copy of it for every student in my class?

Answer: Use Flowchart 6.2 (p. 70) to determine what is allowed.

Question: I want to copy several paragraphs from a site on Hurricane Katrina. How much may I borrow from someone's webpage under fair use?

Answer: The amount you may copy is based on the total amount of material on the site, how much you want to borrow, whether it is the heart of the work, whether it is fact or fiction, published or unpublished, whether such borrowing will affect the marketplace, and how you are going to use what you borrow (see Chapter 2). "When you claim fair use, you take a risk. The wording of fair use language in the Copyright Act is vague and subject to interpretation by the courts!" (Besenjak, 1997: 58).

Question: I found a great photograph of Martin Luther King Jr. on a college website. I want to use it for my eighth-grade advanced history Internet site. However, the college does not answer my queries. Is it all right to use the photograph anyway?

Flowchart 6.1. Web Images

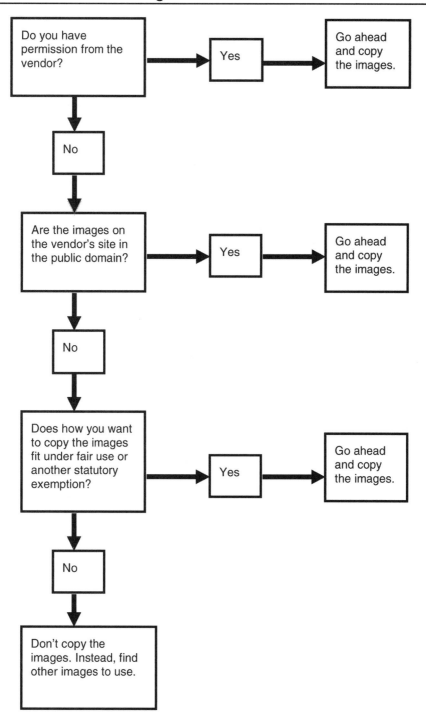

Flowchart 6.2. Printing Webpages

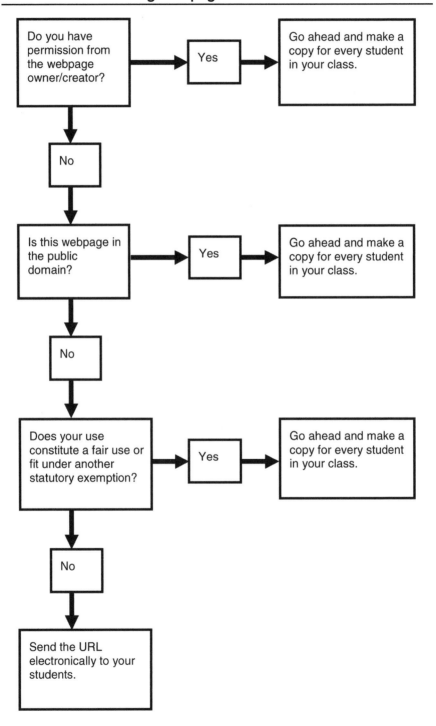

Answer: Use Flowchart 6.3 to decide if it is all right to use the photograph.

Flowchart 6.3. Photographs on the Web

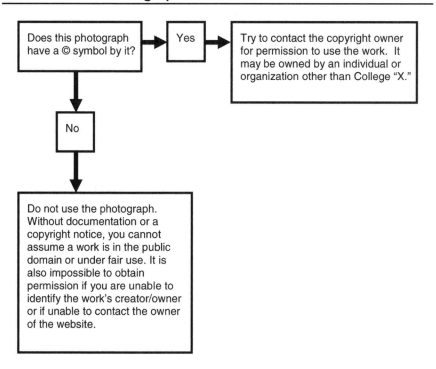

PUBLIC DOMAIN

Question: Is the Internet in the public domain?

Answer: The Internet is a "single worldwide computer network that intercon-nects other computer networks, on which end-user services, such as World Wide Web sites or data archives, are located, enabling data and other informa-tion to be exchanged" ("Internet," 2010). Webpages' content and electronic communications that make up the Internet can be and often are copyright-protected. If the content of any webpage is in the public domain, it should say so somewhere on the site. (*Should* is the operative word here—the site owner or administrator does not have to state whether Internet content is copyright-protected.) However, if there is no statement either way, one should assume that the webpage content is copyrighted.

Question: A student needs an image for a report he is doing. He finds a website with images and chooses one to use. Is the image in the public domain?

Answer: It is possible for anyone who can create a webpage to put it in the public domain, simply by adding a statement to that effect to the page. It is also possible for someone creating a webpage filled with images to borrow some from copyright-protected sites. Thus, you are safest if you borrow public domain images from a reputable site—one where you can trust that the images really are in the public domain. Study Flowchart 6.4 for more help.

Flowchart 6.4. How to Decide Whether an Image Is in the Public Domain

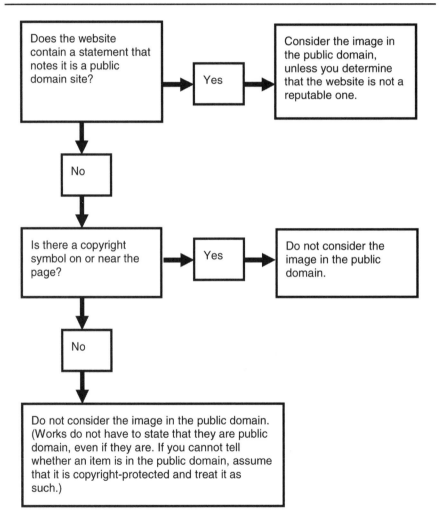

DOCUMENTATION AND LICENSES

Question: Where is the documentation located on a webpage?

Answer: Documentation (that information in most works which states the work's identifying data, such as author, copyright date, publisher, place of publication, etc.) on a webpage is usually at the bottom of each webpage, the beginning or end of the site, or on a special About page. It may be as simple as listing the webmaster or moderator of the site and when the site was last updated. Documentation can also include permissions or restrictions to which the user of the site must agree, copyright information, and other criteria that the moderator or owner of the site has determined must be met for site usage (see Chapter 5). Please remember to read all documentation before agreeing to or checking off on a site. It is to your advantage to know that to which you have agreed.

Question: Do K–12 teachers need to be concerned with licenses for web access?

Answer: In many school situations, licenses are either the responsibility of the technology coordinator or school administrator and apply to the number of computers that use a particular software at one time or in a particular manner, or the responsibility of the librarian and apply to online databases (Hoffmann, 2001) or access to other online information sources, such as online encyclopedias. However, while the classroom teacher may not hold primary responsibility for computer licenses (software) and web access (online databases/online encyclopedias) in that such responsibilities are someone else's job, the teacher needs to be knowledgeable about the terms of licenses, know and abide by these terms, and ensure that the students do the same. In addition, there is always the possibility that a classroom teacher will request a specific website for which a license is required and for which neither the technology coordinator or school librarian is accountable. In such an instance, the license could become the responsibility of the classroom teacher.

Question: Do social and professional websites such as Facebook, Twitter, Shelfari, and LinkedIn have copyright policies and infringement reporting procedures? Does YouTube?

Answer: Yes. While these vary from site to site, a link to copyright policies and procedures is normally found somewhere on the main page, usually at the bottom. Content of these policies and procedures range from providing complaint forms to statements that infringers will be removed from the participating network site to disabling access to infringers to deleting infringing posts or content (Facebook, 2010; LinkedIn, 2010; Shelfari, 2010; Twitter, 2010; YouTube, 2010).

Question: How do database licenses work?

Answer: Read the license, which is usually located at the beginning of the database. In many cases, you are required to click out of it before you can go further into the database. It will tell you what you can copy or print and what you can't. Some databases let you print whole articles. Others allow you to search but not print unless you have purchased a site license. Since database rights vary one to another, make sure that you are aware of exactly what rights you have with each one. There are certain things you should remember about databases, licenses, and copyright:

- Licenses may be more restrictive than fair use; however, when you agree to the license, it is a legal contract and you must abide by it.
- Database material may or may not be from copyrighted publications.
- "Click-on" licenses on the Internet are nonnegotiated contracts. Because of this, there is currently dissent as to whether "clicking away certain copyrights" is actually legal.
- Database collections are not protected by U.S. copyright law. (Torrans, 2003)

PERMISSIONS

Question: I am a physical education teacher. Do I need permission to link my school webpage on soccer to a general sports page?

Answer: No, such linking is usually considered a public domain concept. In fact, this is true for most links. One exception is if the format of the link itself could be copyrighted, such as that of a copyrighted image. However, it is good netiquette (or Internet etiquette) to ask the owner of the webpage if you may link to his or her website.

Question: May I make a deep link to a school-related site without permission? ("Deep linking is . . . used by websites to point a visitor directly to a page within the website instead of the landing page or front page of the site. Deep linking allows visitors to go directly to the information they require, which may be available on a certain page of the website, but not on the web page to which the basic link leads" (Brick Marketing, 2010).

Answer: Some copyright experts and users argue that linking is an address, similar to cross-references in a library catalog. As such, linking, including deep linking, cannot be copyright-protected. Others disagree, saying that linking—especially deep linking, which can bypass advertising pages—may infringe on a copyright owner's rights (American Library Association, 2010). While at the present there is no legal precedent to claim that deep linking infringes on copyright, to avoid the risk of lawsuits and "cease and desist" letters, it may be easier not to deep link. Use Flowchart 6.5 to help make your decision.

Question: May I copy a list of links about the 9/11 disaster that I found on the web to my eighth-grade class's social studies page?

Answer: Use Flowchart 6.6 (p. 76) to decide if you may copy the list.

Flowchart 6.5. Deep Linking

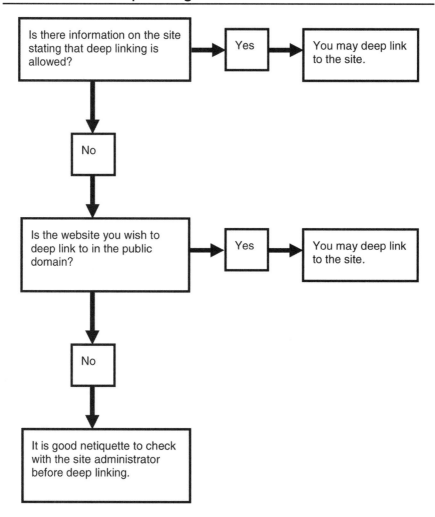

Question: Do I need special permission from Internet authors to borrow or copy parts or all of their webpages?

Answer: Use Flowchart 6.7 (p. 77) to make your decision.

Question: I found a great picture of a wolf on the Wolf Park (http://www.wolf park.net) website. There is a copyright symbol and a person's name at the bottom of the picture. Because our school mascot is the wolf, I would like to use this photograph as a screen saver for the computer lab computers. Is this possible?

Answer: While the photograph is copyright-protected, it may be possible with permission. Please see Flowchart 6.8 (p. 78) for more information.

Flowchart 6.6. Copying Lists

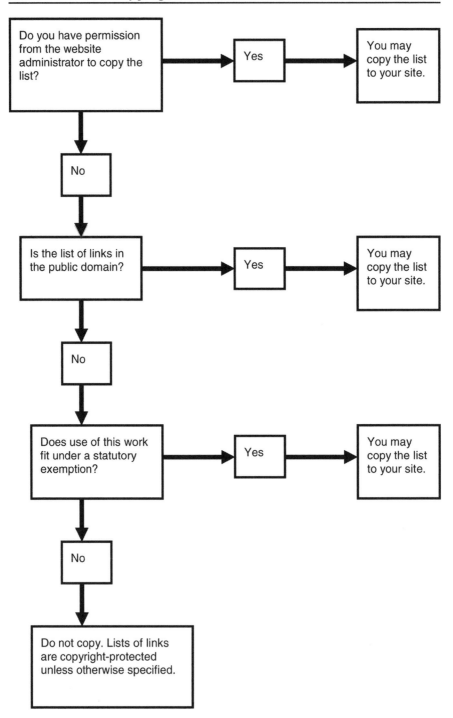

Flowchart 6.7. Borrowing All or Parts of Webpages

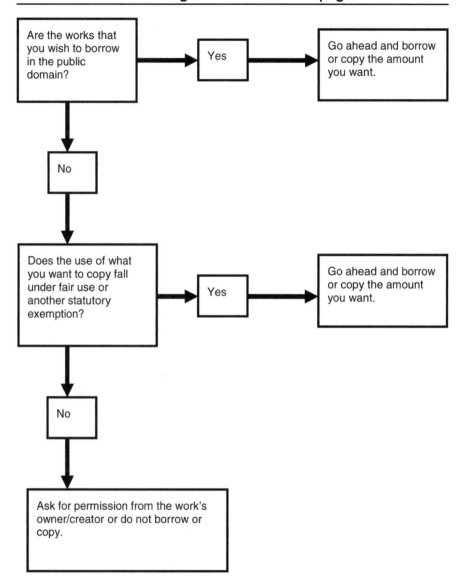

Are the works that you wish to borrow in the public domain? → Yes → Go ahead and borrow or copy the amount you want.

No

Does the use of what you want to copy fall under fair use or another statutory exemption? → Yes → Go ahead and borrow or copy the amount you want.

No

Ask for permission from the work's owner/creator or do not borrow or copy.

YOU CREATE IT, YOU OWN IT

Question: Is it a copyright infringement if someone takes an e-mail attachment you sent and posts it on a blog? Imagine that you sent an e-mail to a group of students. You have information vital to an algebra assignment that you wish them to read before the next class. The information is a piece that you created yourself, just for this class. You attach it to the e-mail and send it out. Weeks

Flowchart 6.8. Using a Photograph from the Web as a Screen Saver

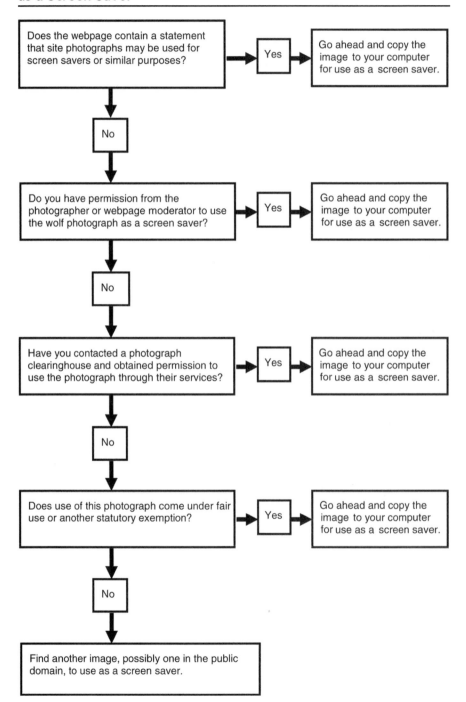

later, a teacher at another school tells you that he found a copy of your work on a student's blog. You are incensed; you did not give permission for this piece to be shared beyond your class. A copy posted to a blogging site means that people you do not know could now have your work.

Answer: The answer to this question is a resounding "yes." Anything you create—and this includes other formats of works as well—is immediately copyright-protected, whether you officially register it with the U.S. Copyright Office or not (U.S. Copyright Office, Library of Congress, 2006). Thus, whoever originally posted it on the blog (since you did not give your permission) is in violation of copyright law. In addition, those on the blogging site who keep and use your work may also be in violation.

Question: Who owns the copyright to a webpage you created for your fourth-grade class, if you worked on it at home, in the evenings, and used your own computer and software?

Answer: If you worked on this webpage using your own equipment and software and all on your own time, then it should be yours, provided you did not sign an agreement with your school that said otherwise. If you worked on it at school using only school equipment and software and on school time, then chances are that it comes under work for hire. Section 201(b) of the Copyright Law of the United States talks about work made for hire. It states, "In the case of a work made for hire, the employer or other person for whom the work was prepared is considered the author for purposes of this title, and, unless the parties have expressly agreed otherwise in a written instrument signed by them, owns all of the rights comprised in the copyright" (U.S. Copyright Law, 1976). This means that "the hiring party steps into the shoes of the creator and becomes the author of the work for copyright purposes" (Jassin, 2010). If you created it partly at home and partly at work, then ownership becomes more complicated. Some school systems have contractual agreements with their employees or policies that cover this issue. These policies vary in identifying the owner of the work. In this case, check with your school system regulations. It is important to remember here that, like so much dealing with copyright, there are a number of factors to consider when determining who owns what, such as where, when, and how the work was created. For example, the U.S. Supreme Court ruling in 1989 on the *Community for Creative Non-Violence (CCNV) v. Reid* is such a case (U.S. Supreme Court, 1989). In brief, this case considers who owns the copyright to a statue: the artist (Reid), who created the statue in his studio after a verbal agreement with the CCNV, or the CCNV, which commissioned it. First, a district court ruled in favor of CCNV, holding that it was "work made for hire." However, a court of appeals reversed that decision, stating that it was not within the scope of employment for Reid, given that he was an independent contractor under agency law, and that the agreement for the statue as a work made for hire had not been in writing. The opinion of the U.S. Supreme Court, delivered by Justice Thurgood Marshall on June 5, 1989, was that it was not work for hire, since Reid was an independent contractor rather than an employee of the CCNV. In delivering this decision, multiple factors were considered by the Court. (Other courts determining who owns the copyright to material on a website could apply these same criteria in their decision process.) The factors to be considered are (1) determining whether a work is created by an employee (work made for hire) within the definition of the 1976 copyright law, Section 101(1); or (2) by an independent contractor within the definition of the 1976 copyright law, Section 101(2); or that of (3) joint authorship, thus copyright co-ownership under Section 201(a) of the Copyright Law of 1976 (U.S. Copyright Law, Sec. 101(1), 101(2), 201(a); U.S. Supreme Court, 1989).

Question: Who owns e-mails?

Answer: The sender/creator owns the e-mail, no matter who receives it.

INFRINGEMENTS AND PENALTIES

Question: Is file swapping/downloading of material to your classroom computer an infringement of copyright law?

Answer: File swapping is an issue that probably happens more in our personal lives than in the educational environment. However, because it is so popular, it is addressed briefly here. File swapping can be an infringement of copyright law, since it involves the sharing of files from one computer to another, usually (1) without obtaining permission from the work's original owners/ producers and (2) without following the fair use factors. What makes the concept of file swapping (and other borrowing of materials) even more confusing is that the software and equipment used to make the copies is often created and obtained legally. Thus, you may be able to purchase file-swapping software, but if you use it in the way it is intended to be used, then you have violated copyright law! This is similar to copying movies, computer software, and other works, which we will discuss in later chapters. While the equipment and software needed to copy works are usually legal, the actual act of copying such works without permission may not be legal.

Question: Is downloading an educational video game from the Internet to your iPad an infringement of copyright law?

Answer: Use Flowchart 6.9 to decide if the copying you want to do is legal according to copyright law. Use the same three criteria in Flowchart 6.9 to decide if you can legally send material to another source electronically.

Question: Is it a copyright infringement to attach a one-page chart from an online professional periodical to a wiki on library information skills that the district librarians are creating?

Flowchart 6.9. Copying from the Internet

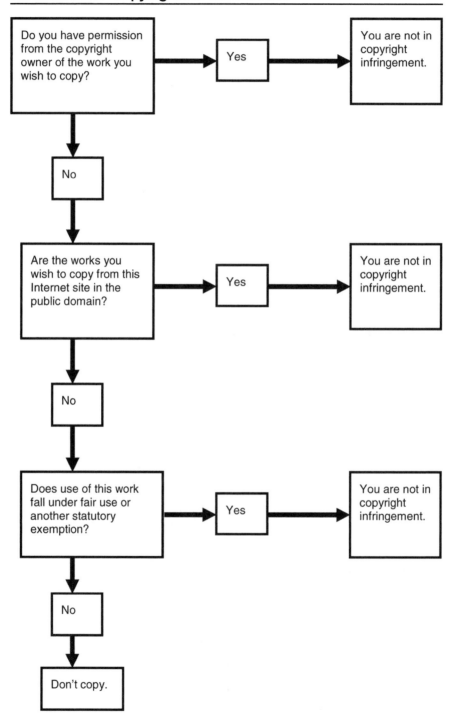

Answer: Use Flowchart 6.10 to determine how to add a chart to a wiki.

Question: Let's suppose that "Helen Avatar" built a building on her own island in *Second Life*, "a 3-D virtual world entirely created by residents" (Botterbusch and Talab, 2009: 9). Helen, an architect in real life, spent a considerable

Flowchart 6.10. Attaching an Online Chart to a Wiki

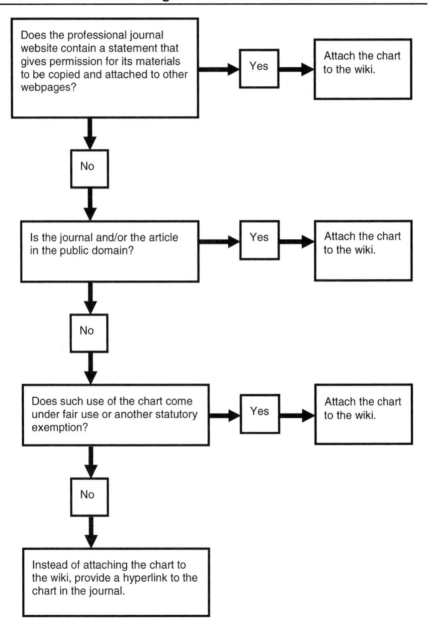

amount of time creating a unique design with which many other *Second Life* users were very impressed. Later, as Helen traveled through the virtual world, visiting friends, she observed an edifice much like hers on another island. The only difference was the color. She believed that another avatar (computer user's alter ego in a web environment) had stolen her design. Can this be considered a virtual world copyright infringement?

Answer: Because avatars in *Second Life* can create, as well as buy and sell goods with their Linden Dollars, it could be possible for copyright infringement to occur. Indeed, *Second Life* has a Digital Millennium Copyright Act page which states in part:

> The DMCA provides a process for a copyright owner to give notification to an online service provider concerning alleged copyright infringement. When a valid DMCA notification is received, the service provider responds under this process by taking down the offending content.... These notifications and counter-notifications are real-world legal notices provided outside of the Second Life environment.... Please note: The DMCA provides that you may be liable for damages (including costs and attorneys fees) if you falsely claim that an in-world item is infringing your copyrights. We recommend contacting an attorney if you are unsure whether an in-world object is protected by copyright laws. (Linden Lab, 2010)

INTERNATIONAL COPYRIGHT LAW

Question: Let's assume your class is studying religions around the world. One of your students finds an excellent site on Druids. However, the site comes from another country. Do we need to be concerned with international copyright law when we use the Internet?

Answer: While the United States belongs to a number of conventions and treaties designed to bring copyright laws worldwide in line (see Chapter 5), in fact, there is no one global copyright law. Each country has its own laws. However, under the Berne Convention, the idea is that the member nations must treat the works of noncitizens the same as they would protect the works of their own citizens. This means that laws that apply to works created in the United States should also apply to works created in other countries—no matter the format (Yu, 2001). Thus, when you use webpages from other countries, you are safest—from a copyright standpoint—if you treat the webpages as if they had been created in the United States. Your other option, which is often more complicated, is to research the copyright laws of the country in which the website was created and abide by them.

Question: Let's assume that you are a school librarian. You and the Spanish teacher decide to collaborate on a literature unit where the students will read picture books from Mexico via VoiceThread. "VoiceThread is a powerful web 2.0 technology that allows language learners the opportunity to interact in an online discussion, while practicing good speaking and writing skills" (Barbara, 2009). During this reading, they will hold up the book and show the pictures as they read. This activity is "in the cloud," i.e., on the web and accessible to the public. Is this legal?

Answer: If such an activity is essential for learning, then it is legal. However, if putting it on the web is not a crucial part of the assignment, then this public performance could be a copyright infringement. Use Flowchart 6.11 to determine whether you can read these books via VoiceThread.

AVOIDING COPYRIGHT PROBLEMS

Question: May I borrow material from a nature website to place on an environment site I am creating for my class? Do I need to cite the owner/creator of the work from which I want to borrow?

Answer: Sometimes the owner of a borrowed work just wants credit for the work. This means that if you are creating a webpage or posting to the web and you want to borrow from a site (or another work) to do so, you should ask the owner/creator of the material for permission to use his or her work (unless your borrowing comes under the fair use factors, another statutory exemption, or public domain). Then, on your webpage, put in a reference crediting the owner/creator of the work that you borrowed. This reference can be at either the beginning or the end of your webpage or at the point of the citation itself. Failure to cite a work, besides possibly making an owner/creator angry, is also plagiarism. So when you borrow anything, cite! Remember that plagiarism is different from copyright infringement. You can cite the owners for something you have copied and still be infringing on their copyright.

Question: Is downloading an online dictionary to my iPad the same as downloading it to my laptop? In other words, do I need to be aware of copyright law when using newer Internet access tools such as iPads, Kindles, Nooks, and similar handheld devices?

Answer: Yes! It does not matter the device. Copyright law is interpreted the same.

Question: Will cloud computing change how we work with copyright law?

Answer: Apply copyright law to cloud computing—a term used because the "set of pooled computing resources and services delivered over the web... resembles a cloud" (Rackspace Cloud, 2011)—the same way that you would apply the law to anything else you use on the web.

Question: Our principal wants to make an electronic toolbox for the faculty and place it on the school intranet. In it, he will place educational materials that he thinks we may need, such as book chapters, lists of Internet links,

Flowchart 6.11. Reading a Book in the Cloud

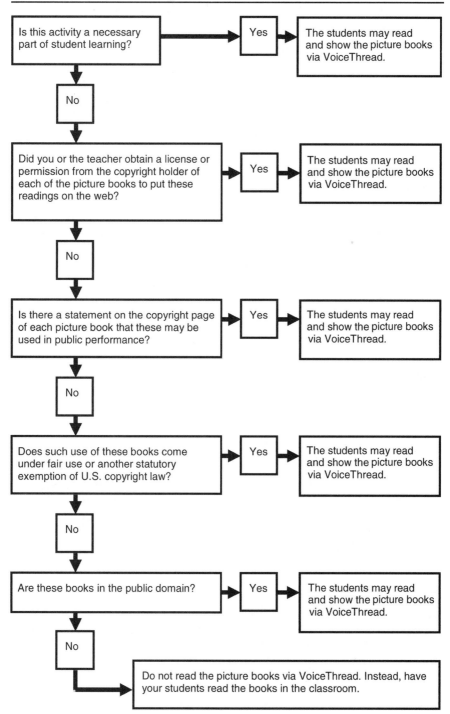

magazine articles, and even books, if he can get them scanned. Since no one will be able to access the electronic toolbox without a password, is there a copyright issue here?

Answer: Any or all of the items mentioned above may be copyright-protected; whether or not there is a password to get into the site makes no difference. In addition, some of the items may originally be in print and some in a digital format. Since the electronic toolbox means that all works must be digital, this venture can become very confusing. Basically, each work will have to be considered separately in terms of copyright law. See Flowchart 6.12 for more information.

CONCLUSION

The 21st century is a challenging period to be a K–12 educator, with digital communication devices becoming the norm, while school budgets remain the same or decrease. Add to that the confusion over copyright law, which in the best of times can be difficult to interpret. As an educator, often trying to do more with less, consider the following questions when borrowing or using another's digital works:

- Does what I want to borrow fit under one or more of the fair use factors?
- Is what I want to borrow in the public domain?
- Can I obtain permission to use all or part of this work from the owner/ author?

If the answer to none of these is yes, then find another work to use or another way to teach the class. Remember that there are ways to work within the law and still have the materials essential for teaching your students. It may be that you just need to be creative, read the works' documentations (sometimes the license or documentation actually lets you do more than you think possible), or learn a few grant-writing skills to legally obtain the necessary works. In addition, when using the material in this chapter, if you do not find your exact question, choose a similar one to use or follow the sample one in Flowchart 5.1 (p. 61). It is possible that the technology you are using now was not available at the publication time of this book because the digital age is evolving so rapidly.

REFERENCES

American Library Association (ALA). 2010. "Hypertext Linking and Copyright Issues." American Library Association. http://www.ala.org/ala/issuesadvocacy/copyright/copyrightarticle/hypertextlinking.cfm.

Barbara. 2009. "Using VoiceThread as a Tool for Language Learning." Technology and Collaborative Creativity in Learning (TaCCL) Lab, University at Albany. December. http://tccl.rit.albany.edu/knilt/index.php/Using_VoiceThread_as_a_Tool_for_Language_Learning.

Flowchart 6.12. Is an Electronic Toolbox Legal?

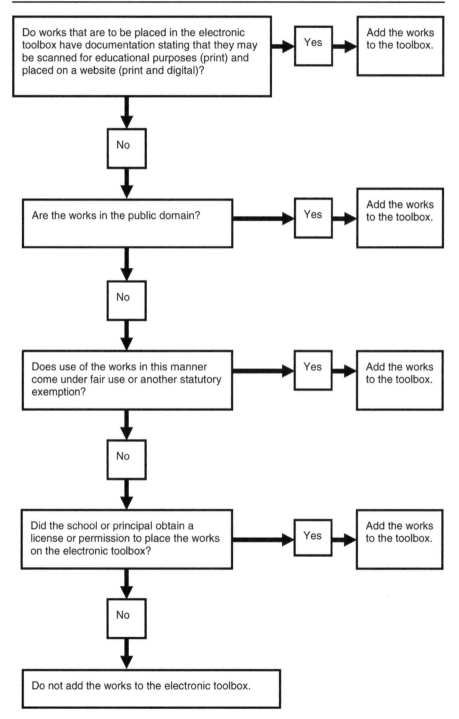

Besenjak, Cheryl. 1997. *Copyright Plain and Simple*. Franklin Lakes, NJ: Career Press.

Bettig, Ronald V. 1996. *Copyrighting Culture: The Political Economy of Intellectual Property*. Boulder, CO: Westview.

Botterbusch, Hope R., and R.S. Talab. 2009. "Copyright and You: Ethical Issues in *Second Life*." *TechTrends* 53, no. 1 (January/February): 9.

Brick Marketing. 2010. "What Is Deep Linking?" Brick Marketing. http://www.brickmarketing .com/define-deep-linking.htm.

Facebook. 2010. "How to Report Claims of Intellectual Property Infringement." Facebook. http://www.facebook.com/legal/copyright.php.

Hoffmann, Gretchen McCord. 2001. *Copyright in Cyberspace: Questions and Answers for Librarians*. New York: Neal-Schuman.

"Internet." 2010. *Collins English Dictionary: Complete and Unabridged*, 10th ed. Harper-Collins. Accessed September 7. http://dictionary.reference.com/browse/Internet.

Jassin, Lloyd J. 2010. "Working with Freelancers: What Every Publisher Should Know about the 'Work for Hire' Doctrine." CopyLaw. http://www.copylaw.com/new_articles/ wfh.html.

Linden Lab. 2010. "DMCA: Digital Millennium Copyright Act." Second Life, Linden Research, Inc. Accessed September 11. http://secondlife.com/corporate/dmca.php.

LinkedIn. 2010. "Copyright Policy." LinkedIn Corporation. March. http://www.linkedin .com/static?key=copyright_policy.

Rackspace Cloud. 2011. "What Is Cloud Computing?" Rackspace, US Inc. http://www .rackspace.com/cloud/what_is_cloud_computing/.

Rubin, Bonnie Miller. 2010. "Teen, Tween Media Use Rising." Section 1. *Chicago Tribune*, January 20: 4.

Shelfari. 2010. "Copyright Policy." Shelfari. Revised August 27. http://www.shelfari .com/CopyrightPolicy.aspx.

Torrans, Lee Ann. 2003. *Law for K–12 Libraries and Librarians*. Westport, CT: Libraries Unlimited.

Twitter. 2010. "Terms of Service." Twitter. Effective November 16. http://twitter.com/tos.

U.S. Copyright Law. 1976. Public Law 94-553, sec. 101, 201.

U.S. Copyright Office, Library of Congress. 2006. "Copyright in General." July. http://www.copyright.gov/help/faq/faq-general.html.

U.S. Supreme Court. 1989. "Community for Creative Non-Violence v. Reid." 490 U.S. 730; Docket Number: 88-293. http://www.oyez.org/oyez/resource/case/1123/.

YouTube. 2010. "Copyright Tips." YouTube. Accessed September 11. http://www.youtube .com/t/howto_copyright.

Yu, Peter K. 2001. "Conflict of Laws Issues in International Copyright Cases." GigaLaw .com. April. http://www.peteryu.com/gigalaw0401.pdf.

CHAPTER 7

Dvds, Cds, Videos, Video Streaming and On Demand, and Copyright Law: Can You Use Such Movie Formats Legally in Your Classroom?

INTRODUCTION

Elementary, middle, and high school teachers sometimes use fiction and nonfiction DVDs, CDs, videos, and/or video streaming in the classroom—this is a given. This often-commonplace activity of showing movies in an educational setting has been under fire for years, however, usually due to misunderstandings about the legal use of such items. As we study how to work within copyright law and show movies in schools, please keep in mind that most questions and answers in this chapter can apply to any of the formats listed in this chapter's title.

In this chapter, we examine the lawful uses of movies in K–12 classrooms. Questions with more than one answer are presented in flowchart form. Remember, as you review the flowcharts in this chapter, you are trying to find any criterion under which you may borrow a work. Therefore, you need only follow each flowchart until you come to that point where you satisfy one of the criteria. When you reach that point, there is no need to go any further. In addition, for more information on each area discussed, please refer to the chapter (Chapters 1 through 5) in which that particular subject is covered.

FAIR USE

Question: You discover that the sex-education videotape that you regularly use to support the unit on sexuality in your introductory health class is falling apart. You ask the library media specialist if she will transfer it to a DVD along with two other deteriorating sex-education tapes that you use all the time. That way, you will have the three easily available when you need them, in a format that should not wear out easily. The original videos can be stored as backup. She suggests that it would be better for one of you to purchase the three programs on DVD or in another format, if available. You feel that such a purchase would be wasted money. What should be done here?

Answer: Use Flowchart 7.1 to decide if you should burn a DVD or purchase a copy of the videos in another format. It is important to note that if you find you are allowed to copy the videos to DVD, you may only show them to your class in the school library. Section 108 of the 1976 Copyright Act, and later expanded upon for digital works in Section 404 of the Digital Millennium Copyright Act (DMCA) of 1998, permits libraries and archives to make up to three copies (including digital) of unique or deteriorating works, provided the newly digitized copies are used only in the library or archive premises (DMCA, 1998). The DMCA also permits libraries and archives "to copy a work into a new format if the original format becomes obsolete—that is, the machine or device used to render the work perceptible is no longer manufactured or is no longer reasonably available in the commercial marketplace" (DMCA, 1998: 15). Such a copy is also to be used only in the library.

Question: Is a teacher allowed to copy a bunch of movie clips, string them together onto a DVD or CD (or videotape), and use it in class?

Answer: Use Flowchart 7.2 (p. 92) to decide if this is allowable under copyright law.

Question: May I show a popular movie clip in my physics class?

Answer: Showing it for an educational purpose should fit under the fair use factors and/or the classroom exemption, Section 110(1) of the U.S. Copyright Law.

Question: I would like to know if there are any alternatives to copyright law when it comes to using video in the classroom and for research.

Answer: A number of groups support a broader view of copyright. Among them are Creative Commons, the Free Software Foundation (see Chapter 5), and Critical Commons. Such organizations provide information for owners of works to create their own licenses (Creative Commons, 2010; Free Software Foundation, 2010), as well as material on the law, showcases for creative productions, and, in some cases, possible alternatives to copyright guidelines (Plumi, 2010).

Question: I am the librarian in a private school. Can I apply fair use or another statutory exemption to the videos in my library?

Answer: Perhaps. All parts of the law still apply, whether you are in a public or private school. The difference is that while the law remains the same, most statutory exemptions address nonprofit educational venues, in which case they do not apply to your school. Thus, it is best to obtain public performance rights, a license, or permission from the copyright owners to use each video in your library.

Flowchart 7.1. Burning Videos to DVDs

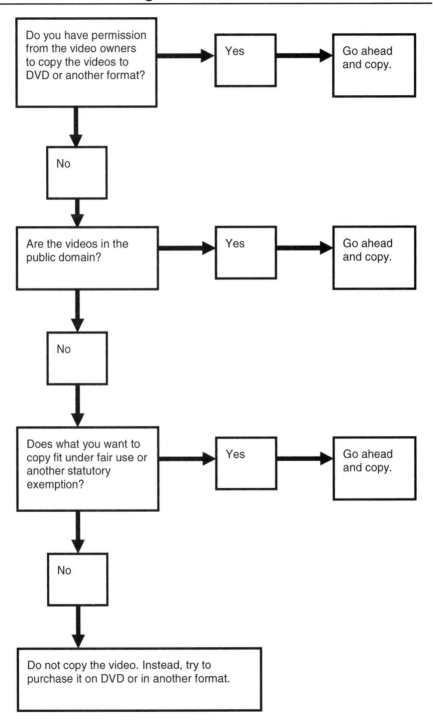

Flowchart 7.2. Copying Movie Clips

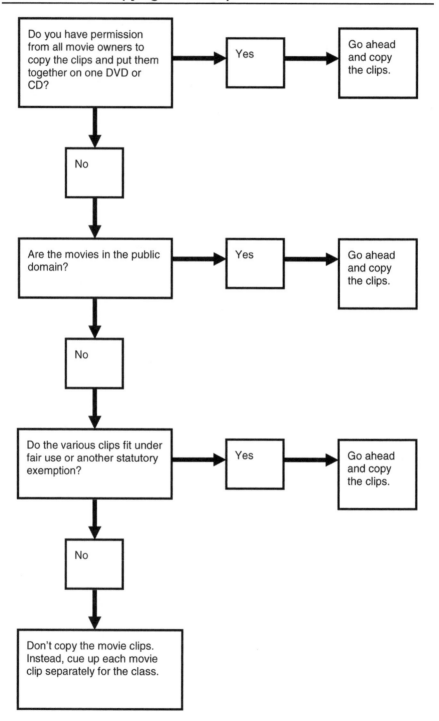

PUBLIC DOMAIN

Question: How do I find out if a movie is in the public domain?

Answer: The U.S. Copyright Office does not maintain lists of works in the public domain. However, for a fee of $165 per hour (two-hour minimum) (U.S. Copyright Office, 2010), they will search their records to see if the work you are interested in is part of the public domain. You may also do your own search, either in person or online, at http://www.copyright.gov/help/faq/faq-services.html#whoowns for free. Note that online records are available only for works registered 1978 and after (U.S. Copyright Office, 2009). Also, refer to Flowchart 7.3 (p. 94).

Question: My high school class is studying the history of our geographic area. I understand that there is a governmental map showing old military sites, which I would like to share with my students. However, I cannot get a hold of it. Since government documents are in the public domain, what gives?

Answer: While most government documents are in the public domain, it does not mean that all are available for public consumption. There are many classified government documents, often denoted as such for security or privacy reasons. In some cases, you may be able to obtain a government document through the Freedom of Information Act, which "requires federal agencies to make certain types of records publicly available" (Fishman, 2010: 47).

Question: Are YouTube videos in the public domain?

Answer: It depends on the video in question. According to the YouTube copyright policy, "YouTube respects the rights of copyright holders and publishers and requires all users to confirm they own the copyright or have permission from the copyright holder to upload content." If such is not the case, YouTube reserves the right to remove offending videos, block use of the site by offenders, and terminate users' accounts (YouTube, 2010).

Question: Can I create a parody of a movie that is in the public domain?

Answer: Yes! See Chapter 3 for more information on public domain.

Question: How do I place a video that the class has made in the public domain?

Answer: Put a statement on the video that it is in the public domain; that is all that you need to do.

DOCUMENTATION AND LICENSES

Question: May I rent an entertainment DVD from a video store and use it in my class?

Flowchart 7.3. Public Domain Movies

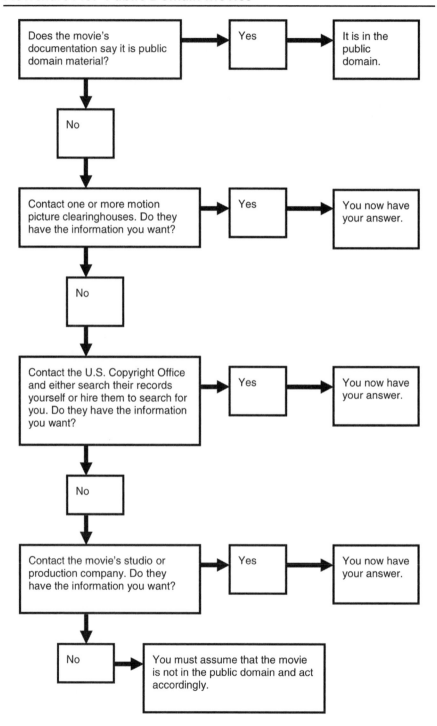

Answer: Section 110(1) of the U.S. Copyright Law states that it is not an infringement for instructors or students to use videos, including those labeled "for home use only," in the classroom, as long as they are using legally obtained videos and the use is for face-to-face instruction in a nonprofit educational institution (U.S. Copyright Law, 1976). This section of the law can also be applied to DVDs, CDs, and other movie formats. Use Flowchart 7.4 to decide whether you can show a video to your class.

Flowchart 7.4. Using Entertainment DVDs in Class

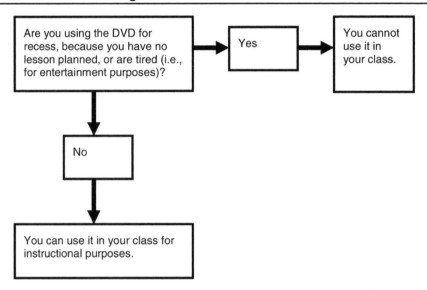

Question: The elementary school art teacher paints Disney characters, based on her memory of a Disney video, on the lunchroom walls. The kids love it and ask for more. Is this an infringement?

Answer: Yes. Unless you have purchased a license from a company to use their works or otherwise have permission, such use is an infringement of copyright law.

Question: The parent-teacher organization in my children's school is having a movie night in the learning center, showing *Harry Potter and the Sorcerer's Stone*. They are charging three dollars per person, proceeds to go toward purchasing more learning-center materials. They tell me that they have purchased public performance rights, so it is okay. What are public performance rights?

Answer: When users purchase public performance rights, they have purchased the rights to display the work in a public forum. Public performance rights for a movie might be purchased from a vendor, a clearinghouse, or the owner/creator of the work. (See also Chapter 4.)

Question: The eighth grade in my middle school has won recognition for volunteer work in our community. I would like to reward them with a movie in the school auditorium on Friday afternoon. Can I legally do this?

Answer: Use Flowchart 7.5 to decide if such a showing of the movie is legal. You may find that you have to purchase performance rights. There are also companies that specialize in acquiring permissions from motion picture studios. These companies then sell the school or school district a license to use all or some (usually listed) of the movies produced by each studio. One example of this type of company is Movie Licensing USA. This organization offers licenses for such studios as Disney, Columbia, DreamWorks, Warner Bro., and others (Movie Licensing USA, 2010).

Please note that, in Flowchart 7.5 as well as in several other flowcharts throughout this book, there is more than one way for the borrower to ask for permission to use a work. You can ask the owner(s) of the work directly for permission, contact a clearinghouse, or purchase a license to borrow the work. If you satisfy the conditions of one of the permission questions, there is no need to follow the flowchart any further.

Question: Can the school librarian make a copy of a DVD for a teacher to use if the school owns the original and two teachers want to use the DVD at the same time?

Answer: Probably not. However, there are some instances where this might work. See Flowchart 7.6 (p. 98).

Question: Do schools need to purchase public performance rights for videos if they are educational videos?

Answer: If the videos support the class curriculum, they do not need public performance rights. Such rights are needed, however, if the video is used for entertainment or reward purposes.

Question: A colleague wishes to order a DVD of a classic movie to use in a high school English class. The vendor says that she must purchase a specific licensing agreement. What is going on? Shouldn't such use be legal under the classroom exemption?

Answer: The owner of the DVD's copyright can determine how it is used. If that individual or group wishes to state specific uses via a license, then the teacher needs to obtain the license in order to use the movie. If no license is required, then the classroom exemption (Section 110 of U.S. Copyright Law) will apply.

PERMISSIONS

Question: As the new algebra teacher at the high school, you conceive the idea of having your freshman students create a website dealing with basic algebraic

Flowchart 7.5. Using Movies as Rewards

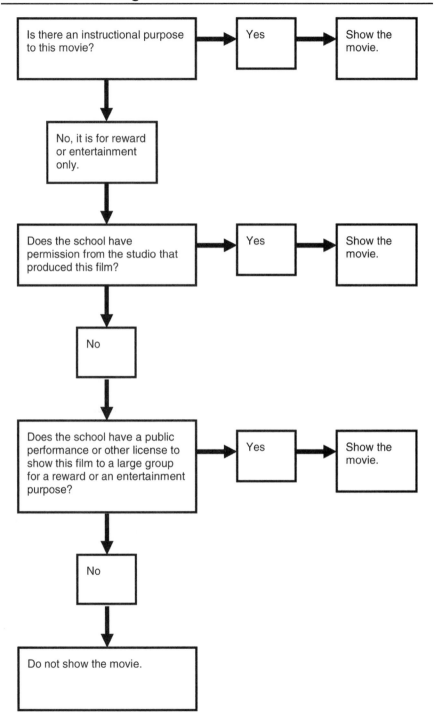

Flowchart 7.6. Copying a DVD

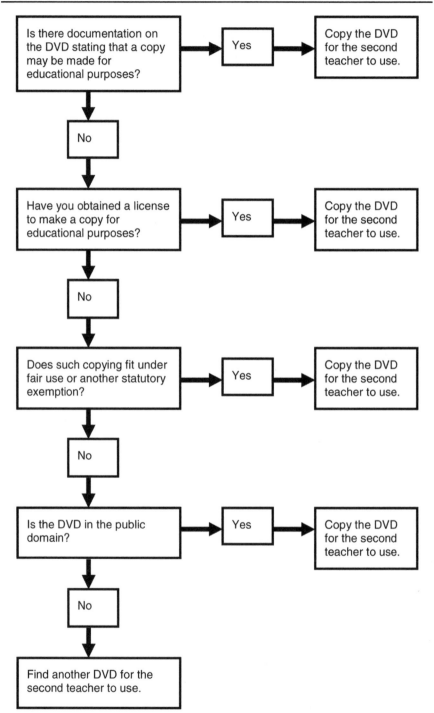

equations. To catch the viewer's eye, you want to add clips from popular movies that have a math or numerical theme. How do you obtain clearance to use videos and DVDs on school websites?

Answer: Use Flowchart 7.7 (p. 100) to decide which clips— if any—you can use legally.

Question: Am I allowed to show a DVD over a closed-circuit system to the whole school?

Answer: Possibly. Use Flowchart 7.8 (p. 101) to decide.

Question: What is "video on demand," and can I ask the librarian to obtain a movie for me to use in my classroom this way?

Answer: "Video-on-demand...make(s) it possible...to select...motion pictures...and order them and receive them instantly...over the Internet...or satellite broadcast" (Donaldson, 2008: 431). For example, it may be possible for your librarian to go to an Internet source, such as Blockbuster or iTunes, and obtain a movie (free, for rent, or for sale) for you to show in your classroom via a computer and projection device. In such a case, he or she and you need to be aware of any specific licenses or copyright policies on these sites that might determine how the film can be used. For more information, see Flowchart 7.9 (pp. 102–103).

Question: Can a student copy images found through a Google search from the Internet for use in a film he is creating without getting permission to use the works?

Answer: If such use is for a learning purpose, such as a class assignment, and the images will be used only in the classroom or for the student's personal portfolio, then yes, such use is possible.

YOU CREATE IT, YOU OWN IT

Question: Imagine that you are a middle school technology teacher. You have just finished a unit on copyright law, so your students are focused on borrowing legally. You assign the students, in groups of four, to make a short movie. All groups elect to use original materials in their movies. They figure that this way they will own the whole work and thus no copyright violations will occur. One group chooses to film its movie outside city hall in front of a new statue the city purchased a year ago. While the sculpture, an unusual piece by a new female artist, is very prominently displayed in their film, it is not the subject of said film. Is there a copyright violation here?

Answer: If the artist has chosen to retain her copyright of the sculpture, even though she sold the sculpture to the city, it is possible there is a violation here: "It is a fundamental tenet of copyright that certain pieces of art, including sculpture,

Flowchart 7.7. Borrowing Movie Clips

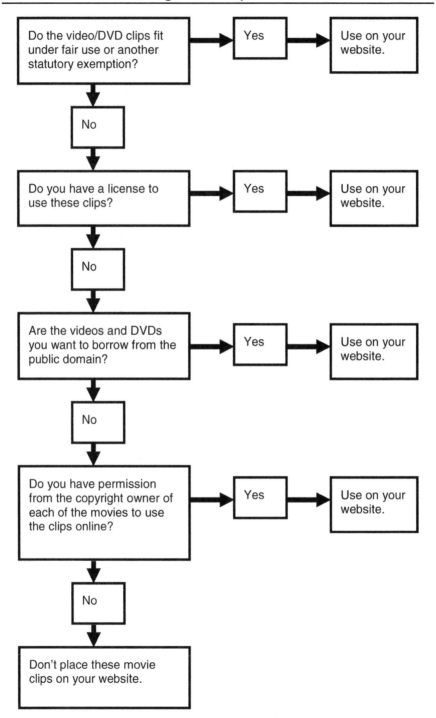

Flowchart 7.8. Closed-Circuit Systems and DVDs

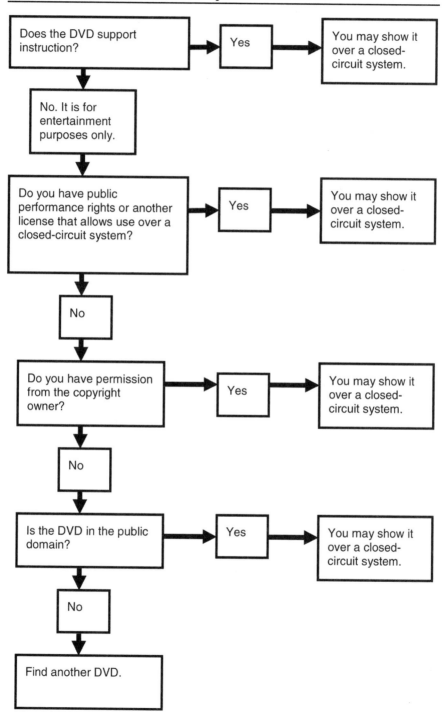

Flowchart 7.9. Using Video On Demand

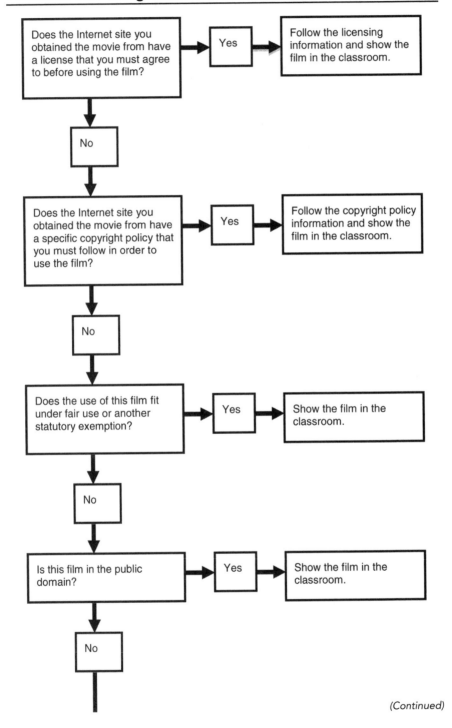

Does the Internet site you obtained the movie from have a license that you must agree to before using the film? → Yes → Follow the licensing information and show the film in the classroom.

No

Does the Internet site you obtained the movie from have a specific copyright policy that you must follow in order to use the film? → Yes → Follow the copyright policy information and show the film in the classroom.

No

Does the use of this film fit under fair use or another statutory exemption? → Yes → Show the film in the classroom.

No

Is this film in the public domain? → Yes → Show the film in the classroom.

No

(Continued)

Flowchart 7.9. Using Video On Demand *(Continued)*

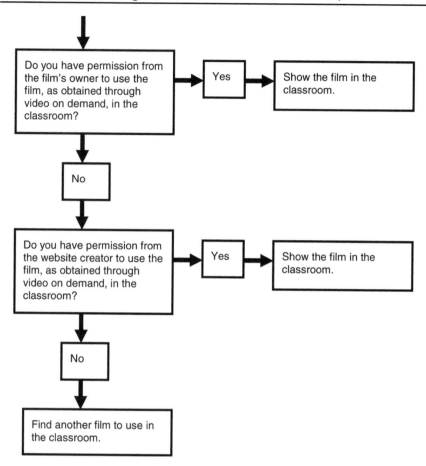

are eligible for copyright protection.... Consequently, permission must be obtained from the copyright holder in order to reproduce images of the sculpture" (Copyright Website, 2010). A possible exception might be if the sculpture were the subject of the movie. In such a case, it might constitute fair use. See Chapter 2 for a discussion of fair use. Students often "get away" with copyright violations that occur as part of a school assignment. However, it is best to follow copyright law in all instances. Flowchart 7.10 (p. 104) provides more direction.

Question: Assume that you are an elementary school teacher. You are about to teach a unit on folk and fairy tales, and you decide to have your students put on a program for the rest of the school. The idea is for your students to act out the stories of "Cinderella," "Aladdin," and "The Three Little Pigs" after they have read and interpreted the stories. There will be no written script. You decide that you will record this program to show to future classes, and you want to intersperse your students' story interpretations with excerpts from

Flowchart 7.10. Statues, Filming, and Copyright

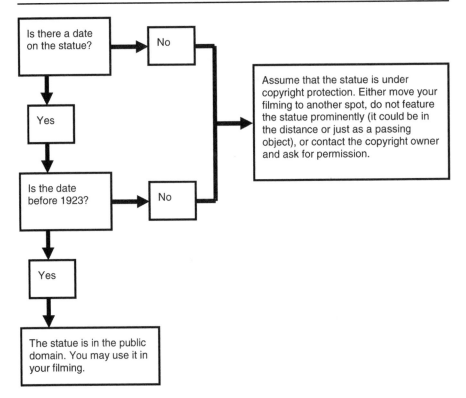

Is there a date on the statue? → No

Yes ↓

Is the date before 1923? → No

Yes ↓

The statue is in the public domain. You may use it in your filming.

Assume that the statue is under copyright protection. Either move your filming to another spot, do not feature the statue prominently (it could be in the distance or just as a passing object), or contact the copyright owner and ask for permission.

commercial movie adaptations of "Cinderella," "Aladdin," and "The Three Little Pigs." Is it a copyright infringement to read and interpret the original stories on a DVD or video? And to add the commercial excerpts?

Answer: Classical stories and characters, including the three mentioned in this question, are in the public domain and are frequently borrowed by motion picture companies, book publishers, musicians, and others. So, no, it is not an infringement to tape your students' interpretations of public domain folk and fairy tales. However, derivative pieces of public domain works can once again attain copyright protection when the borrower puts his or her "stamp" on those revised parts of the work. For example, when an illustrator chooses to draw Snow White as an African American and the seven dwarfs as Asian, this new interpretation of old work places the interpretation under copyright protection for the illustrator or owner of the work. Thus, while the classroom exemption may apply for the use of the excerpts, it is still in your best interest to make sure that the excerpts of commercial movies you borrow are fair use, under public domain, or that you have the needed permissions or licenses. Flowchart 7.11 will help you decide if you can legally add excerpts from commercial movies to a class DVD or video.

Flowchart 7.11. Adding Commercial Film Excerpts to Class-Created DVDs and Videos

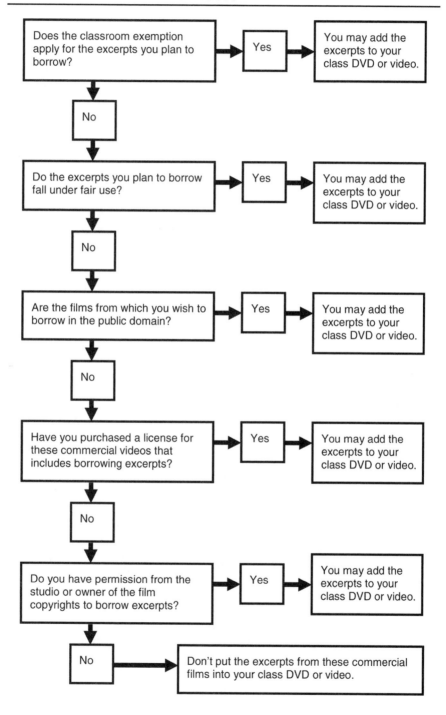

Question: The school technology specialist has just purchased a VHS-to-DVD converter. He wants to take all of the library videos and transfer them to DVD. He says that since such conversions would be for education, this process is legal. Is this true?

Answer: Absolutely not! There is no such thing as a legal blanket policy that allows the transferring of a work from one format to another—even for educational purposes. Essentially, by using the converter in this manner, he would be creating any number of derivative works. However, if not available for purchase or rent—on a case-by-case basis—you and he may be able to determine which videos can be copied and which cannot. See Flowchart 7.12 for additional directions.

Question: I am the librarian in a middle school with a large population of high-interest, low-reading-level students. I have hit on the idea of videotaping volunteers reading first chapters from selected novels in the library. My idea is that the students can view the videos and decide if they want to read the rest of the book or not. I think it will get some of the students to take on books that they might not otherwise pick up. Can I do this legally?

Answer: It depends. Remember that you must consider each novel separately. See Flowchart 7.13 (p. 108) for help.

INFRINGEMENTS AND PENALTIES

Question: It is recess time, and it's five degrees below zero out. You make the decision to keep your third-grade class indoors. However, your students need something to do, and you are exhausted. One of your students has brought his favorite DVD to school. Would it be a copyright infringement if you were to show it to your class?

Answer: Use Flowchart 7.14 (p. 109) to guide your decision.

Question: Suppose your biology class is studying bird beaks. You find a great CD on birding in South America, which you check out from the public library. Can you use it in class without violating copyright law?

Answer: Yes, you can use this CD in class without committing copyright infringement because you are using it for an instructional purpose.

Question: Suppose you teach science in a very conservative area. You know of a great movie that supports your unit on planets. However, you are afraid to purchase it because it talks about evolution (of the planets), and any mention of evolution is anathema in your district. You decide to purchase a special DVD player that can mute or skip over objectionable parts of DVDs as they are played. Your administrator refuses to fund your purchase, stating that such a player is in violation of copyright law. Is it?

Flowchart 7.12. Transferring Videos to DVDs

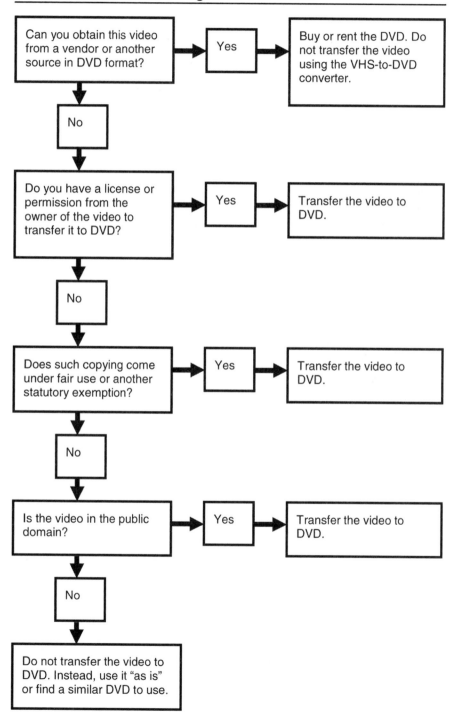

Can you obtain this video from a vendor or another source in DVD format? → **Yes** → Buy or rent the DVD. Do not transfer the video using the VHS-to-DVD converter.

No

Do you have a license or permission from the owner of the video to transfer it to DVD? → **Yes** → Transfer the video to DVD.

No

Does such copying come under fair use or another statutory exemption? → **Yes** → Transfer the video to DVD.

No

Is the video in the public domain? → **Yes** → Transfer the video to DVD.

No

Do not transfer the video to DVD. Instead, use it "as is" or find a similar DVD to use.

Flowchart 7.13. Videotaping Volunteers Reading from a Novel

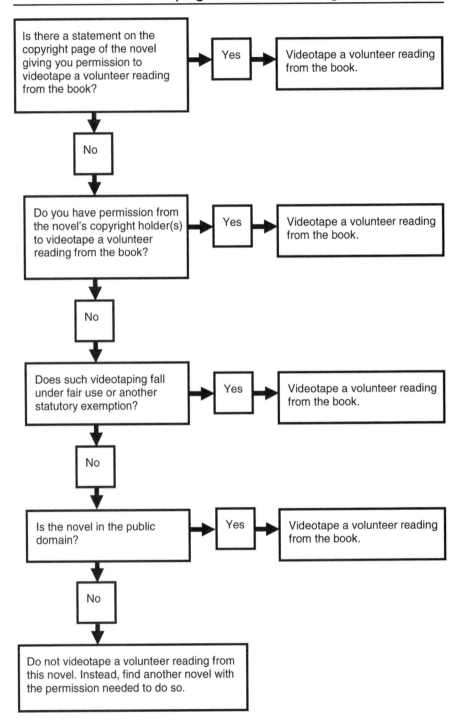

Flowchart 7.14. Showing Student-Owned Works during Recess

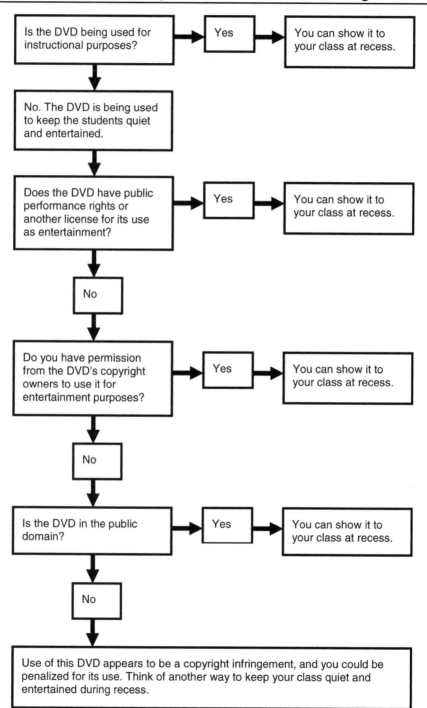

Answer: There are filtering DVD players available, such as ClearPlay and TV Guardian, which can block or skip unacceptable DVD content as it is viewed (ClearPlay, 2010; Family Safe Media, 2010). Use of such equipment is legal, since you have retained the original item and are just not using selected parts of it.

Question: Within the last year, your administration has obtained (1) several recordable DVD drives and copying software; (2) CD burners for all teachers' computers and half of the lab computers; (3) more DVD and CD players; and (4) more audio-recording devices. The idea behind all this is that with these recording devices, the school will be able to record more material from popular television, movies, CDs, and the Internet, copy it for use in the school, and eventually save money by purchasing less media. At the moment, the focus in your school is on burning films to DVDs. Overall, your administration feels that they will save money. Do such actions infringe on copyrights?

Answer: Yes! While the past few years have seen a flood of hardware and software that can be used for copying become available on the market, that does not mean that the copies made from such media are legal. Under copyright law, in this case, fair use, public domain, permissions, and licensing of materials still apply. Therefore, do not use the items purchased for your school for illegal copying. It is in violation of copyright law and subject to penalty.

Question: How does a school library replace a DVD that has been lost or stolen? (See Section 108 of the copyright law: Limitations on Exclusive Rights: Reproduction by Libraries and Archives.)

Answer: This is a confusing piece of the law. For this question, look to part (d) of Section 108: "The rights of reproduction and distribution under this section apply to a copy, made from the collection of a library or archives where the user makes his or her request or from that of another library or archives of no more than one article or other contribution to a copyrighted collection" (U.S. Copyright Law, 1976). In layman's terms, you can borrow the item in question from another library and create a copy.

INTERNATIONAL COPYRIGHT LAW

Question: The father of one of your students has just returned home from a business trip to Southeast Asia. While there, he purchased a DVD copy of a movie, one that has recently come out in the theaters in the United States. The DVD's jewel case has no movie photograph on the cover, there is no copyright information anywhere on the case or DVD, and only the name of the movie is on the DVD. Furthermore, your student tells you that the quality of the DVD is not good. To make things more complex, you search the Internet and find the same movie there as well. What's going on?

Answer: Chances are that the DVD and Internet copies of the movie are pirated. Piracy, the unauthorized replication or use of media, is not part of copyright law, but it is often associated with it, since pirated items are frequently found to be in copyright violation. Film piracy occurs when an individual or group (1) obtains a copy of a movie on disk or tape from someone in the film distribution area before the authorized release date or (2) actually sneaks into a theater and records the movie as it is shown. The stolen copy is then brought to a clandestine production area where it is mass-produced on disk or digitally broken into file pieces easy enough to put on the Internet. At that point, it is then distributed. Some such organizations pirate for monetary purposes; others, especially those who place such films on the web, do it because they feel such media should be free for all consumers (Munoz and Healey, 2003). Since the movie is still in the theaters in the United States, it is highly likely that use of your student's movie would violate U.S. copyright law. In addition, the United States belongs to several international organizations with treaty agreements in the area of copyright (see Chapter 5). Depending on who produced the pirated film and in which country, this means that such pirating could also be in violation of copyright in other countries. Movie piracy is expensive. For example, it caused the U.S. motion picture industry to lose approximately $6.1 billion in potential income in 2005 (L.E.K. Consulting, 2010). The bottom line is: don't use the DVD that your student brought to class or the movie you found on the web.

Question: I teach at an American school in Germany. I recently found a fantastic video clip on the web that I would like to use in my class. It appears to have a Creative Commons license. Exactly what does that mean for my use of the clip?

Answer: It does not matter where you teach; the same Creative Commons license will apply. What does matter is what rights the original owner of the video specified under the license. In order to use the video, you will need to follow the exact stipulations that the original owner placed on the work through the Creative Commons agreement.

Question: Can we stream a video on a Japanese website to our language lab for use with students?

Answer: Japan belongs to several of the same copyright conventions as does the United States. Thus, treat a video from a Japanese website the same as you would treat one from a U.S. website.

Question: I teach in a private K–9 international school with an American curriculum. Can we apply fair use and the classroom exemption in our use of DVDs and videos?

Answer: No. Just because you have an American curriculum does not mean that you can apply U.S. laws to the works you use in your schools. Instead, apply the copyright laws for the country in which the school resides.

AVOIDING COPYRIGHT PROBLEMS

Question: I am taking 30 sixth-graders to a natural history museum for the day. This is a full-day school-sponsored outing. The ride each way is two hours long. I would like to take some of my personal DVDs (commercial entertainment films) along for them to watch on the bus, which has a TV and DVD player. Can I do so legally?

Answer: Use Flowchart 7.15 to decide if you can legally show your personal DVDs on the bus.

Question: I purchased this DVD from a local store. May I use it in class?

Answer: As has been shown throughout this chapter, that depends on how you want to use it. See Flowchart 7.16 (p. 114) for more information.

Question: A teacher has a favorite video that she shows yearly in her class. Her enthusiasm about this video has caused several other teachers to want to use it also. As a favor to the media specialist, the teacher burns the video to a CD. She then donates the CD to the media center. Is there a copyright problem here?

Answer: In all probability, she has created an unauthorized copy. (Please note that libraries can sometimes make copies of works that are deteriorating, damaged, or missing, if no replacements can be found, or replacements are not at a fair price. This exemption can be found in Section 108 of the Copyright Law of the United States.)

Question: Your principal informs all teachers in the school that they may not use any videos or DVDs unless they have been purchased by the learning center. You argue that there are many places videos and DVDs can come from and still be used in the school. Who is right?

Answer: You are. As long as the film is being shown for an instructional purpose, you can rent it from a video store, check it out from the public library, borrow it from a student, purchase it from a discount store, or get it from other sources.

Question: Can the technology specialist legally stream an educational video he found on the web to more than one science classroom at the same time?

Answer: Video streaming, which "allows for Internet access to entire copies of motion pictures...subject to whatever constraints the streaming source places on access" (Lutzker, 2010: 1), must follow copyright law the same as the use of any other video. In addition, the streaming source, as Lutzker (2010) notes, may have a license or grant specific permissions to the users of the video in question. Follow the Internet source's license/specific permissions first, if these are available. See also Flowchart 7.17 (p. 115).

Flowchart 7.15. Using Personal DVDs on a School Outing

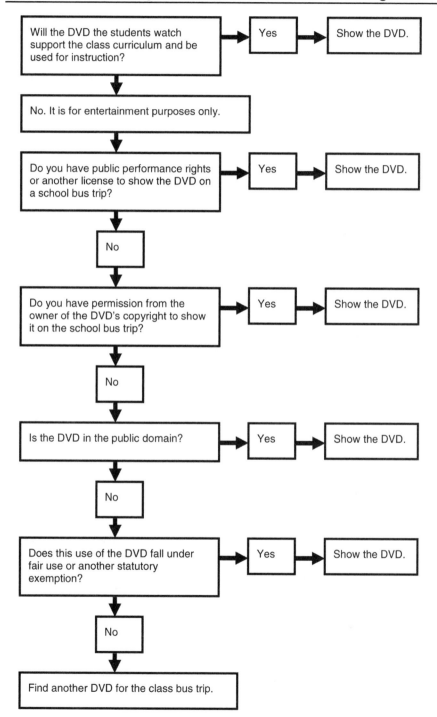

Flowchart 7.16. Using Locally Purchased DVDs in Class

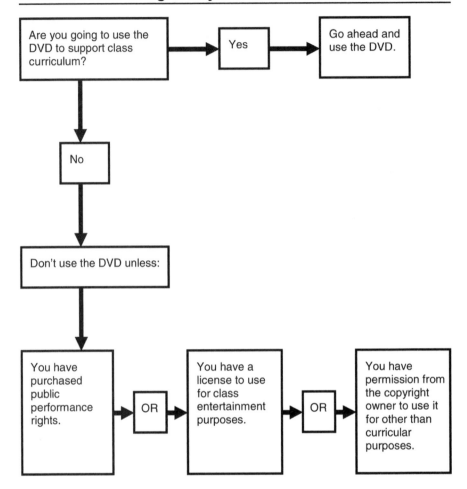

CONCLUSION

In the average K–12 school district today, more than half of all copyright questions deal with the use of DVDs, CDs, videos, and/or video streaming. Because copyright law is so gray, although there are general rules, the critical answers to DVD/CD/video streaming use in the schools are often missing. The questions, answers, and flowcharts in this chapter are designed to help you as you use both instructional and entertainment media in your classroom. While we are more likely in the 21st century to be using DVDs and films obtained via the web, examples using videotapes and movie DVDs have been kept in this chapter for those schools where the technology may be less current. Please remember that, for the purposes of this chapter, all of the mentioned media are used interchangeably for any movie/film format used in K–12 schools.

Flowchart 7.17. Streaming Video and Copyright

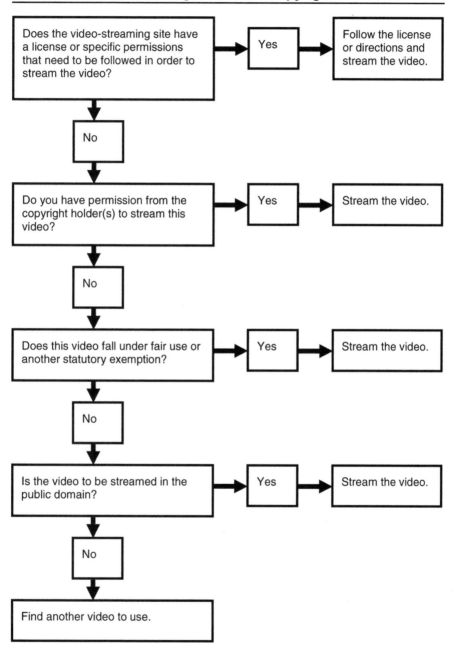

REFERENCES

ClearPlay. 2010. "Home." ClearPlay, Inc. http://www.clearplay.com.

Copyright Website. 2010. "Copyright Casebook: Batman Forever and the Water Vampire." Copyright Website LLC. http://www.benedict.com/Visual/Batman/Batman.aspx.

Creative Commons. 2010. "About." Creative Commons Corporation. Accessed June 7. http://creativecommons.org/about/what-is-cc.

The Digital Millennium Copyright Act of 1998 (DMCA). 1998. U.S. Copyright Office Summary. Washington, DC: U.S. Copyright Office.

Donaldson, Michael C. 2008. *Clearance & Copyright: Everything You Need to Know for Film and Television.* Los Angeles: Silman-James Press.

Family Safe Media. 2010. "TV Guardian: Profanity Filtering Tools." Nextphase, Inc. http://www.familysafemedia.com/tv_guardian_summary.html.

Fishman, Stephen. 2010. *The Public Domain: How to Find & Use Copyright-Free Writings, Music, Art & More.* 5th ed. Berkeley, CA: Nolo.

Free Software Foundation (FSF). 2010. "GNU Operating System." http://www.gnu.org.

L.E.K. Consulting. 2010. "The Cost of Movie Piracy." PerfSpot.com LLC. http://www.perfspot.com/docs/doc.asp?id=1098.

Lutzker, Arnold P. 2010. "Educational Video Streaming: A Short Primer." *AIME News* 24, no. 1 (Spring): 1–4.

Movie Licensing USA. 2010. "Studios We Represent." Movie Licensing USA. Accessed October 8. http://www.movlic.com/studios.html.

Munoz, Lorenza, and Jon Healey. 2003. "Studio Waging Uphill Fight against Bootlegging." *Chicago Tribune*, Arts & Entertainment, December 7: 16.

Plumi. 2010. "Critical Commons: About Us." Critical Commons. Updated May 24. http://criticalcommons.org/about-us.

U.S. Copyright Law. 1976. Public Law 94-553.

U.S. Copyright Office, Library of Congress. 2009. "Copyright: Can I Use Someone Else's Work? Can Someone Else Use Mine?" U.S. Copyright Office. Revised October 6. http://www.copyright.gov/help/faq/faq-fairuse.html.

———. 2010. "Copyright: Fees." U.S. Copyright Office. Revised September 24. http://www.copyright.gov/docs/fees.html.

YouTube. 2010. "What Is Your Policy on Copyright Infringement?" YouTube. http://help.youtube.com/support/youtube/bin/answer.py?hl=en-GB&answer=55772.

CHAPTER 8

Television and Copyright Law: TV Is Free, Isn't It?

INTRODUCTION

Recordable DVDs and digital video recorders, cable channels, satellite TV, streaming video, TV recording/computer software—television viewing and recording have come a long way from the three channels and black-and-white vision of a half century ago. As such new technologies evolve, so too do the questions surrounding them, especially as they pertain to use by K–12 educators and others who work with children, tweens, and teens.

Activities such as using streaming video in the classroom, making a copy of a show from a cable network for class, stringing together a video of television advertisements for an assignment, or saving and using a copy of a popular television program year after year create the possibility of copyright infringement, whether you realize it or not. Sometimes administrators become so concerned with television pirating that they request no copies of television programs be used in the classroom. However, there are ways to borrow from television without violating copyright law. How do you discern legal from illegal use of television programs in our classrooms? The discussion in this chapter will help with this endeavor.

The questions that follow cover television programs, educators, and copyright. Questions with more than one answer are presented in flowchart form. Remember that when you use the flowcharts in this chapter, you are trying to find any criterion under which you may borrow a work. Therefore, you need only follow each flowchart until you come to that point where you satisfy one of the criteria. Once you reach that point, there is no need to go any further. For more information on each area discussed, please refer to the chapter (Chapters 1 through 5) in which that particular subject is covered.

FAIR USE

Question: When you record a television show for curricular use in your school, what rules apply?

Answer: That depends. Let's assume you are recording from a major broadcast network (i.e., a network that can be received via cable or not). Called "off-air" recording, there are several guidelines that apply to this type of instructional taping of television broadcasts. These are publicly recognized as the "Guidelines for Off-Air Recording of Broadcast Programming for Educational Purposes" (Congressional Record, 1981). Be aware that these guidelines, which as listed here, are in effect only "in the course of relevant teaching activities" (U.S. Congress, 1984). Most copyright guidelines are meant to interpret the fair use factors found in the 1976 Copyright Act, Section 107. One of the ways to access these guidelines is through the U.S. Copyright Office's website at http://www.copyright.gov.

- During the first ten days after taping, the programs may be viewed by the class for instruction once and repeated once for reinforcement.
- Off-air recorded programs may be retained for 45 days. The last 35 days, the teacher may view the recording for evaluation purposes only.
- Programs may be recorded at individual teachers' requests but not for anticipated requests.
- After 45 days, the recording should be erased.
- Location for performance of the off-air recorded program should be either in classrooms or other areas used for instructional purposes; in one building, cluster of buildings or a campus; or in the residences of those students who receive formal home instruction.
- The recorded program may not be edited. However, you do not have to use the whole thing in class.
- This is a one-time-only opportunity. Teachers may not ask for the same program to be recorded more than once.
- Recorded programs must be used for educational use only.
- In some cases, more than one copy may be made of a recording if it is necessary to meet teachers' needs. In such a case, rules for the extra copies are the same as those for the original.
- All off-air copying must include the copyright notice found on the broadcasted program.
- Ask the copyright holder if you need more rights than those normally assigned to educators. Copyright holders often say yes to educational purposes.
- Some channels, such as PBS, give to educators more rights than those already noted. Check with the individual networks for this information (Torrans, 2003).

Question: Now, let's assume that the television program you wish to record for curricular purposes is from either a cable or satellite network. What rules apply in these cases?

Answer: In both cases, you now need to follow the specific educational copying criteria as determined by the cable or satellite channel. (Such criteria is often found on a website for the particular network or in network publications.) With these types of broadcasts, there is no one set of copying rights available. All rights are determined by the individual copyright owners.

Question: Last Monday night one of the major networks aired a special on social networking. You recorded it to use in your class. Before showing it to the students, you delete the commercials from the recording. Can you legally cut the commercials out of a recorded network broadcast without obtaining permission from the network?

Answer: No, you cannot. By cutting out the commercials, you have created a derivative work. This does not constitute a fair use (see Chapter 2). However, you can show the social networking special basically as you wish by using the remote to fast-forward through each commercial. You may also show a fair use portion of the recording, which does not include a commercial. In other words, while you may not alter a program, you do not have to use all parts of it.

Question: Let's imagine that you are teaching a high school psychology class. There are several popular daytime talk shows that feature people chatting about their problems. You decide to record short segments that are all aired during a single week from these programs and compile them into one DVD for class discussion the following week. Is this legal?

Answer: No. Once again, you have prepared a derivative work. Under copyright law, you may not do this without permission. What you can do—although it is more cumbersome—is tape each segment (assuming each use fits under the fair use factors) on a different DVD. Then pop each taped segment into the video player as you need it. (For information on permissions and obtaining licenses for such use, please see Chapter 4 as well as the sections Documentation and Licenses and Permissions in this chapter.)

Question: Can I just copy the visual track from a TV program for use with my students?

Answer: No. By taking the sound away, you have created a new work. However, you can overcome this by turning down the sound on the TV/monitor when showing the students the program.

Question: I understand that after 45 days, I may no longer use a television program I have recorded. However, it is a great program. I want to use it every semester. Therefore, I plan to ask my grandmother, aunt, best friend, and neighbor to also tape it. I will then use one of their tapes each semester. That way, I can keep using the program for at least four semesters. Is that okay?

Answer: No, it is not okay. Off-air recordings cannot be recorded more than once for use by the same teacher, no matter who records them or how many times the program is broadcast (Congressional Record, 1981). In this case, it would be best if you purchased the recording from the network.

PUBLIC DOMAIN

Question: I teach social studies and government at the local high school. I want to show my government class the U.S. House of Representatives in action. Can I tape a portion of the House activities from C-SPAN for this class?

Answer: Yes. Floor proceedings for both the House and Senate are in the public domain (C-SPAN, 2010).

Question: Martin Luther King Jr.'s birthday is coming. I'd like to show my students his "I Have a Dream" speech. One of the major networks has a version. May I use it?

Answer: Use Flowchart 8.1 to decide if you can show the speech you have recorded from network television.

DOCUMENTATION AND LICENSES

Question: You are teaching high school history, and you have found a great special about the Holocaust on a cable channel. Are you allowed to use it in your class?

Answer: You may be allowed to. Flowchart 8.2 (pp. 122–123) will help you decide. Many cable networks automatically provide educational rights for a selected period of time, at their determination. For example, Cable in the Classroom (CIC) grants rights for at least a year from the airdate of the program (CIC, 2010). Numerous cable networks post copyright guidelines and taping rights on the Internet. It is in your best interest to search the web for such procedures before making your recording.

Question: I was reading the educator's guide for a cable network program, and I see a show on vocations that I would like to show to the seniors on career day. Since we have cable at our school and this network is on our cable system, I assume that we can show this live to the seniors. Am I correct?

Answer: Unless there is a statement to the contrary at the beginning and/or end of the program or in the cable network's educator's guide, then yes, you may show the program live to the seniors.

Question: I am a new school librarian. There is a TiVo system in my library, and teachers are requesting that I use it to tape shows for them to use in the classroom. They really like the idea that they can skip the ads with this system, making it easier to teach. I am concerned that they are now working with derivative works, and these are illegal. What should I do?

Answer: Essentially, a TiVo system works as a digital video recorder; i.e., the ads are there, whether the teacher fast-forwards through them or not. Thus, there is no derivative work involved in using this system. Consider each

Flowchart 8.1. Recording from a Major Network

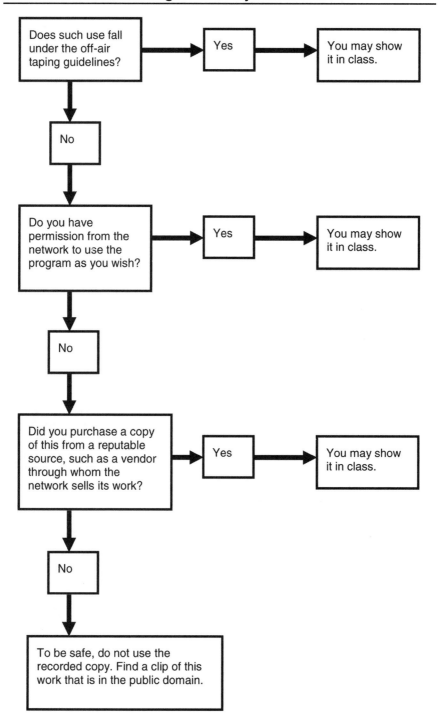

Flowchart 8.2. Using Recorded Cable Programs in the Classroom

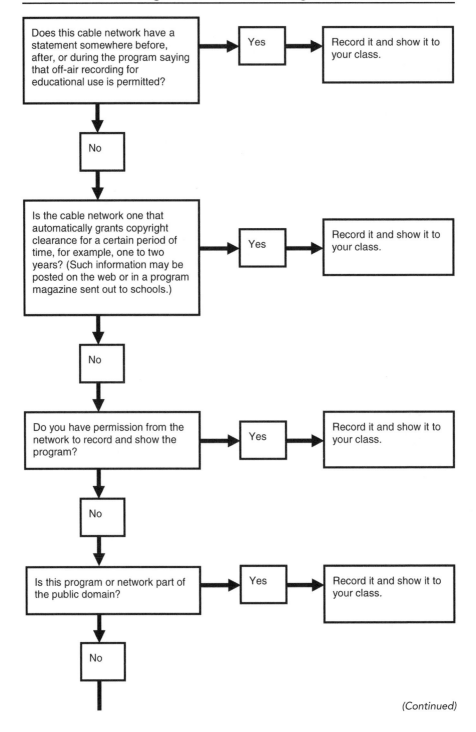

Does this cable network have a statement somewhere before, after, or during the program saying that off-air recording for educational use is permitted? → **Yes** → Record it and show it to your class.

No

Is the cable network one that automatically grants copyright clearance for a certain period of time, for example, one to two years? (Such information may be posted on the web or in a program magazine sent out to schools.) → **Yes** → Record it and show it to your class.

No

Do you have permission from the network to record and show the program? → **Yes** → Record it and show it to your class.

No

Is this program or network part of the public domain? → **Yes** → Record it and show it to your class.

No

(Continued)

Flowchart 8.2. Using Recorded Cable Programs in the Classroom (Continued)

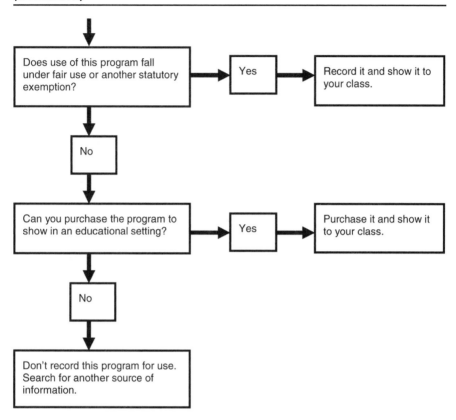

program recorded through TiVo as you would the off-air taping of any show. If it is a major broadcast or from cable or satellite, then act accordingly (see previous questions in this chapter about major broadcasts and cable and satellite networks).

PERMISSIONS

Question: Is it okay to tape a television program for instructional use in my classroom?

Answer: The answer varies with the source of the program. Use Flowchart 8.3 (p. 124) to determine what you may do.

Question: I'm a school librarian. May I make more than one copy of an off-air recording if two or more of my teachers need it at the same time?

Answer: Yes. Just follow the "Guidelines for Off-Air Recording" (Congressional Record, 1981).

Flowchart 8.3. Recording Television Programs for Instructional Use

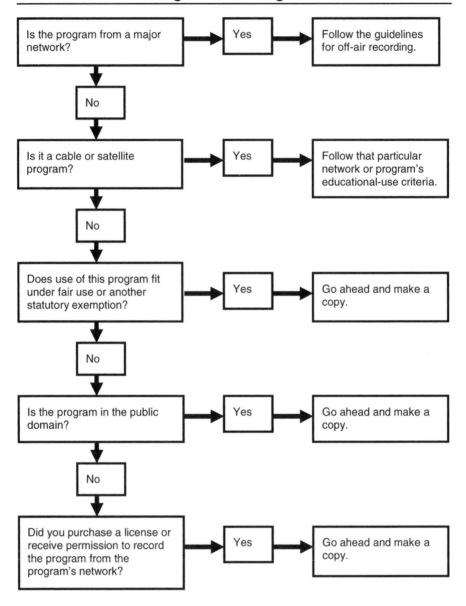

Question: The school has a satellite dish. Since the administration pays for this piece of equipment and the television access it provides, as a teacher you feel that taping programs from it should be free. Are teachers allowed to copy programs off-air from satellite transmissions? What about from cable networks?

Answer: Satellite and cable have equivalent copyright limitations. See Flowchart 8.4.

Flowchart 8.4. Recording Off-Air from Satellite or Cable Transmissions

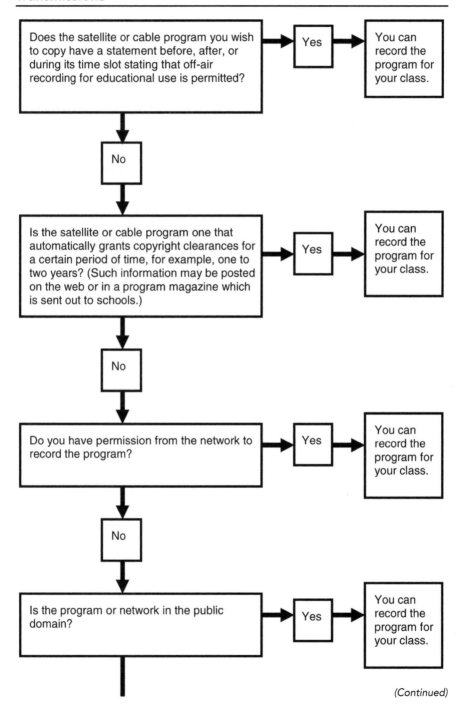

Does the satellite or cable program you wish to copy have a statement before, after, or during its time slot stating that off-air recording for educational use is permitted?

Yes → You can record the program for your class.

No

Is the satellite or cable program one that automatically grants copyright clearances for a certain period of time, for example, one to two years? (Such information may be posted on the web or in a program magazine which is sent out to schools.)

Yes → You can record the program for your class.

No

Do you have permission from the network to record the program?

Yes → You can record the program for your class.

No

Is the program or network in the public domain?

Yes → You can record the program for your class.

(Continued)

Flowchart 8.4. Recording Off-Air from Satellite or Cable Transmissions *(Continued)*

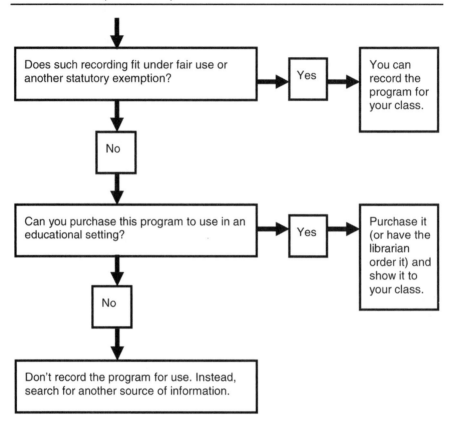

YOU CREATE IT, YOU OWN IT

Question: Several students in your video-production class have prepared short videos about their school, with student and teacher interviews and shots of the school, inside and out. As the video-production teacher, you would like to retain their videos to show as "best examples" to future classes. May you do so?

Answer: If students created their own videos, whether for your class or not, they own the copyrights to these videos. As a result, you will need the students' permissions to use such videos in future classes. Although the students are the owners of their own works, if the students are minors it may also be helpful to obtain their parents' permissions.

To this permission request, you might also add how long you plan to use the work and in what capacity (see Chapter 4). Remember that it is important to get these permissions in writing and specify each student's name, the particular work, and the class for which the work was originally completed.

Question: I want to digitize a televised version of *Hamlet* and put it on our English-class website. This way my students can access it at home. Can I legally do this, since I am essentially creating a derivative work?

Answer: That depends on where you obtained the original version of the work. See Flowchart 8.5 (p. 128) to decide what television programs you can digitize and place on a class website.

INFRINGEMENTS AND PENALTIES

Question: I'm an educator, and I'm recording certain television shows because our school can't afford to purchase them. I haven't asked for permission, and I know it could be in violation of copyright law, but the kids need this information and this is the only way I know of to get it to them. Will I get caught? Will I get punished? What can happen to me?

Answer: You may never get caught. However, not getting caught doesn't make copyright infringements legal. For example, a disgruntled fellow employee, a parent, or anyone else could report your illegal recording to the network. Penalties for illegal television taping vary, and can include (1) schools' being forced to purchase all illegal tapes; (2) teachers losing their jobs (or other disciplinary actions); (3) school districts paying fines; (4) educators receiving cease-and-desist letters; (5) librarians being required to purchase a license; and/or (6) adverse publicity for your school community. While you may not get caught, be aware that there are schools and teachers who do, and they are penalized. Thus, illegal taping is a gamble. How badly do you want to risk it?

Question: Your class is discussing how the media influences our culture. To demonstrate this, a colleague brings a DVD to school on which he has strung together several television commercials. Is he in copyright infringement?

Answer: Perhaps. The simplest answer is that it is possible he has infringed on copyright law since commercials are protected under this law and he has made copies of them. In addition, by stringing them together, he may have created a derivative work (see previous discussion on derivative works). However, since advertisers want people to see what they are selling, chances are that no company will care that he has copied these and is showing them in class. In addition, one could argue, since this is for an educational purpose, that fair use or the classroom exemption may apply. See Flowchart 8.6 (p. 129) for more information.

Question: I hear that there is new technology available that lets us view our televisions remotely. The possibilities for utilization in the school sound endless! For example, we could access the school television when taking a class on a retreat! Can we use such technologies to support our curriculum? Would using such a technology be considered a copyright violation?

Flowchart 8.5. Digitizing a Television Program

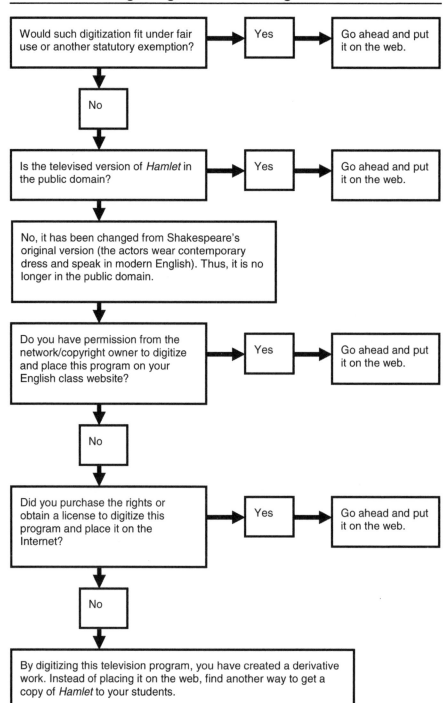

Would such digitization fit under fair use or another statutory exemption? → Yes → Go ahead and put it on the web.

No

Is the televised version of *Hamlet* in the public domain? → Yes → Go ahead and put it on the web.

No, it has been changed from Shakespeare's original version (the actors wear contemporary dress and speak in modern English). Thus, it is no longer in the public domain.

Do you have permission from the network/copyright owner to digitize and place this program on your English class website? → Yes → Go ahead and put it on the web.

No

Did you purchase the rights or obtain a license to digitize this program and place it on the Internet? → Yes → Go ahead and put it on the web.

No

By digitizing this television program, you have created a derivative work. Instead of placing it on the web, find another way to get a copy of *Hamlet* to your students.

Flowchart 8.6. Stringing Commercials Together to Use in Class

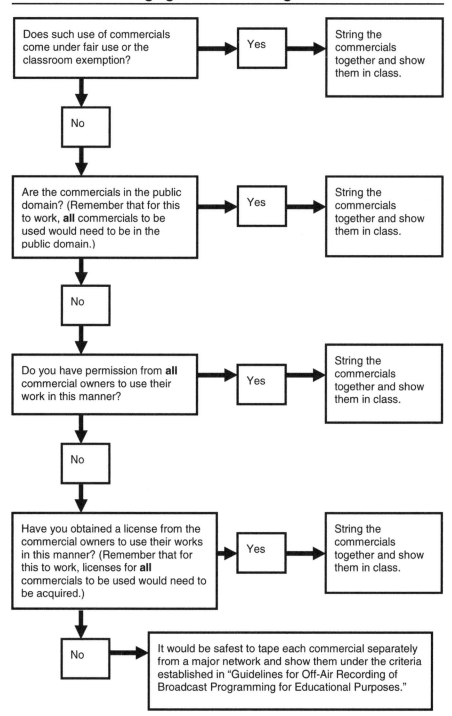

Does such use of commercials come under fair use or the classroom exemption?

→ Yes → String the commercials together and show them in class.

No

Are the commercials in the public domain? (Remember that for this to work, **all** commercials to be used would need to be in the public domain.)

→ Yes → String the commercials together and show them in class.

No

Do you have permission from **all** commercial owners to use their work in this manner?

→ Yes → String the commercials together and show them in class.

No

Have you obtained a license from the commercial owners to use their works in this manner? (Remember that for this to work, licenses for **all** commercials to be used would need to be acquired.)

→ Yes → String the commercials together and show them in class.

No

It would be safest to tape each commercial separately from a major network and show them under the criteria established in "Guidelines for Off-Air Recording of Broadcast Programming for Educational Purposes."

Answer: You are talking about place-shifting technology or video streaming, which "allows anyone with a broadband Internet connection to have video streams from their home television set, DVR or other video source... forwarded for viewing remotely on a computer, netbook or mobile phone at any location where they have a high-speed Internet connection or cellular data network" (Sling Media, 2010a, 2010b). If you purchased the place-shifting technology with a specific license, then you must abide by that license "even if the copyright law would allow for a more liberal exploitation in the absence of a license" (Lutzker, 2010: 3–4). Use Flowchart 8.7 as you consider such a technology.

INTERNATIONAL COPYRIGHT LAW

Question: I live near the Canadian border, and we pick up Canadian television stations all the time. Can I tape one of their programs and use it in my classroom?

Answer: Use Flowchart 8.8 to find out if you can tape a program for class use.

Flowchart 8.7. Using Place-Shifting Technologies/Video Streaming in the School

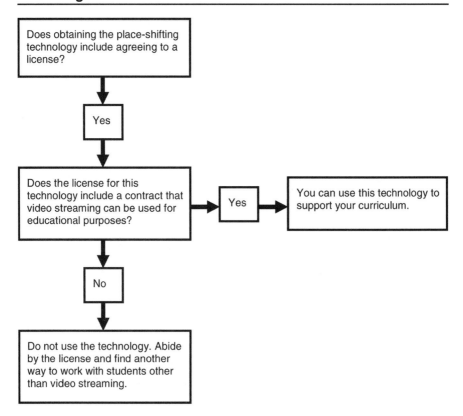

Flowchart 8.8. Recording Foreign Television

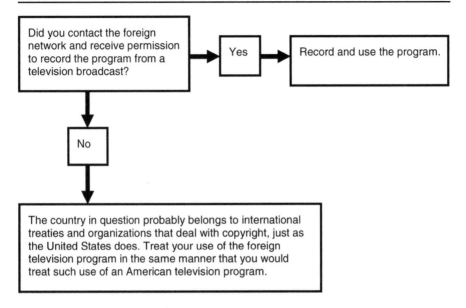

Question: These recordable DVDs are really great! When I visit my mother in Ecuador, I am going to tape my favorite South American soap opera to use with my high school advanced Spanish class. Since it is from a different country, I can ignore copyright laws when using this, right?

Answer: No, you may not! Ecuador and the United States belong to several of the same international copyright organizations (United States Copyright Office, 2010: 4). Therefore, you are safest if you treat the soap opera as if it were one that you had recorded in the United States.

AVOIDING COPYRIGHT PROBLEMS

Question: How can I make sure that we never violate copyright law when working with television programs?

Answer: The only "for sure" way to *always* avoid copyright problems when using television programming is to find something other than this format with which to work.

CONCLUSION

So, can you copy a television program for use in the classroom? Yes, no, maybe, sometimes, it depends. As we have seen, when it comes to copyright law each work must be considered on its own merit. There is often no one answer for any specific medium.

REFERENCES

Cable in the Classroom (CIC). 2010. "Copyright & Recording Guidelines." Cable in the Classroom. October 2. http://www.ciconline.org/Legal/CopyrightRecordingGuidelines.

C-SPAN. 2010. "C-SPAN Copyright Policy." National Cable Satellite Corporation. October 2. http://www.c-span.org/About/C-SPAN-Copyright-Policy/.

Congressional Record. 1981. "Guidelines for Off-Air Recording of Broadcast Programming for Educational Purposes." 1981. *Congressional Record* 127, no. 145 (October 14): E4750-E4752.

Lutzker, Arnold P. 2010. "Educational Video Streaming: A Short Primer." *AIME News* 24, no.1 (Spring): 1–4.

Sling Media. 2010a. "Legal Information: Web Site Terms of Use." Sling Media. http://www.slingmedia.com/get/terms-of-use.

Sling Media. 2010b. "What Is Placeshifting?" Sling Media. http://www.slingmedia.com/go/placeshifting.

Torrans, Lee Ann. 2003. *Law for K–12 Libraries and Librarians*. Westport, CT: Libraries Unlimited.

United States Copyright Office. 2010. "International Copyright Relations of the United States." Washington, DC: United States Copyright Office.

U.S. Congress. 1984. "Guidelines for Off-Air Taping for Educational Purposes." *Congressional Record* (14 October). Washington, DC: United States Congress.

CHAPTER 9

Computer Software and Copyright Law: Why Is Documentation Important?

INTRODUCTION

Unauthorized copying of computer software, whether available on a disk or the web, is illegal. This is supported by the 1976 U.S. Copyright Law, updated and expanded upon in 1980 (Stern, 1985), and revised to include piracy in 1992 (Simpson, 2005). Most of us realize this and can verbalize it readily. However, where do other computer-based and digitized technologies, for example, DVD encyclopedias, CD dictionaries, and e-books, fit in when it comes to copyright? What about computer software codes, software available on the Internet, databases, and digital rights management—is there a connection to all of these and copyright? The answer to all is a resounding yes. This chapter will take a look at a number of these computer-based technologies available to K–12 educators in order to answer questions of copyright law as it applies to various uses. Please be aware that the term *computer-based technologies* is used here in a very broad sense to identify a number of things associated with educational technologies that K–12 teachers use and that are in some way associated with computer use. More computer-based technologies, such as the Internet and multimedia, are addressed in other chapters.

It is so tempting and often easy to copy software—and, in many cases, who will know? The following questions cover a variety of computer-based technologies and copyright of use to K–12 educators. Questions with more than one answer are presented in flowchart form. Remember that when you use the flowcharts in this chapter, you are trying to find any criterion under which you may borrow a work. Therefore, you need only follow each flowchart until you come to that point where you satisfy one of the criteria. Once you reach that point, there is no need to go any further. For more information on each area discussed, refer to the chapter (Chapters 1 through 5) that covers that particular subject.

FAIR USE

Question: May I print an article from a DVD or CD-ROM encyclopedia and copy it for each member of my class?

Answer: Use Flowchart 9.1 to determine whether you can print copies of an article from a DVD or CD-ROM encyclopedia. The "Guidelines for Classroom Copying" (see Chapter 5) may also be applied to this question.

Question: May I borrow material from commercial software on plant regeneration and put it on a webpage? We are studying this subject in biology, and I want the students to access it from home.

Answer: Use Flowchart 9.2 (p. 136) to decide if you can put the material on a webpage.

Question: Is computer software code copyright-protected?

Answer: Unless the copyright owners say otherwise, it is safest to assume that borrowing or cracking computer software code is an infringement of copyright law.

PUBLIC DOMAIN

Question: If computer software that I purchased on the web does not have a copyright notice on it, does that mean it is in the public domain?

Answer: No, it does not. It just means that the software's creators did not put a copyright notice on it. While Internet works are often viewed as if they were in the public domain, in reality they should be treated the same as any other work. If it doesn't state that it is in the public domain, you should presume that it is not. Thus, assume it is copyrighted, unless the documentation says otherwise.

Question: When working in your math classroom, you come across a CD on multiplication and division skills. On the jewel-box lid is a statement from the publisher saying that this CD is in the public domain. How can you use the CD?

Answer: Any way you want! You can make copies to send home with your whole class, print out parts of it for worksheets, or use sections on a webpage you are designing. It is yours to use as you see fit.

DOCUMENTATION AND LICENSES

When using computer software, it is extremely important to read all documentation first. The documentation may include a contract or license, and if that is the case, it is your responsibility to follow the contract in your use of the software. Reading documentation is a step that many users skip. Their reasoning includes that it takes too long, the words are in too fine a print, it's boring, and so on. What such users often do not recognize is that by not reading the documentation, they may eventually break the law without realizing it. Ignorance is no excuse. If the law has been broken, you are liable. With this in mind, consider the following questions about documentation and computer software.

Flowchart 9.1. Printing from a DVD or CD-ROM

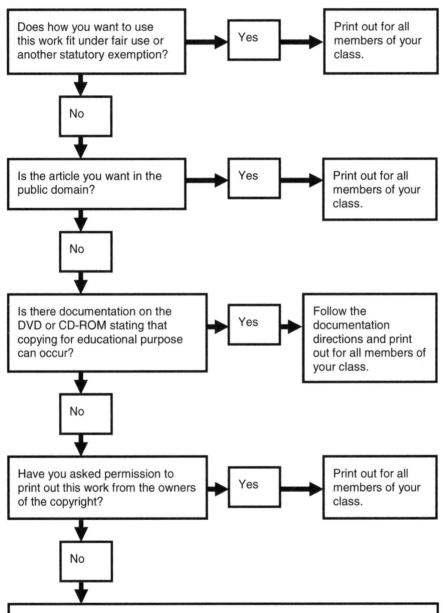

Does how you want to use this work fit under fair use or another statutory exemption? → **Yes** → Print out for all members of your class.

No

Is the article you want in the public domain? → **Yes** → Print out for all members of your class.

No

Is there documentation on the DVD or CD-ROM stating that copying for educational purpose can occur? → **Yes** → Follow the documentation directions and print out for all members of your class.

No

Have you asked permission to print out this work from the owners of the copyright? → **Yes** → Print out for all members of your class.

No

Don't print out the article for each member of your class. Assuming that the work's license and/or documentation does not prohibit such use, you may instead show your students the article in class by printing out one copy and passing it around, displaying it on a computer monitor, or projecting the article to a screen for the whole class to see at the same time.

Flowchart 9.2. Borrowing from Software

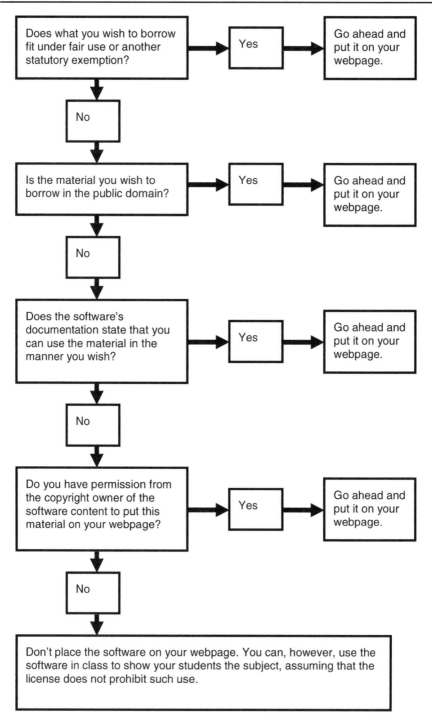

Does what you wish to borrow fit under fair use or another statutory exemption?

Yes → Go ahead and put it on your webpage.

No

Is the material you wish to borrow in the public domain?

Yes → Go ahead and put it on your webpage.

No

Does the software's documentation state that you can use the material in the manner you wish?

Yes → Go ahead and put it on your webpage.

No

Do you have permission from the copyright owner of the software content to put this material on your webpage?

Yes → Go ahead and put it on your webpage.

No

Don't place the software on your webpage. You can, however, use the software in class to show your students the subject, assuming that the license does not prohibit such use.

Question: Can I copy a favorite computer program that I own to my classroom computer for use with students?

Answer: Use Flowchart 9.3 (p. 138) to determine if you can copy personal software.

Question: Can Mr. Brown's third-graders use the same word-processing program on the 25 machines in the computer lab at the same time?

Answer: Flowchart 9.4 (p. 139) gives the steps for making this decision.

Question: How can I tell what copyrights the computer software I checked out from the school library media center has?

Answer: The documentation, whether in print format, accessible via the Internet, or on the software, should state whether it is under copyright or in the public domain. In addition, when copyrighted, there is usually a copyright notice on the software. You can also ask your school library media or technology specialist for his or her records regarding this software. The software may have a license by which you must abide. It, too, is part of the documentation material. If there is a license, remember that it is a contract, and when you obtain a license to use a copyrighted work, you are essentially contracting to use certain copyrights afforded that work. (See Chapter 5 for more information on documentation and licenses.)

Question: I just bought a used computer from the school for my home use. There is still a copy of some of the lab software on it. Can I use it?

Answer: That depends on the license or documentation that the school originally purchased with the software. Ask the school for clarification.

Question: I wrote a grant to purchase five iPads. I want to download several e-books to each for students to use in the library. Am I to consider copyright of the e-book in terms of software or as if it were in print?

Answer: First of all, protection of copyright is the same for all works, regardless of format. Second, the documentation/license of where you purchased such e-books will tell you how you can use your e-books. For example, iTunes has a "Terms and Conditions" section which states how media it sells, including e-books, may be used (iTunes Store, 2010). Remember that you must abide by the license (see Chapter 5), even if what it states is different from copyright law. Bear in mind, however, if there is no license, that all rights and exemptions under the copyright law apply, and that what the copyright owner may state on media he or she owns is basically a reiteration of some of these terms.

Question: I found some software on the web that I would like to purchase for use in my industrial arts class. It says that it has a Creative Commons License. Exactly what does that mean for me?

Flowchart 9.3. Copying Personal Software to a Classroom Computer

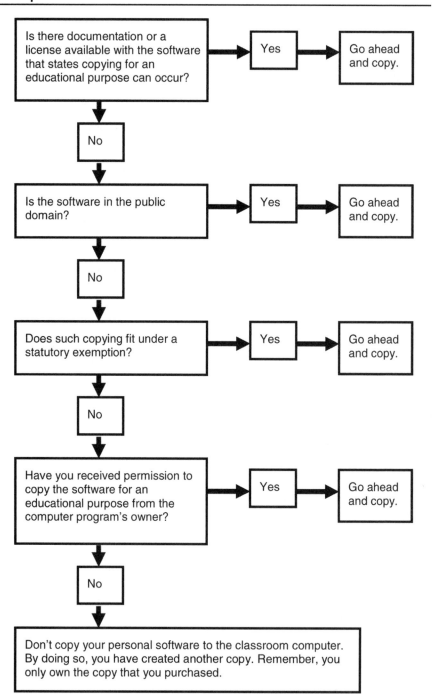

Is there documentation or a license available with the software that states copying for an educational purpose can occur? → Yes → Go ahead and copy.

↓ No

Is the software in the public domain? → Yes → Go ahead and copy.

↓ No

Does such copying fit under a statutory exemption? → Yes → Go ahead and copy.

↓ No

Have you received permission to copy the software for an educational purpose from the computer program's owner? → Yes → Go ahead and copy.

↓ No

Don't copy your personal software to the classroom computer. By doing so, you have created another copy. Remember, you only own the copy that you purchased.

Flowchart 9.4. Placing Software on Multiple Computers

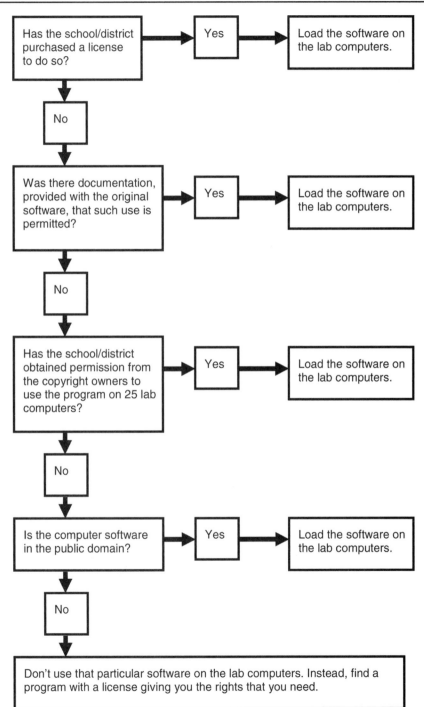

Answer: It means that you are to follow the license, the same as you would for any other software license. In other words, the owner of that specific software has chosen to identify what rights users may have to his or her work and has done so using this particular license.

PERMISSIONS

Question: Can I burn a CD of software I purchased from a computer store to a DVD for safe-keeping purposes? I will then use the copy, and keep the original in a secure place.

Answer: Use Flowchart 9.5 to decide if this is allowed.

In addition to the information in Flowchart 9.5, libraries—including school libraries—may make copies of a number of works for preservation, interlibrary loan, and some private study purposes (U.S. Copyright Law, 1976). Let's look at preservation copying. Could it apply to the software in Flowchart 9.5? It could apply if:

- the software is deteriorating, damaged, lost, stolen, or in an obsolete format;
- and the user is willing to use the DVD version only on the school library premises;
- and the library has already conducted an investigation and discovered that a replacement cannot be obtained at a fair price;
- so, therefore, with those conditions satisfied, up to three preservation copies of the software may be made (U.S Copyright Law, 1976; Digital Millennium Copyright Act [DMCA], 1998).

While this gets complicated, it is possible that, if the individual is willing to work with the school librarian, they could find a way to copy the software.

Question: May I make copies of school software available via the Internet for my students so that they can get their assignments done?

Answer: Use Flowchart 9.6 (p. 142) to guide your decision.

Question: My school owns an old version of a software program featuring newspaper templates. We would like to upgrade to a newer version, but we can't find one. Can we just copy the old for use in the computer lab?

Answer: Assuming that this program really can't be found, under the preservation copying exemption (see previous discussion about library copying for preservation purposes) your school library media specialist could make a copy for use in the media center. Before doing this, however, search widely for upgraded software and ask permission from the copyright holder.

Question: What is Digital Rights Management (DRM), and how might this affect us as educators?

Flowchart 9.5. Copying Software to Another Format

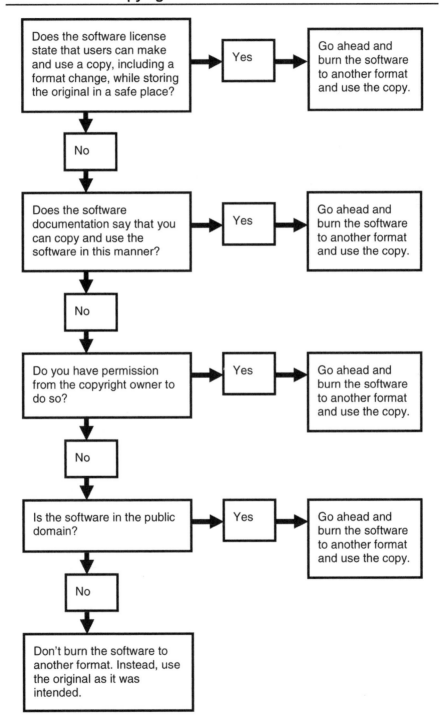

Flowchart 9.6. Making School Software Available for Students

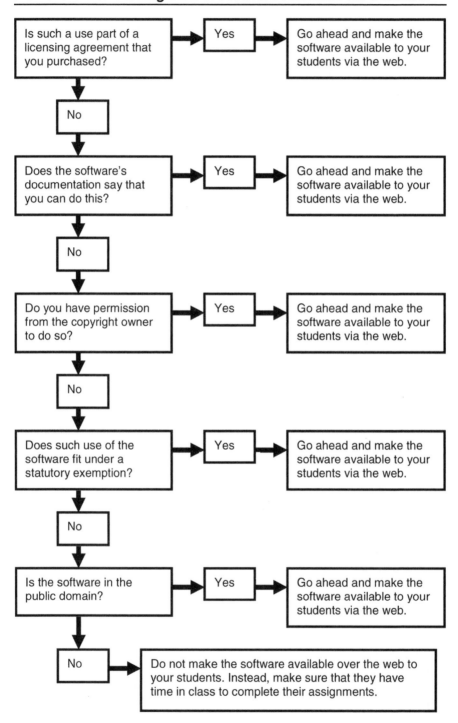

Answer: DRM is any technology that can control how we use digital works. As the American Library Association (ALA) states, "DRM has uses far beyond simply enforcing traditional and long-standing protections extant in current law. By embedding controls within the product, providers can prevent the public from use that is non-infringing under copyright law as well as enforce restrictions that extend far beyond those specific rights enumerated in the Copyright Act (or other laws)" (2010). What this means for us as K–12 educators is that the placing of such technology in any computer-based software that we purchase for school use might mean that we could not use the item to its full potential under law. Thus, DRM technologies may well alter such concepts of copyright law as the first sale doctrine and fair use/other statutory exemptions, as well as implement time, preservation, and archival limits and/or dissemination of software needed in the schools (ALA, 2010). The main thing to be aware of here is that while DRM technologies are not illegal, their placement in educational software could change what we present to our students, as well as how often.

YOU CREATE IT, YOU OWN IT

Question: Two students in my high school technology class are writing a piece of gaming software as extra credit. They wish to give the software "to the world" and hope that gamers everywhere will eventually be able to use their finished work as a basis for developing future action adventure games—as long as the new users also share their derivative works "with the world." Is copyright law a concern here?

Answer: It sounds like they are trying to create open-source software, which "allows... input of differing agendas and ideas to the development of software... making (the software)... stronger and more feature-rich" (Abram, 2009: 2). As such, they are offering gamers everywhere certain rights to their software, for example, the ability of users to work with the software without asking for permission to use and/or change it, as long as the users do what the creators ask of them. Thus, this is actually a contractual issue. (See Chapter 5 of this book for a more detailed explanation of open sourcing and contracts/licenses.)

Question: My word processing program has clip art available. Can I use this in a brochure that I am making to advocate for the school library?

Answer: Read the license and documentation accompanying the word processing program. It will tell you exactly how you can use the program, including the clip art.

INFRINGEMENTS AND PENALTIES

Question: A student in your English class brings in a piece of software that creates footnotes for term papers. He says that it is freeware (software placed by its owner/creator into the public domain). You suspect that it is pirated. How can you tell?

Answer: Illegal copies of software usually have one or more of the following characteristics:

- No documentation is available.
- There are no rebates or guarantees included with the software.
- If the software is labeled, the label looks unprofessional.
- There is no shrink-wrap license.
- The disk it is on is a copy.
- The software is already loaded on a used machine you purchased. (Butler, 2002b)

Question: Who is liable if a student is caught illegally downloading a program at school: the student who infringed, the teacher who assigned the unit on which the student was working, the librarian who unwittingly provided the equipment used in the infringement, the technology coordinator who provided the software needed for the infringement, the principal of the school, or the school district superintendent?

Answer: All could be held liable under copyright law. This is because liability follows the "pecking order." There are three categories of copyright infringement. They are listed here, using our example of the student illegally downloading software.

- Direct Infringement—This is what the student, who knowingly violates the rights of the copyright owner by downloading the software, is doing.
- Contributory or Indirect Infringement—This is where we find the teacher, the librarian, and the technology coordinator. Any or all of these people may have assisted indirectly in the downloading of the software:
  ○ by providing the hardware or software, and/or
  ○ by assigning a project that needed that software, etc. In addition, these people either knew, or should have known, that they were assisting the student in violating copyright law.
- Vicarious Infringement—This is where the principal and the superintendent could fit in if they, in some way, derive a financial benefit from downloading the software from the Internet. This is because these individuals control, directly or indirectly, the direct and contributory infringers (Simpson, 2005).

Question: So I've pirated some software. No one will ever know. Besides, they are after the big copier, not "little ol' me," right?

Answer: That may be true. Maybe no one will ever find out that you illegally copied software. Although by copying software illegally, you may be violating your professional ethics and modeling undesirable behavior to your students.

Moreover, software producers and copyright owners usually are after those who violate in a big way, those who copy many programs many times. Be aware, however, that some computer software watchdog organizations and copyright owners offer confidential Internet sites or phone numbers through which infringements may be reported. An example is the Business Software Alliance which provides an online form, a phone number, and a chance to chat live for those who wish to report an infringement (Business Software Alliance, 2010). Another organization that will take your privacy reports is the Software and Information Industry Association, which states on its website, "Report piracy here and you may be eligible for a reward of up to $1 million" (Software and Information Industry Association, 2010). Remember that no one can guarantee you will not be caught. If you are planning on copying software illegally, make sure that you haven't made any enemies who might report you!

Question: I don't believe you! Give me an example of a teacher getting caught copying software. What were the penalties?

Answer: In a Chicago suburb, an individual who worked at a school down-loaded Adobe Acrobat software illegally onto several computers used by school administrators. A lawsuit ensued, brought about by a software group that pursues copyright infringements. The penalties can be extreme. For example, in this case, the school district paid $50,000 to the watchdog organization, the offending employee resigned, and the school district's principals were required to purchase their own computers and software ("School District Pays Copyright Penalty," 2001). Penalties vary from case to case depending on the infringements, the court overseeing the lawsuit, those involved in the lawsuit, and so on.

INTERNATIONAL COPYRIGHT LAW

Question: A former student of mine who is traveling in Hong Kong has sent me a CD compilation of computer-assisted drafting (CAD) software. It is so much cheaper than buying it in the States! Is it pirated?

Answer: Flowchart 9.7 (p. 146) will help you evaluate the situation. In this case, the flowchart steps are not definitive; however, they will guide you in determining whether the software is pirated.

Question: Can I use it anyway?

Answer: Since it was so cheap, it is probably pirated. The United States is a signatory to several international copyright treaties (see Chapter 5). Your pirated software could easily be a copyright infringement in the country of origin as well as in the United States. Don't use the CAD software that your student sent you.

Flowchart 9.7. Pirated Software

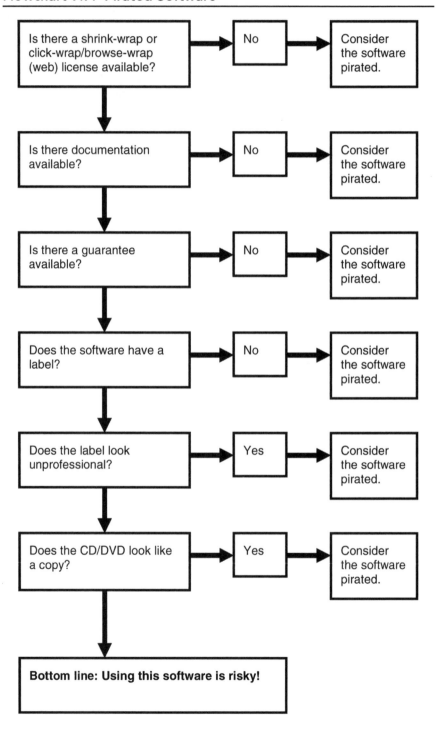

Question: My library has purchased a license for a database that provides newspaper articles worldwide. Do I need to make sure that my students follow international copyright law when they use articles from a newspaper published in another country?

Answer: First of all, there is no such thing as "international copyright law." There are, however, a number of conventions, treaties, and agreements on copyright to which the U.S. and various other countries belong, for example, the World International Property Organization (WIPO) Treaty, the Trade-Related Aspects of Intellectual Property Rights (TRIPS) Agreement (dealing with international trade), and the Berne Convention. In addition, a contract law international convention (the EC Convention on the Law Applicable to Contractual Obligations) does have a database directive providing that all such compilations are under copyright law (Goldstein and Hugenholtz, 2010). The bottom line is that the easiest thing for you to do is to follow the licensing agreement for the database, as well as any other documentation posted for database users. This information will tell you exactly what you and your students may do with the database material.

AVOIDING COPYRIGHT PROBLEMS

Question: We have an older piece of software on CD that a fifth-grade teacher uses faithfully every semester. While it is still in good shape, the librarian believes it would be prudent to make a backup copy. Can she do so for archival purposes?

Answer: If the software was legally obtained, then yes, one archival copy may be made under Section 117 of the U.S. Copyright Law (Russell, 2005).

Question: Our school's Internet filtering software is set to block YouTube. One of my teachers found several videos on the YouTube site that he would like to use to support the middle school history curriculum. Is it legal to convert the files and save them to the desktop using a program such as Zamzar or Vixy?

Answer: Using an online file conversion program (e.g., Zamzar, Vixy, TillaWire, Freecorder 4, Replay Media Catcher 4) changes videos, music, images, and other media into formats such as avi, mp3, MPEG-4, and wmv. One of the main staples of copyright ownership is the ability to create derivative works, and it could be argued that a file conversion program does just that. Many sites providing videos and other media (for example, YouTube and TeacherTube), while often assumed by users to be featuring public domain media, may have policies or copyright statements announcing that illegal use of the media on their sites will result in penalties and/or the infringer being removed from said website. Therefore, it is best to use the videos in their original formats. See Flowchart 9.8 (p. 148) for more information concerning this matter.

Flowchart 9.8. Using File Conversion Programs

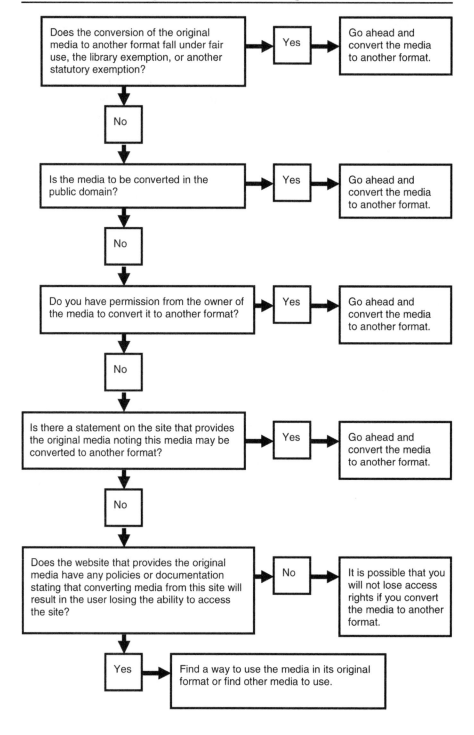

CONCLUSION

In addition to the previous information in this chapter, here are some steps toward making copyright compliance easier:

- Make sure that all documentation is available to the users.
- Consult the documentation. Yes, you need to actually read it!
- Ensure that any archival copies of software or other computer-based technologies are kept in a secure place. You may even wish to lock the copies up so that others will not be tempted to borrow them.
- Be sure that your school has a software/computer-based technologies' policy and ethics code. If not, encourage your school library media specialist, technology specialist, or school administrator to create one. Within the code include a written policy for the use of personal software on school computers, whether in a lab, classroom, or at a teacher's desk. Have this policy/ethics code accessible to all who use computer software and other computer-based technologies. (For example, it might be placed in your school's copyright policy.)
- Be aware of any licenses for the computer-based technologies you use. Some licenses may let your students copy and take home software programs or parts of them for educational purposes. Your school library media specialist or technology specialist or coordinator should have a log of these.
- Read all warning notices, such as copyright notices, licensing restrictions, and terms of use. Software and other computer-based technologies may contain such notices, for example, during start-up, and these may be in addition to the work's documentation.
- Be diligent in following all licensing restrictions.
- Understand that not all computer-based technologies' documentation and licenses are the same. For example, some computer software may let you install a copy on your home machine as well as on a school machine, while others may not (Butler, 2002a).

This Chapter 9 conclusion is based largely on an article first published in *Knowledge Quest* (Butler, 2002a).

REFERENCES

Abram, Stephen. 2009. "Integrated Library System Platforms on Open Source." White Paper. Provo, UT: SirsiDynix.

American Library Association. 2010. "Digital Rights Management (DRM) & Libraries." American Library Association. http://www.ala.org/ala/issuesadvocacy/copyright/digitalrights/index.cfm.

Business Software Alliance. 2010. "Report Piracy Now! Your Report Is Confidential." Business Software Alliance. https://reporting.bsa.org/usa/report/add.aspx.

Butler, Rebecca P. 2002a. "Computer Software and Copyright Law—Read This First." *Knowledge Quest* 31, no. 1 (September/October): 32–33.

————. 2002b. "Software Piracy: Don't Let It Byte You!" *Knowledge Quest* 31, no. 2 (November/December): 41–42.

Digital Millennium Copyright Act (DMCA). 1998. Public Law 105-304.

Goldstein, Paul, and Bernt Hugenholtz. 2010. *International Copyright.* New York: Oxford University Press.

iTunes Store. 2010. "Terms and Conditions." Apple Inc. Updated June 21. http://www .apple.com/legal/itunes/us/terms.html.

Russell, Carrie. 2005. "The Long and Short of It." *School Library Journal* 51, no. 12 (December): 31.

"School District Pays Copyright Penalty." 2001. *Chicago Tribune*, Section 2, September 12: 3.

Simpson, Carol. 2005. *Copyright for Schools: A Practical Guide.* 4th ed. Worthington, OH: Linworth.

Software and Information Industry Association. 2010. "Report Piracy." Software and Information Industry Association. http://www.siia.net/piracy/report/soft.

Stern, Richard H. 1985. "Section 117 of the Copyright Act: Charter of the Software Users' Rights or an Illusory Promise?" *Western New England Law Review* 7: 459–485.

U.S. Copyright Law. 1976. Public Law 94-553, sec. 108.

CHAPTER 10

Music/Audio and Copyright Law: Who Will Know If You Copy It?

INTRODUCTION

The purpose of this chapter is to cover, as simply as possible, information—for K–12 educators—on U.S. copyright law and music/audio in a variety of formats. Copyright information for music can be extremely complex. For example, a single music CD might have at least three copyright registrations: one for the song's sheet music, one for the lyrics, and one for the performer's version of the song. In the past few years, the advent of online stores, such as iTunes, which sell music for downloading to computers, cell phones, iPads, and other digital devices, has made borrowing and using music legally more commonplace. However, obtaining music for educational, as well as personal, use can still be confusing. This chapter attempts to clarify some of the more common questions surrounding music and other sound recordings found in school settings.

First, it is important to define, as does the U.S. Copyright Office, the differences between musical compositions and sound recordings. In "Circular 56a," the U.S. Copyright Office does exactly that. According to its definition, a musical composition consists "of music, including any accompanying words. . . . A musical composition may be in the form of a notated copy (for example, sheet music) or in the form of a phonorecord (for example, cassette tape, LP, or CD)." The U.S. Copyright Office further defines the creator/author of the musical compo- sition as "generally the composer, and the lyricist, if any" (U.S. Copyright Office, Library of Congress, 2009b: 1). "Circular 56a" further defines a sound recording as resulting from "the fixation of a series of musical, spoken, or other sounds," and the sound recording author as "the performer(s) whose perfor- mance is fixed, or the record producer who processes the sounds and fixes them in the final recording, or both" (U.S. Copyright Office, 2009a: 1). Sound recordings do not include the sounds accompanying motion pictures or other audiovisual works (U.S. Copyright Office, 2009a). It may be worded in more "legalese" than we like to read when we are searching quickly for a simple answer to our copyright questions, and it may be more confusing than we would like it to be; however, "Circular 56a" states that there are two separate kinds of audio works: musical compositions and sound recordings. They are not the same, they do not necessarily have the same owners or authors (although they can), and their rights under copyright law can be different as well. It is possible, for example, for the score of a musical to be in the public domain, while a CD version of the same musical is registered under copyright. It is also possible that the copyright owners of a recording of country-western music that your students want to perform for a parent-teacher organization night are actually the performer of the work and the recording company who produced the work. With this in mind, who owns what or whom to ask for permission to use the works can sometimes get quite confusing. (This is one of the places where clearinghouses and other organizations that help users obtain the correct permissions for use of works come in. They may save you a lot of time and exasperation! See Chapter 4.)

You should also be aware that while the right to copy applies to both musical compositions and sound recordings, the right to perform applies only to musical compositions. However, like most things dealing with copyright, there are exceptions. Thus, if you want to perform a particular song, unless it is in public domain, you need the permission of the owner(s) of its musical composition. If you want to copy the sheet music of this song (again, unless it is in public domain), you also need the permission of the owner(s) of the musical composition. However, if you want to copy a version of this song, which you own on CD, to a webpage, then, assuming the work is not in the public domain, you need permission of the owner(s) of the sound recording. Are you still following? Now, let's talk about rights.

While the best way to find out about rights to musical compositions and sound recordings is to study the U.S. Copyright Law of 1976, especially Sections 106, 114, and 115 (Sections 107 through 121 also have information on the topic), chances are that this is not feasible for you in the regular school day. However, it is best to be aware that the rights afforded musical compositions and sound recordings under law are not necessarily always the same. For example, if CDs, music available legally from an Internet site, or other musical compositions have been distributed to the public, then a compulsory license is required to duplicate these works. A compulsory license operates in a similar manner to fair use. In the case of music, this means that the owner of a copyrighted song can be compelled to let someone else perform it, as long as the new performer does not change the song in any way. In addition, it is highly likely that the new performer will have to pay a royalty fee for the use of the song (Ferrara, 2005).

However, for reproductions of sound recordings, no mention is made of a compulsory license; nonetheless, their rights include the right to reproduce the original music or other sounds (Bell, 2004; U.S. Copyright Office, Library of Congress, 2008). To take a more specific example, suppose you wrote a song. You created the sheet music, including the notes and lyrics. You also created a CD version in which you sing this song. What you have created is the musical composition. Now, say that you sell the rights to perform your song to Neil Diamond and Columbia Records. The CDs, digital online music files, etc., that Diamond performs and that Columbia produces are owned by them—depending on their agreement, it may be owned by either one or by both. These are the sound recordings, and the owner of the copyright (Diamond, Columbia, or both) has the right to reproduce the music. Websites to go for helpful information on music/audio copyrights include the U.S. Copyright Office at http://www.copyright.gov and Tom W. Bell's "Music Copyrights Table" at http://www.tomwbell.com/teaching/Music(C)s.html.

Another important point that is mentioned often in this chapter is that of licenses (for general information on this subject, see Chapter 5). For musical works, there are four types of licenses:

1. Mechanical
2. Performance (how the owners of the works can collect royalties for public performances)
3. Synchronization (for reproducing and distributing a work via non-print and movies)
4. Print (for reproducing and distributing print musical compositions) (Frankel, 2009)

For the purposes of this chapter, unless otherwise noted, we are discussing the mechanical license, which "allows for the reproduction and distribution of a musical work as a recording in return for royalties paid to the copyright holder" (Frankel, 2009: 23).

You now know that illegally copying music and other audio is not limited to file sharing (see Chapter 6) or transferring music from one format to another. The following questions cover musical recordings and sheet music, other audio recordings, educators, and copyright. Questions with more than one answer are presented in flowchart form. Remember that when you use the flowcharts in this chapter, you are trying to find any criterion under which you may borrow a work. Therefore, you need only follow each flowchart until you come to that point where you satisfy one of the criteria. Once you reach that point, there is no need to go any further. For more information on each area discussed, please refer to the chapter (Chapters 1 through 5) that covers the particular subject.

FAIR USE

Question: Students in my journalism class are creating webpages as part of a class assignment. Several want to add audio clips from popular rap songs. How can they do this without it being an infringement of copyright law? (Remember that even very small parts of a song—for example, a bar or two, or several notes—can be an infringement if uploaded to the web without the proper permissions, licenses, etc.

Answer: Use Flowchart 10.1 to determine what the students can legally do with the rap songs.

Question: I teach students who are blind. As a necessity, all materials I use with them are either oral or in Braille. Can volunteers read books and record them digitally for my students to use?

Answer: First, check to see if the selected books can be purchased in an audio format. If not, then yes, the books may be read and recorded for the blind students to use. Such digitization needs a notice identifying the original copyright owner and copyright date as well as a notice that the copies will not be reproduced or distributed in another format (Legislative Branch Appropriations, 1997, Sec. 121).

Question: I am a vocal music teacher. I like to use popular music in my classes to demonstrate different vocal arrangements. Sometimes I take songs from the web or CDs and burn them to a class CD for curricular use. Am I violating copyright law?

Answer: Use Flowchart 10.2 (pp. 156–157) to decide if this is a violation of copyright law. There may be exceptions, so be sure to check the U.S. Copyright Office's website, http://www.copyright.gov, for further information.

Question: I am teaching a unit on diet to my third-graders. I want to take a well-known tune from *Sesame Street* and change the words to make a song about healthy eating. This is for a teaching purpose, so there should be no problem with copyright, should there?

Answer: The answer here is very gray, and essentially you may have two choices. First of all, it is possible that such a use might fall under the classroom exemption. In this case, yes, you may use the song as described in your question. However, because you have just created a derivative work, this use might also be considered an infringement of copyright law. It all depends on who is defining it. Therefore, unless you can argue that this is a parody, you may be safer finding another work to use—preferably one you wrote yourself or perhaps from a company that provides public domain and royalty-free music for purchase, such as RoyaltyFreeMusic.com (2010) or Soundzabound (2010). In addition, there are some websites, such as GMP Music, which will let you "temporarily (short term) place the music track you selected in a production for the purpose of determining the acceptability of the music for that specific application" (GMP Music, 2010).

PUBLIC DOMAIN

Question: If I don't register the fight song I wrote for the sports team, is it automatically in the public domain?

Flowchart 10.1. Adding Popular Music to Webpages

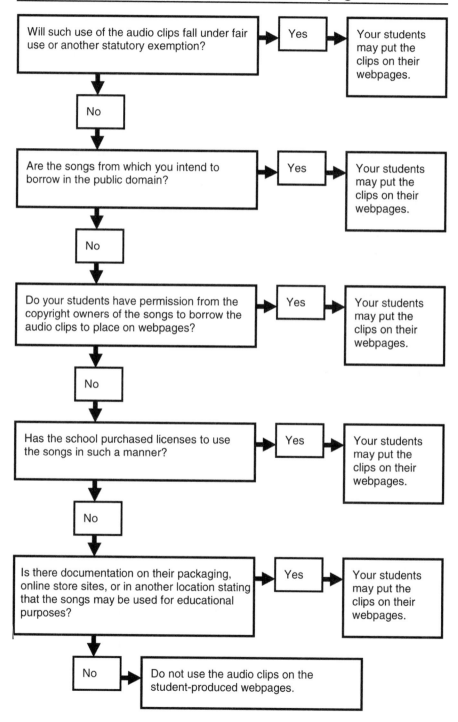

Flowchart 10.2. Copying Popular Music for Class Use

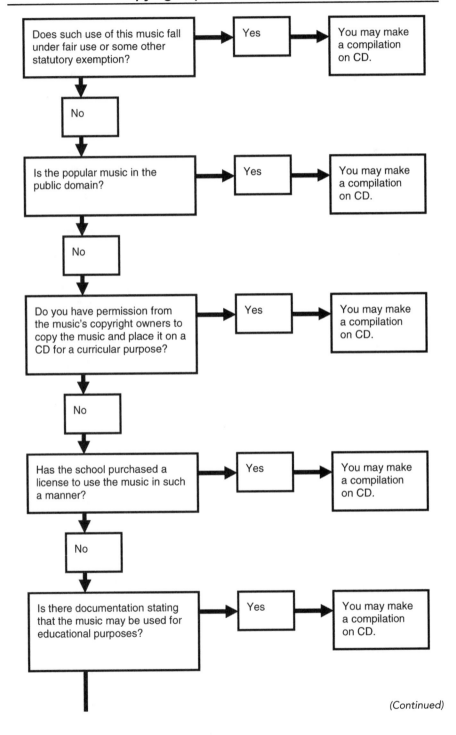

(Continued)

Flowchart 10.2. Copying Popular Music for Class Use *(Continued)*

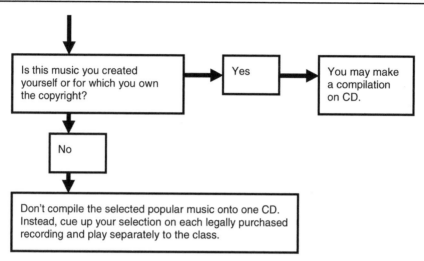

Answer: No, it is not in the public domain unless you choose to place it there. Copyright registration is voluntary. Nonetheless, all works become copyrighted the instant they are created. If you wish to file a lawsuit against an infringer, however, it is helpful to have your work officially registered with the U.S. Copyright Office (U.S. Copyright Office, Library of Congress, 2006).

Question: My music class is studying the history of American and European music. I want to model good copyright behavior for my students and, at the same time, provide them with a variety of music genres that they can download to their iPods and other handheld devices. Where are some websites that I can go to find public domain music?

Answer: A number of websites offer users "free" (e.g., public domain), music for download. These include Classic Cat (http://www.classiccat.net) and Musopen (http://www.musopen.org). In addition, some sites offer public domain sheet music, for example, PD Info (http://www.pdinfo.com), as well as Musopen. Be aware that these sites normally sell the public domain materials and/or ask for donations in terms of time, money, or more music (Classic Cat, 2010; Musopen, 2010; PD Info, 2010). Other possible music sites of interest include Grooveshark (http://listen.grooveshark.com), which offers listeners the ability to hear music online for free (Grooveshark, 2010) and MyBytes, which lets users create and register (similar to the open-source concept discussed in Chapter 5) their own music with a "music mixer" and "showcase" (MyBytes, 2010). Check out all music download sites very carefully. Some may not be licensed distributors and, while appearing legitimate, offer illegal works (Sohn, 2008).

Question: I have been collecting public domain songs in a variety of audio formats for many years. I would like to take all these songs, transfer them to a digital format, and then create a CD with the collection on it for use in my music history class. Since I am creating any number of derivative works, with a final derivative work in mind, is this a legal use of these songs?

Answer: It sure is! You can transfer these songs to any format you want and place them in a collection. Since the original songs are in the public domain, you can even sell the final compilation, if you should so desire. Relax and have some fun with this project!

DOCUMENTATION AND LICENSES

Question: The band director is always photocopying sheet music for the marching band. He says he does this to keep the originals in good shape, to be able to use the sheet music for many years to come. I say he is violating copyright law. Can he do this?

Answer: Without the proper permissions, he cannot legally copy sheet music for the marching band. Sheet music has been copyright-protected since 1831 (Justia, 2010). Flowchart 10.3 walks you through the process of deciding when it is permissible to copy sheet music.

In addition, there are guidelines for the copying of classroom materials and music that might apply, given the right parameters. See Chapter 5 for more information on this or visit the U.S. Copyright Office at http://www.copyright.gov for possible exceptions.

Question: When the music department purchases a license to perform a song in public concert, exactly what rights do they purchase?

Answer: The music department purchases the rights that the copyright owner licenses to them, which are the specific rights that the copyright owner agrees the music department can have. These rights vary; they may include the right to charge admission fees for the concert, photocopy the accompanying sheet music, perform the song a specific number of times, videotape the performance, and so on. It is important that you make sure you obtain the license or permissions for the specific rights that you need. Fines are often levied on those who infringe on licensing rights (Webster, 1996).

Question: When is it legal to play recorded music in the library? Students and teachers—individually, in small groups, and in classes—come and go throughout the day.

Answer: There are a number of possible answers to this question. See Flowchart 10.4 (pp. 160–161) for information. Be aware that what is true in this flowchart would also work for playing musical recordings in a classroom.

Question: We are very proud of the musical that the high school performed this past year and would like to post a video of a performance of one of the

Flowchart 10.3. Copying Sheet Music

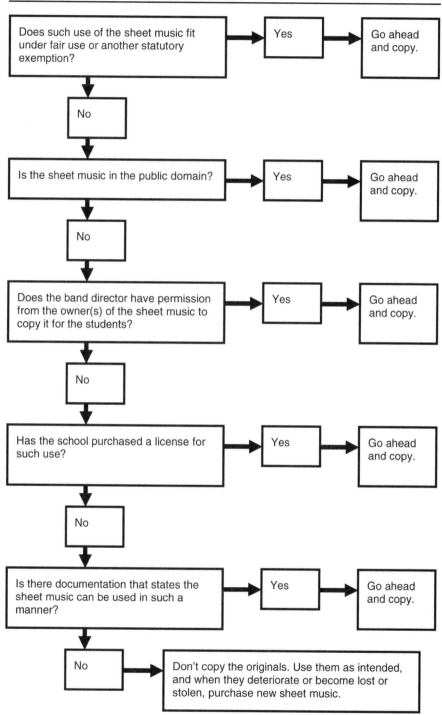

Does such use of the sheet music fit under fair use or another statutory exemption? → Yes → Go ahead and copy.

No

Is the sheet music in the public domain? → Yes → Go ahead and copy.

No

Does the band director have permission from the owner(s) of the sheet music to copy it for the students? → Yes → Go ahead and copy.

No

Has the school purchased a license for such use? → Yes → Go ahead and copy.

No

Is there documentation that states the sheet music can be used in such a manner? → Yes → Go ahead and copy.

No → Don't copy the originals. Use them as intended, and when they deteriorate or become lost or stolen, purchase new sheet music.

Flowchart 10.4. Playing Recorded Music in the Library

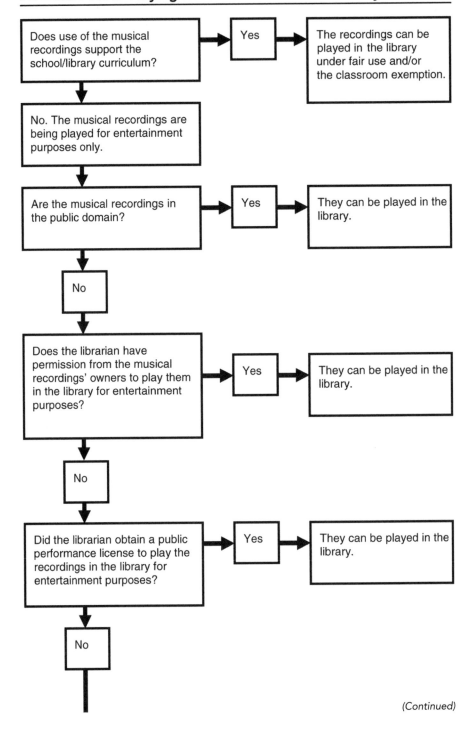

(Continued)

Flowchart 10.4. Playing Recorded Music in the Library *(Continued)*

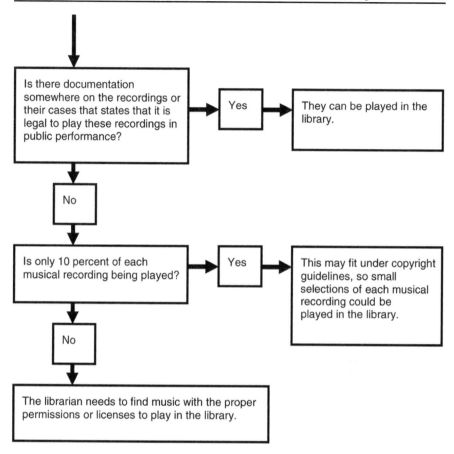

songs from it on SchoolTube, which is "the nation's largest K–12 moderated video sharing website that provides students and educators with a safe and FREE video sharing website that is exclusively endorsed by leading education associations" (SchoolTube, 2010), or a similar site. Can we do so legally?

Answer: Perhaps. The first thing you need to do is to access the copyright guidelines for the site on which you would like to post. For example, School Tube copyright guidelines are available at http://www.menc.org/resources/view/copyright-guidelines-for-schooltube. According to these guidelines, posting a song from the high school musical via video on SchoolTube constitutes a public performance, as well as the creation of a derivative work. This means that you need to consider whether the song from the musical:

1. is copyright-protected or in the public domain;
2. is performed at a MENC: The National Association for Music Education event, all of which "are covered under a blanket license paid each year by

MENC to ASCAP and BMI for compositions licensed by those agencies" (MENC, 2010); or

3. has a license for reproduction attached to its use (MENC, 2010).

For more information, please refer to Flowchart 10.5.

Question: Many varieties of digital handheld devices, such as iPads, iPods, Droids, Nooks, Kindles, Playaways, and MP3 players, are available in today's world, and more are being developed every day. Reading an e-book with one of these devices may impact a physically disabled or learning disabled student's reading in a positive way. How can we be sure that we are using these items in a legal manner?

Answer: The best way to legally use these new tools and the audio that can be or is downloaded on them is to follow the documentation of the downloaded item (or of the device, if the download is already available on it; e.g., Playaways). For example, Apple's "Legal Information & Notices" informs users how they can and cannot legally use works downloaded from iTunes (Apple, 2010). An example of a site offering free text-to-speech downloads, developed solely for disabled students, is Bookshare (http://www.bookshare.org). This site also has a legal area specifying how the works on it may be used (Bookshare, 2010).

PERMISSIONS

Question: I have a very creative student in my music class. He wants to take a well-known line from a Beatles song and make a new song out of it. His idea, then, is to play the song at a school assembly. Does he need any special permission to do this? After all, what he borrows is such a small piece that it should be fair use.

Answer: First of all, given that this is a well-known line, it may be considered the "heart of the work," which means that, under the fair use factors, borrowing it would be too much. Second, what your student is doing is called "sampling." Sampling is essentially when someone borrows a small part of already-existing music and uses that bit as the basis for new music (Home Recording Connection, 2010). Sampling could violate copyright law for either the music's lyrics or the tune or both. Thus, your student needs to obtain permission from the owner of that particular Beatles song before creating his new song. Under no circumstances should this new song be played in an assembly unless permissions for creating and performing the new song were granted to the student.

Question: Is it all right for our cheerleaders to perform routines to popular music at games and other public events? (They like to bring their own CDs and a boom box.)

Flowchart 10.5. Posting a Song on a Video-Sharing Website

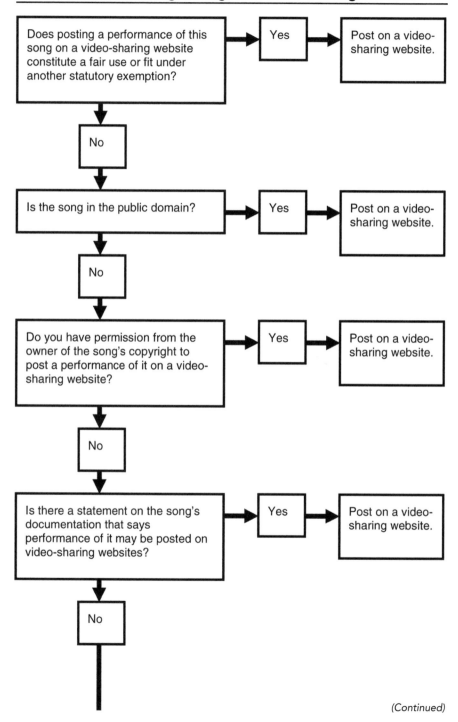

Does posting a performance of this song on a video-sharing website constitute a fair use or fit under another statutory exemption? → Yes → Post on a video-sharing website.

No

Is the song in the public domain? → Yes → Post on a video-sharing website.

No

Do you have permission from the owner of the song's copyright to post a performance of it on a video-sharing website? → Yes → Post on a video-sharing website.

No

Is there a statement on the song's documentation that says performance of it may be posted on video-sharing websites? → Yes → Post on a video-sharing website.

No

(Continued)

Flowchart 10.5. Posting a Song on a Video-Sharing Website
(Continued)

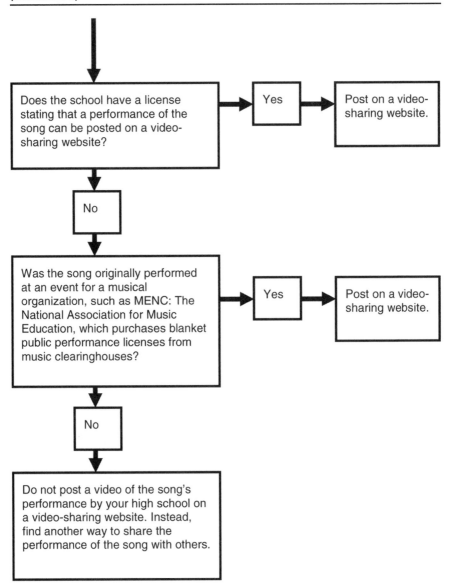

Answer: To be sure that the use of the music your cheerleaders choose for their public performances is not a copyright infringement, your school can purchase a license to use royalty-free music. Such music is obtained through clearinghouses and similar organizations (see Chapter 4) or, more simply, from vendors who deal in this kind of music. These vendors either obtain permissions from copyright owners or find public domain music. The vendors then put this music into collections, which they sell for a fee to schools and other groups who need public performance music. Often, these royalty-free music vendors have educational prices and sell schools blanket permissions to use the music any way they wish, from public performances to multimedia productions (RoyaltyFreeMusic.com, 2010). There are other options as well for obtaining the use of music for public performances, so check the U.S. Copyright Office's website (http://www.copyright.gov). For example, the school could directly contact one of the clearinghouses that deals in licenses for popular music performances. Some of the organizations that represent such groups as songwriters, composers, music publishers, and recording labels are the American Society of Composers, Authors and Publishers (ASCAP), Broadcast Music, Inc. (BMI), the Harry Fox Agency, and the Recording Industry Association of America (RIAA). See also Flowchart 10.6 (p. 166) for guidance in making your decisions.

Question: Can my students print the words to popular songs from an Internet site? They are using the lyrics as poetry examples for my English class.

Answer: Use Flowchart 10.7 (p. 167) to guide your decision.

You may also check the website of the U.S. Copyright Office (http://www.copyright.gov) for possible exceptions.

Question: For a school project organized by our principal, several local celebrities, including the mayor and our state senator, read stories to our elementary school classes. The stories were digitally recorded and uploaded to a library computer. No attempt was made to discover if there were already audio versions of these stories available for purchase. Now, when a student wishes to check out one of these books, he or she can bring along a personal handheld digital device and download the audio version as well. I am the media specialist, and I am very concerned about this. I think that we may be violating copyright law. Am I right?

Answer: Do not presume that these books can be recorded, stored in the media center, and used for circulation purposes, no matter who is reading them or what the project is. Each book must be individually studied to determine whether such a use is legal. Use Flowchart 10.8 (pp. 168–169) to decide if this is a violation of copyright.

In addition there may be other issues with which to be concerned when dealing with local celebrities, including politicians, who are reading picture books and recording them. One issue would be the right of publicity: "The Right of Publicity prevents the unauthorized commercial use of an individual's name, likeness, or other recognizable aspects of one's persona. It gives an individual the exclusive right to license the use of their identity for commercial promotion" (Legal Information Institute, 2010). For the purposes of this particular question, however, we assume the local celebrities are volunteering their names and likenesses, as well as their time.

Flowchart 10.6. Performing Popular Music at Public Events

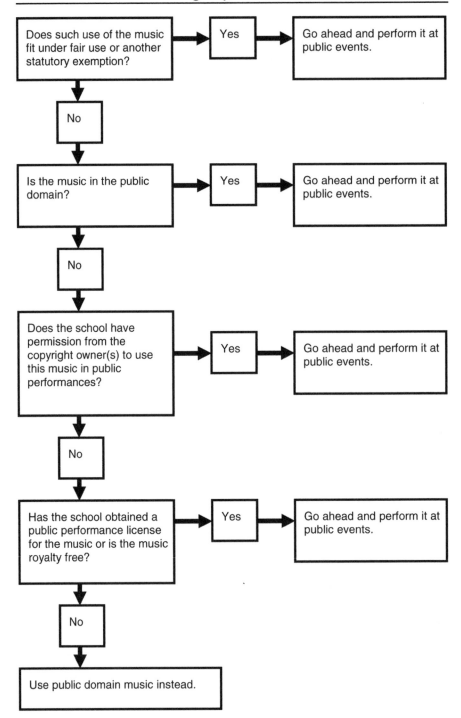

Flowchart 10.7. Printing Lyrics from the Internet

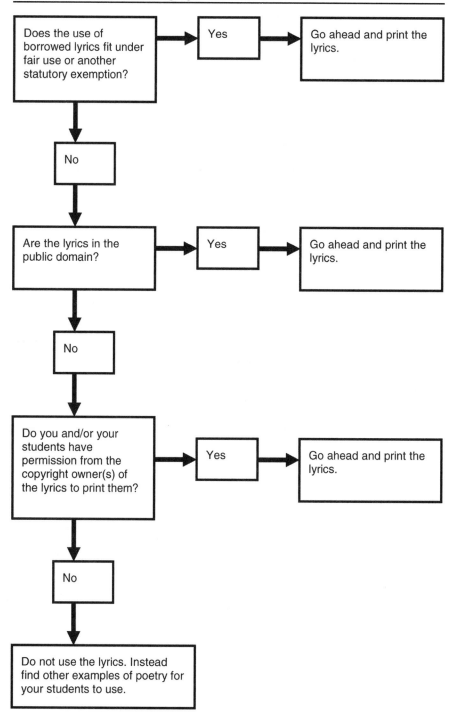

Flowchart 10.8. Audio-Recording Picture Books

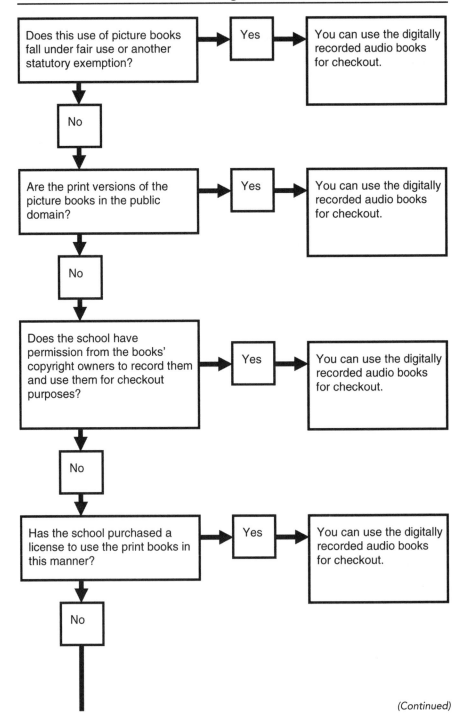

(Continued)

Flowchart 10.8. Audio-Recording Picture Books *(Continued)*

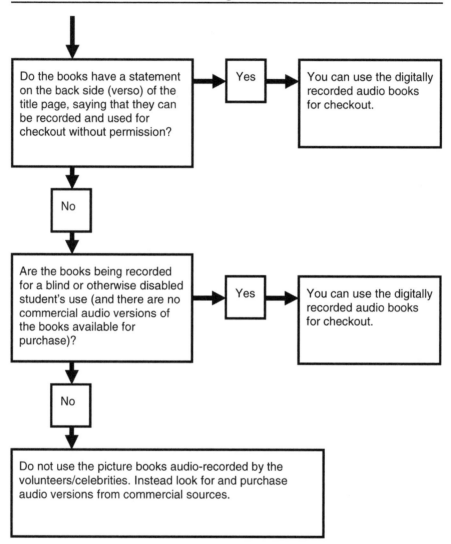

YOU CREATE IT, YOU OWN IT

Question: One of my students wrote and performed an original song for a school holiday concert. She says that her parents told her about something called a "poor man's copyright." Should she use this to copyright her song?

Answer: It is a fallacy that sending a copy of your original work to yourself is a legitimate "poor man's copyright." This method of trying to protect your work has never stood up in court (Frankel, 2009) and is meaningless under current copyright law because works are copyright-protected from the moment they are created. You can, however, officially register your work with the U.S. Copyright Office (see Chapter 1).

INFRINGEMENTS AND PENALTIES

Question: One of my library aides wants to take the 1960s' song "You're No Good" and create a satirical song about cheese titled "You're No Gouda." Is this an infringement of copyright law?

Answer: No, if the use of the original song fits under the fair use factors. Although it appears that she has created a derivative work, what she has done is to make fun of the original work. As long as such use fits under fair use, you don't need permission to make a parody. Section 107 of the U.S. Copyright law states that "the fair use of a copyrighted work . . . for purposes such as criticism [or] comment . . . is not an infringement" (U.S. Copyright Law, 1976, Sec. 107, 16).

Question: I have asked a technologically astute student to create a webpage for our class. He wants to borrow music from another site and put it on our site. Is this an infringement of copyright law?

Answer: Use Flowchart 10.9 to decide if this is an infringement of the law. Remember that it is always important to read the documentation on Internet sites. As can be seen from the flowchart, it is possible that a specific site will provide a statement saying that works from that site can be used, with or without acknowledging the original site, on school or other educational webpages (FA©E, 2010).

Question: Help! Part of the school's sheet music collection was damaged in last night's rainstorm. The leak in the roof destroyed all but one piece of the altos' part. We have a concert tonight. Can we legally copy the altos' part several times for the concert?

Answer: Yes, it can be copied for the concert only. Include the copyright notice, found on the original sheet music, on the copy, as well as any appropriate recognition to the sheet music source. Destroy the copies after the concert and purchase more originals, if they are available (Harper, 2005).

Question: Can a teacher download an e-book to his computer and play it aloud for the whole class to hear?

Answer: That actually depends on *how* he is going to use the e-book, for example, to support the curriculum or for entertainment or reward. See Flowchart 10.10 (p. 172) for more information.

Question: I have been a school librarian for a long time. Every year it seems that I once again need to remind administration, faculty, staff, and students about music copyright infringements and penalties. Comments I hear include

Flowchart 10.9. Borrowing Music from One Website for Another

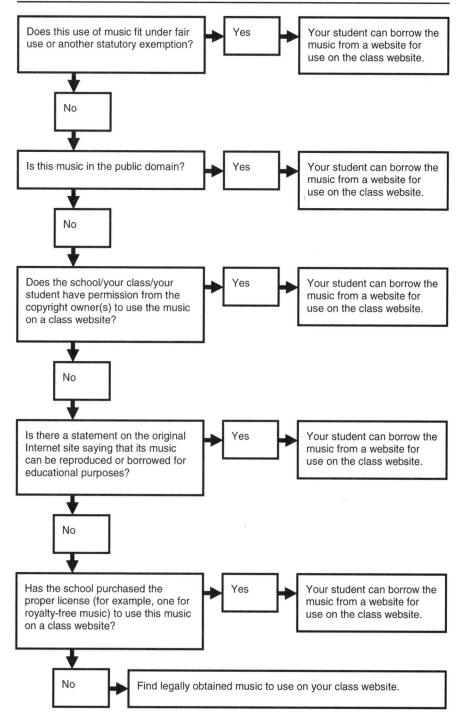

Flowchart 10.10. Playing an E-book Aloud for a Class

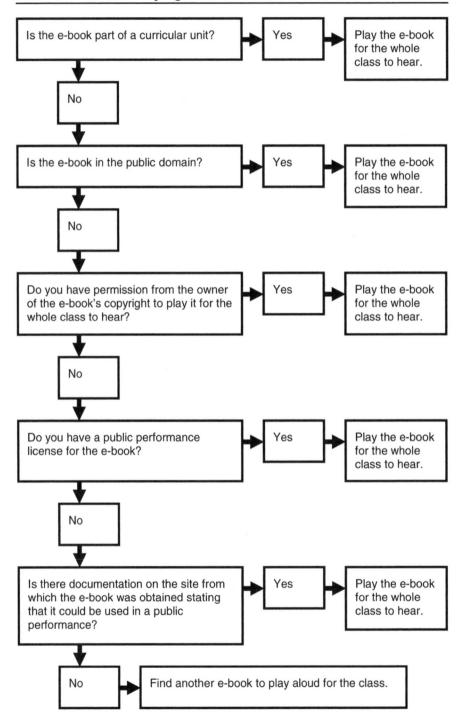

"Why does it matter?" and "We do it all the time, and we don't get caught" and "Everyone downloads music from the web and copies CDs and DVDs." How do I help them understand copyright infringements can happen to, and be done by, anyone, and that some infringers do get caught?

Answer: Perhaps one of the easiest ways to posit the notion that copyright law violations are recognized, at least part of the time, is to give popular culture examples, found in media sources ranging from trendy to more educational arenas. With that in mind, a few copyright infringement examples, all dealing with music or audio, include the following:

- Rush, a Canadian rock band, accused Rand Paul, U.S. Senator from Kentucky, of playing two of their songs without permission in his recent U.S. Senate campaign (*The Courier-Journal*, 2010).
- Burning CDs checked out from the library to your personal computer is a copyright infringement (Caro, 2009).
- Between 2003 and 2008, the U.S. music industry filed lawsuits against 35,000 alleged downloaders for copyright infringement (Skates, 2008).
- In 2005, an Indiana songwriter accused Britney Spears of infringing on his copyright with her song "Sometimes" (*People*, 2005). The lawsuit was later dismissed; Spears was able to prove it had not been copied (Silverman, 2005).
- George Harrison was sued for copyright infringement because his song "My Sweet Lord" allegedly infringed on the song "He's So fine" as performed by the Chiffons (Copyright Website, 2010).

INTERNATIONAL COPYRIGHT LAW

Question: For the middle school variety show, you have asked a student to dress up like Elvis Presley, mimic his movements, and lip-synch the words to one of his songs. The student in question purchased a recording of Presley's works when he and his family went to Europe last summer, and you notice that the recording has a European copyright on it. Can you use this recording in your variety show?

Answer: Much of Europe belongs to the same international copyright treaties and organizations as the United States. Thus, you should treat the Elvis recording purchased in Europe in the same manner that you would treat one purchased in the United States. See Flowchart 10.11 (p. 174).

Question: I purchased a CD of traditional Tibetan music when I was in China. Can I place it in the library for student checkout when my class is studying international music?

Answer: Sure, this CD can be checked out from the library. This comes under the first sale doctrine; this piece of U.S. Copyright Law states that the owner

Flowchart 10.11. Using a Foreign Recording for a Public Performance

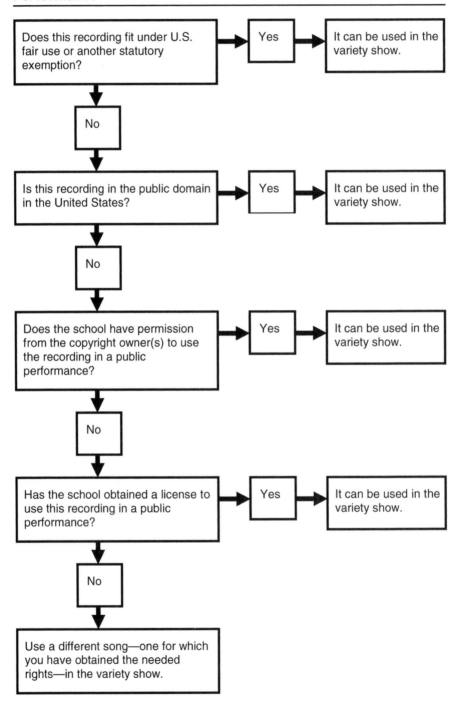

of a legal copy of a phonorecord (sound recording) can use the copy as he or she sees fit (Lipinski, 2006). This would include making the item available for circulation in a school library.

Question: I found some popular music on the web that I would really like to download to my iPod. Then when I take my vocal students on a field trip to a regional choral contest, I can play these over the bus loudspeaker for fun while we are traveling. I am thinking that if I download the music from foreign websites, rather than U.S. ones, I will not have to worry about U.S. copyright infringement. What do you think?

Answer: Be concerned about U.S. copyright law no matter where the downloaded music was obtained from, given that "it is still illegal for someone in the United States to download a recording that is copyrighted in the United States, even if the download comes from an Internet server in a foreign country" (Fishman, 2010: 122). Instead, look for music to use on the bus trip that has a public performance license, is in the public domain, or which you have permission to use for entertainment.

AVOIDING COPYRIGHT PROBLEMS

Question: Can the school library record multiple copies of a school orchestra concert for distribution in student homes? They will not charge for doing this.

Answer: Use Flowchart 10.12 (p. 176) to decide if the recordings are allowed under copyright law. Consult the U.S. Copyright Office's site (http://www .copyright .gov) for exceptions and further information.

Question: Can a local business record an elementary choral concert, edit it, and sell it to parents and the local community?

Answer: In all probability, such a moneymaking scheme is a copyright infringement. Yet there are some instances—however unusual—in which it would be possible for the local business to do this. See Flowchart 10.13 (p. 177).

Question: We charge admission to our high school basketball games. Are we allowed to play popular music over the loudspeaker at intermission or before the game starts?

Answer: Use Flowchart 10.14 (p. 178) to determine whether the music may be played.

Question: I want to assign my students to make lip dub videos, using popular songs. Once the videos are created, I plan to put them up on the web to show the students' parents, friends, the surrounding community, etc. Is this legal?

Flowchart 10.12. Free-of-Charge Recording of School Concerts for Home Distribution

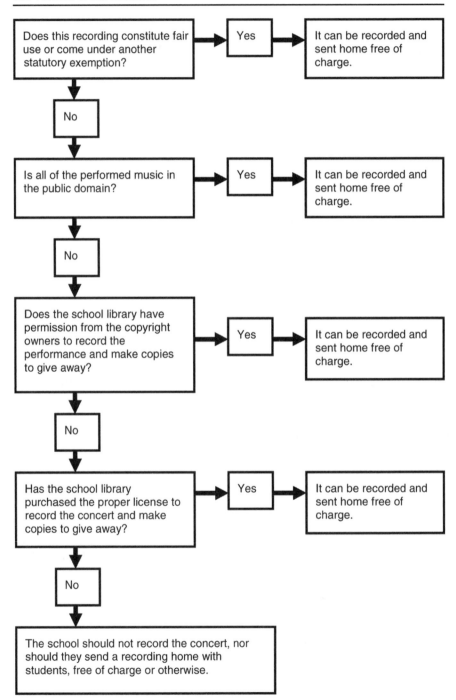

Flowchart 10.13. For-Profit Recording of School Concerts for Home Distribution

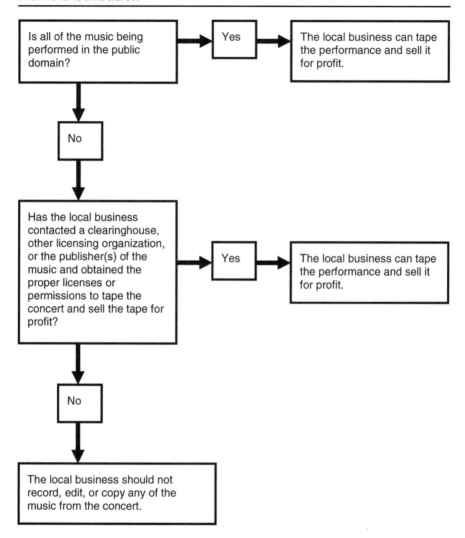

Answer: A lip dub video, "filmed with the song dubbed over the footage during editing, which lends theatrical heft and volume to what would otherwise be a routine lip-sync" (Vimeo, 2011), could be considered a public performance once it is available for public consumption via the web. Therefore, refer to Flowchart 10.15 (p. 179) to determine whether placing lip dub videos using popular songs on the web is a legal use.

Question: I am a school principal, and the technology teacher in the middle school at which I work has just approached me with a possible project. He wants to teach the eighth-graders how to use Windows Movie Maker. His idea

Flowchart 10.14. Playing Popular Music at School Sporting Events

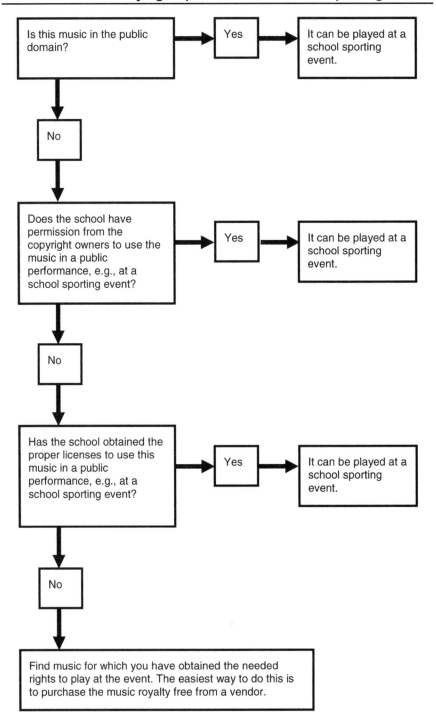

Flowchart 10.15. Placing Lip Dub Videos That Feature Popular Songs on a Website

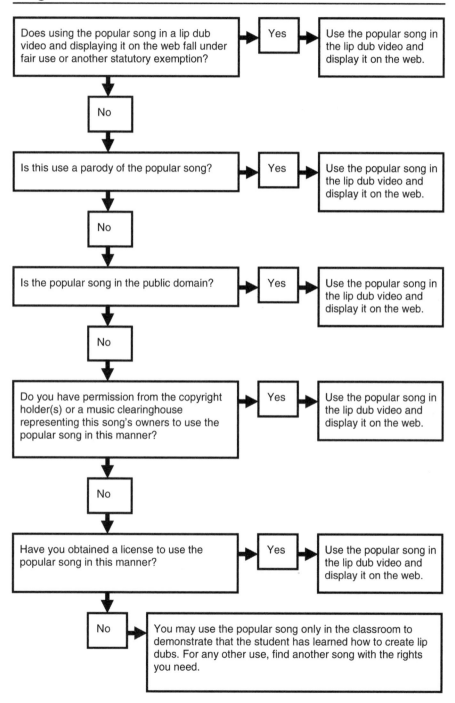

is that small groups of students will create an idea, develop a storyboard, record a short video, and add music to the final product, which will then be presented in class. I am concerned about adding music. Music copyright is so complicated. Can he do this?

Answer: As long as this use of music supports the curriculum (part of the lesson is teaching the students how to embed music into Movie Maker), then the students can legally do what the teacher proposes. Just make sure that this use of the music is for a curricular purpose, that project presentations stay in the classroom, and that the students understand the only other way they can use the project is for a portfolio.

CONCLUSION

When using audio formats—including musical recordings, sheet music, and copyright—the following are particularly important to investigate: fair use, public domain, permissions, documentation, licenses (for example, public performance), and royalty-free music companies. All, at one time or another, will help users employ audio materials without copyright infringements. In addition, while purchasing royalty-free music from a vendor, obtaining licenses, or contacting clearinghouses may all involve spending a little money, pursuing these alternatives is usually worth it. All three will obtain consent for you to use musical works in specific ways. Essentially, they obtain/provide permissions for you. Last, because confusion abounds in this area, if you have questions that this chapter does not cover or does not cover in the manner that you require, consult your school's copyright attorney.

REFERENCES

Apple. 2010. "Legal Information & Notices." Apple Inc. http://www.apple.com/legal/terms/site.html.

Bell, Tom, W. 2004. "Music Copyrights Table." TomWBell.com. http://www.tomwbell.com/teaching/Music(C)s.html.

Bookshare. 2010. "Legal Information." Benetech. http://www.bookshare.org/_/aboutUs/legalInformation.

Caro, Mark. 2009. "Crime Scene?" *Chicago Tribune.* Section 3. October 28: 1, 5.

Classic Cat. 2010. "Classic Cat: The Free Classical Musical Directory." Classic Cat. http://www.classiccat.net.

Copyright Website. 2010. "Copyright Casebook: George Harrison and the Chiffons." Copyright Website LLC. http://www.benedict.com/Audio/Harrison/Harrison.aspx.

The Courier-Journal. 2010. "Rand Paul Accused by Rock Band of Violating Music Copyright Laws." *The Huffington Post.* June 3. http://www.huffingtonpost.com/2010/06/03/rand-paul-accused-by-rock_n_599372.html.

FA©E. 2010. "Friends of Active Copyright Education." Copyright Society of the U.S.A. Accessed September 9. http://www.csusa.org/face/index.htm.

Ferrara, Lawrence. 2005. "What Is a Compulsory License?" Artists House Music. October. http://www.artistshousemusic.org/videos/what+is+a+compulsory+license.

Fishman, Stephan. 2010. *The Public Domain: How to Find & Use Copyright-Free Writings, Music, Art & More.* 5th ed. Berkeley, CA: Nolo.

Frankel, James. 2009. *The Teacher's Guide to Music, Media, and Copyright Law.* New York: Hal Leonard Books.

GMP Music. 2010. "Thank You for Selecting TEMP." Gene Michael Productions, Inc. Accessed October 31. http://www.gmpmusic.com/album/?category=8&save=.

Grooveshark. 2010. Homepage. Escape Media Group. http://listen.grooveshark.com.

Harper, Georgia. 2005. "Fair Use of Copyrighted Materials." University of Texas. Updated March 30. http://www.utsystem.edu/ogc/intellectualproperty/copypol2.htm.

Home Recording Connection. 2010. "Frequently Asked Questions." http://www.home recordingconnection.com/faq.php#q13.

Justia. 2010. "White-Smith Music Pub. Co. v. Apollo Co., 209 U.S. 1 (1908)." Justia U.S. Supreme Court Center. http://supreme.justia.com/us/209/1/case.html.

Legal Information Institute. 2010. "Right of Publicity: An Overview." Cornell University Law School. Accessed September 9. http://www.law.cornell.edu/topics/publicity .html.

Legislative Branch Appropriations Act of 1996. 1997. Public Law No. 104-197, sec. 110, 121.

Lipinski, Tomas A. 2006. *The Complete Copyright Liability Handbook for Librarians and Educators.* New York: Neal-Schuman.

MENC: The National Association for Music Education. 2010. "Copyright Guidelines for SchoolTube." MENC. August. http://www.menc.org/resources/view/copyright-guidelines-for-schooltube.

Musopen. 2010. "About." Musopen. Accessed October 31. http://www.musopen.org.

MyBytes. 2010. Homepage. Microsoft. Accessed October 31. http://www.mybytes.com/ index.html.

PD Info. 2010. "Public Domain Music. Royalty Free Music." Public Domain Information Project. Haven Sound, Inc. http://www.pdinfo.com.

People. 2005. "Passages." *People Magazine.* May 30, 2005: 101.

RoyaltyFreeMusic.com. 2010. Homepage. Jupiterimages Corporation. http://www.royalty freemusic.com.

SchoolTube. 2010. "About Us." SchoolTube, LLC. http://www2.schooltube.com/About Us.aspx.

Silverman, Stephen M. 2005. "Judge: Britney Didn't Steal Song." *People.* November 9. http://www.people.com/people/article/0,,1127686,00.html.

Skates, Sara. 2008. "RIAA Changes Strategy in Fight Against Illegal Downloading." SESAC News. December 23. http://www.sesac.com/News/News_Details.aspx?id=882.

Sohn, David. 2008. "Music Download Warning List." Center for Democracy and Technology. July 1. http://www.cdt.org/copyright/warninglist.

Soundzabound. 2010. Homepage. Soundzabound Music Library, Royalty Free Music for Schools. http://www.soundzabound.com/.

U.S. Copyright Law. 1976. Public Law 94-553.

U.S. Copyright Office, Library of Congress. 2006. "Copyright in General." July. http:// www.copyright.gov/help/faq/faq-general.html#register.

———. 2008. "Circular 73: Cumpulsory License for Making and Distributing Phonorecords." Washington, DC: U.S. Copyright Office.

———. 2009a. "Circular 56: Copyright Registration for Sound Recordings." Washington, DC: U.S. Copyright Office.

———. 2009b. "Circular 56a: Copyright Registration of Musical Compositions and Sound Recordings." Washington, DC: U.S. Copyright Office.

Vimeo. 2011. "Lip Dub Stars on Vimeo." Vimeo, LLC. Accessed March 4. http://vimeo.com/channels/lipdub.

Webster, Kathy. 1996. "Copyright Violation Cases." LM_NET. September 24. http://www.eduref.org/lm_net/archive/LM_NET-pre1997/1996/Sep_1996/msg01457.html.

CHAPTER 11

Multimedia and Copyright Law: How Confusing! Can You Borrow a Variety of Works for Your Production?

INTRODUCTION

Multimedia is "interactive text, images, sound, and color. Multimedia can be anything from a simple PowerPoint slide show to a complex interactive simulation" (Utah Education Network, 2010). Works can be used equally in face-to-face and/or online teaching (synchronous or asynchronous). Because multimedia productions may contain a number of separate items, each with its own copyright protection, multimedia is addressed in this book separately from the works that it may encompass. The questions that follow cover multimedia productions, educators, and copyright law. Questions with more than one answer are presented in flowchart form. Remember, when you use the flowcharts in this chapter, you are trying to find any criterion under which you may borrow a work. Therefore, you need only follow each flowchart until you come to that point where you satisfy one of the criteria. Once you reach that point, there is no need to go any further. For more information on each area discussed, refer to the individual chapter that covers that particular subject in depth.

FAIR USE

Question: A technology teacher assigns a multimedia production as a group project. One group borrows liberally for their multimedia assignment: a song from a music CD, a clip from a video, a cartoon from a newspaper Internet site, a poem from a print anthology, and a graphic from a website. Can they borrow these works under copyright law?

Answer: Yes, they can, if the use fits Flowchart 11.1 (p. 185). Fair use is defined quite broadly when student projects are involved. Therefore, as long as the work borrowed is the smallest amount needed to cover the assignment, said work will come under fair use. However, if more than the minimum is borrowed, then public domain, permissions, and licenses may come into play. Thus remember, the smallest amount you need is the amount you should use. In addition, such multimedia projects should be used for in-class presentations or student portfolios only.

Question: Is it okay for my students to put photographs in their multimedia project?

Answer: Use Flowchart 11.2 (p. 186) to determine if the students may use photographs. Obtaining permission of the subjects of a photograph is a privacy issue. This ethical matter, in addition to copyright, should be addressed when using photographs of human subjects for multimedia and other presentations, projects, and publications.

Question: When creating multimedia projects, do I have to use the "Fair Use Guidelines for Educational Multimedia"?

Answer: No. While some educators use the "Fair Use Guidelines for Educational Multimedia" (see Chapter 2) to measure how much of protected works can be used in multimedia projects, in this chapter I primarily use the four fair use factors found under Section 107 of the 1976 copyright law (see also Chapter 2). Under Section 107 of the U.S. Copyright Law (1976), the four fair use factors are

1. the purpose and character of the use, including whether such use is of a commercial nature or is for nonprofit educational purposes;
2. the nature of the copyrighted work;
3. the amount and substantiality of the portion used in relation to the copyrighted work as a whole; and
4. the effect of the use upon the potential market for or value of the copyrighted work.

You can find the law in a number of places, including U.S. Copyright Office's website at http://www.copyright.gov. Under fair use, more can be borrowed than is allowed under the conservative interpretation of the four fair use factors, the "Fair Use Guidelines for Educational Multimedia." In addition, in the preamble to the "Fair Use Guidelines for Educational Multimedia" (2003), the authors make the following observations:

> While only the courts can authoritatively determine whether a particular use is fair use, these guidelines represent the participants' consensus of conditions under which fair use should generally apply and examples of when permission is required. Uses that exceed these guidelines neither may nor may not be fair use...the more one exceeds these guidelines, the greater the risk that fair use does not apply.

PUBLIC DOMAIN

Question: I found a multimedia work on the web. There is no copyright notice on it. Therefore, it is in the public domain, and I can use it any way I want, correct?

Flowchart 11.1. Borrowing a Variety of Works for a Multimedia Production

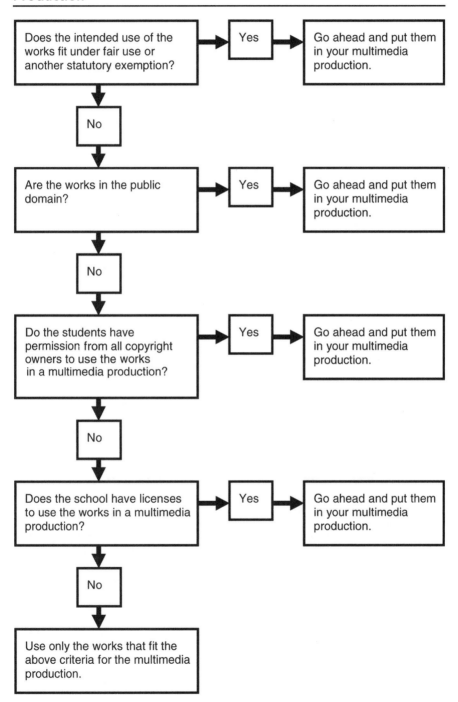

Flowchart 11.2. Using Photographs in Multimedia Projects

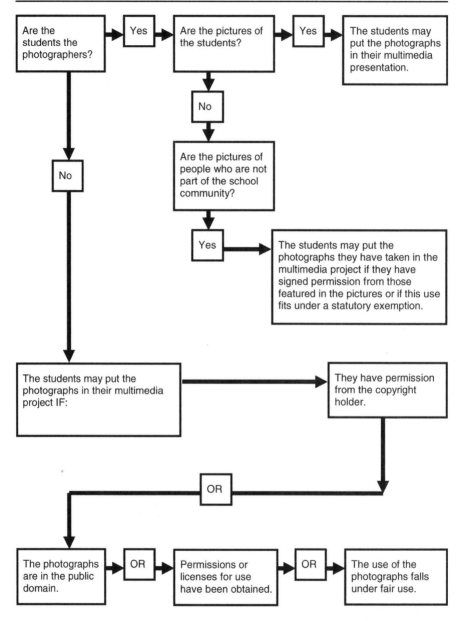

Answer: No, that is not correct. It just means that the owner/creator did not put a copyright notice on it. Unless the website specifically states that the multimedia work is in the public domain, you must assume that it—and/or its pieces—is copyrighted and treat it accordingly.

Question: How do I put my multimedia work into the public domain?

Answer: If you are the owner of your multimedia work, and all contents of the multimedia product also belong to you, it is easy to transfer your rights (U.S. Copyright Office, Library of Congress, 2006). In the case of public domain, you just label your work, "public domain." If you have borrowed some or all of the contents of the multimedia work from others, then you cannot put it into public domain unless, or until, you obtain permission to do so from the owners of the content pieces.

Question: Can a multimedia work, created entirely of public domain items, be copyright protected and/or licensed?

Answer: Yes. The intermingling of the public domain items to make a new whole can be protected under copyright law and/or licensed. For example, the creator of "A Fair(y) Use Tale," a video made up entirely of clips from Disney movies, is licensed under a Creative Commons license (The Center for Internet and Society, 2010). However, the original public domain pieces are still in the public domain.

DOCUMENTATION AND LICENSES

Question: I'm planning on giving credit to everyone from whom I borrow for my PowerPoint project. I believe that since I am citing the owners and showcasing their work, I will not need to purchase any licenses or obtain permission for using these works. Am I right?

Answer: No! You are wrong. By giving credit, you will not be committing plagiarism. However, you could still be infringing on someone's copyright ownership. Thus, the same rules apply as for borrowing any copyrighted works.

Question: Can I, as a teacher, produce my own computer-based presentation for class instruction using a combination of student and commercial works?

Answer: Use Flowchart 11.3 (p. 188) to determine which materials you can use in your presentation.

Question: What is the first sale doctrine? How does it affect multimedia works?

Answer: The first sale doctrine gives the owner of a particular copy of a work the right to dispose of that copy as she or he sees fit (United States Copyright Law, 2010b). This means that someone who purchases a lawfully made computer-generated presentation has the right to display it, keep it, resell it, give it away, or dispose of it. However, the owner of the copy does not have the right to make copies of his or her one copy, prepare derivative works, permit other borrowing of the work, or place the original in the public domain. Such rights belong only to the copyright holder of the original work.

Question: Imagine that you are an economics instructor for a class that is taught at two high schools, one site face to face and the other site via the web.

Flowchart 11.3. Using Student or Commercial Works in Computer-Based Presentations

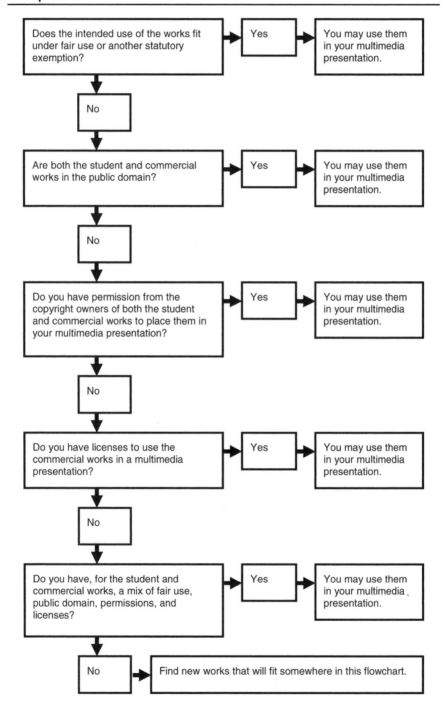

You find a video in a vendor's catalog that fits the subject area of one of your class units. What really is appealing about this video is the catalog statement, which says that this video has copyright clearance to be used in both online and televised distance-education classes. You purchase the video and insert it into a multimedia project that you created for your class. Within a week, the video's copyright owner contacts you. This person states that you have violated copyright law and must pay royalties to him for using his video for distance education. You point out the statement in the vendor's catalog, and the copyright owner tells you that it is a misprint. Have you really infringed on copyright law? Are you liable?

Answer: Yes, even though you used the work in good faith and according to the documentation that you found, you are in copyright violation. Cease using the video for distance education.

PERMISSIONS

Question: Can an instructor show students examples of multimedia projects to illustrate assessment concepts over a distance-education network?

Answer: Multimedia works can be used for face-to-face teaching, library reserve, and distance education (Harper, 2007). While all multimedia works can be used in these ways, they have the same limitations that are placed on uses of works in general. For example, does the use of the work fit under fair use? Is the work in the public domain? Does the borrower have permission or a license for such use? For distance-education courses, certain criteria must be met, as illustrated in Flowchart 11.4 (p. 190). Please also see discussion of the TEACH Act in Chapter 13.

Question: How can I get permission to use a piece of animation for a multimedia presentation when the animation is credited "from the Internet"?

Answer: You can't. Find another animation for which permission is available or the copyright owner identified, or both, and then ask for permission.

Question: If you write for permission to use a newspaper cartoon in a multimedia presentation and don't get a response, can you use the cartoon in your project if you cite the work?

Answer: No, you cannot legally do so. By citing the work, you will not have plagiarized, however.

Question: Our high school students are required to create a professional portfolio for their senior class project. With all the new technologies available, these portfolios have morphed from print only into multimedia projects with PowerPoint presentations, music, websites, video, you name it. What kinds of permissions do the students need to obtain as they put together their portfolios?

Flowchart 11.4. Using Student Examples in Distance Education

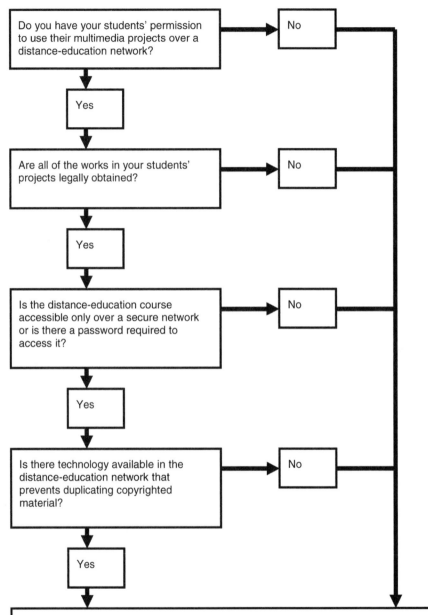

Do you have your students' permission to use their multimedia projects over a distance-education network? → No

Yes ↓

Are all of the works in your students' projects legally obtained? → No

Yes ↓

Is the distance-education course accessible only over a secure network or is there a password required to access it? → No

Yes ↓

Is there technology available in the distance-education network that prevents duplicating copyrighted material? → No

Yes ↓

If you answered "Yes" to **all** of the questions above, you may show your students' work over a distance-education network. If you answered "No" to **any** of the questions above and use of the work does not fall under any statutory exemptions, don't show your students' multimedia projects over a distance-education network. Find another way to illustrate assessment concepts.

Answer: That depends on how the students plan to use the portfolios they are creating. If they plan to use them for the senior class project assignment, as examples of their work for employment interviews, or as unpaid presentations at professional organization meetings or conferences, then they do not need to get permissions for pieces they have borrowed from other sources (as long as they borrowed the least amount needed in each case). However, should they wish to earn money from their portfolio materials—for example, by displaying the portfolio at a paid presentation—then any materials borrowed from sources other than those created by the seniors themselves need permissions or licenses for use.

YOU CREATE IT, YOU OWN IT

Question: Somebody already copyrighted the name that I wanted to use for my multimedia project. Can I still use it?

Answer: Names cannot be copyrighted. Therefore, you can use a name, unless it is trademarked. "A **trademark** is a word, phrase, symbol or design, or a combination of words, phrases, symbols or designs, that identifies and distinguishes the source of the goods of one party from those of others" (United States Patent and Trademark Office, 2010).

Question: I created a very detailed multimedia project for a home economics class that I teach. I am now moving to a new district, and I want to take my project with me. My current school district says that I have to leave it with them. Who should get control of my multimedia project?

Answer: Use Flowchart 11.5 (p. 192) to determine if you own the project or if it is work for hire.

Question: I want to protect my ownership of a multimedia project that I created and presented over real-time television to a middle school class in another state. What do I need to do?

Answer: Register it with the U.S. Copyright Office. (See Chapter 1.)

Question: Two of my high school students—on their own time—created a PowerPoint (PPT) presentation on how to write a term paper, using material from print sources and the web, as well as sound and video clips from popular media. It is really done very well. They are proud of their work and would like to post it to the web. However, they are afraid, with the amount of information being added daily to the web, that their work will not be easily found. Therefore, in addition to checking to ensure that they have obtained all necessary copyright permissions for their work, they want to give it a "catchy" domain name—one that others will want to access. They have chosen TwilightTermPaper.com as their domain name, even though the PPT has nothing to do with this popular vampire series. Does this matter, since they are not charging for use of the PPT?

Flowchart 11.5. Who Owns Teacher-Created Multimedia?

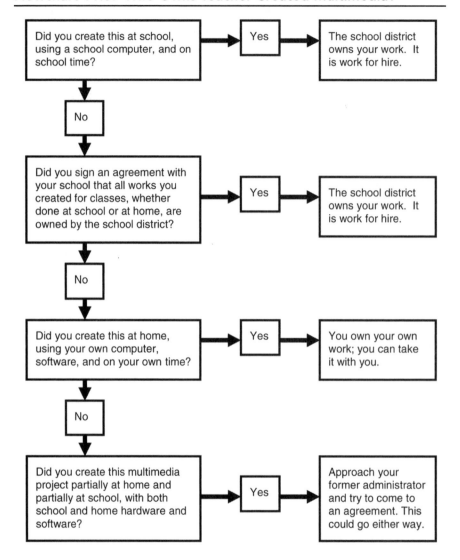

Answer: Yes, it can matter. Make sure that a domain name fits the subject of the multimedia project; do not delude those who might access your work (Donaldson, 2008).

INFRINGEMENTS AND PENALTIES

Question: How do I know if I am allowed to use Internet clip art in my multimedia project?

Answer: Use Flowchart 11.6 to answer this question.

Remember that there are many instances in which webpages provide clip art to users. While clip art is most often in the form of images, animations and sound can also be clip art. The problem is that sometimes the creators/owners of the webpage borrow copyrighted images, etc., from other sites, place these on their site, and then inform users that their site is in the public domain. Unless you know more about a piece of clip art, you might not know whether it is really in the public domain. Therefore, when using clip art that has been identified as public domain material, it is best to obtain it from a site that you consider reputable, such as a prominent computer software site.

Flowchart 11.6. Using Clip Art in Multimedia Projects

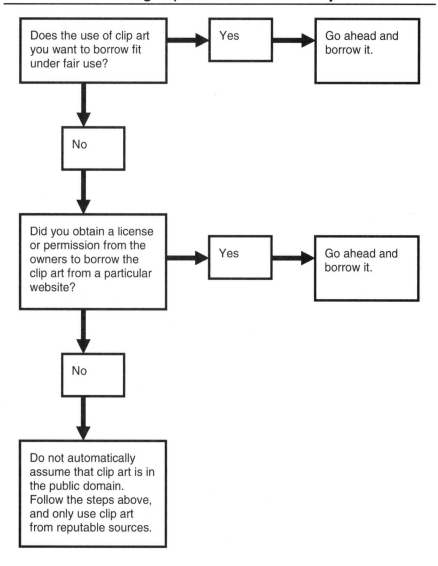

Question: I teach online. May I place an instructional video in my multimedia presentation for class?

Answer: Use Flowchart 11.7 to determine whether you are allowed to use the video.

Question: Can I change a digitized image enough that it becomes my work? Can I then place it in my multimedia production without worrying about copyright infringement?

Answer: No. A derivative work is a derivative work.

Question: Two of my seventh-grade students are Harry Potter fanatics. They have created a keynote presentation about the boy wizard, including a list of Harry Potter website hyperlinks. I have heard that lists can violate copyright law, and I don't want them to get into any trouble. What's the deal here?

Answer: It is not a copyright violation if your students make their own list of Harry Potter links and put them in their keynote presentation. It could be an infringement if they borrowed a list of Harry Potter links created by someone else.

INTERNATIONAL COPYRIGHT LAW

Question: I am a history teacher. As part of a class multimedia presentation, I have created a list of links to historical sites worldwide. If I put the presentation on my webpage and make my links "live," will my students be copyright compliant if they use the links?

Answer: Yes. However, it would be good netiquette to ask for permission from those sites before you provide their links to your students. It may not always be practical, on the other hand, to ask for permission to link to others' Internet sites. You will need to use your own judgment on this issue.

Question: The library has an extensive collection of foreign-language tapes, DVDs, CDs, videos, and multimedia. They were purchased in several foreign countries by some of our students who were living in Europe at the time. We believe that all items were legally obtained. We would like to copy these to a server in order to stream them into classrooms when they are needed for curricular support. Can we do so legally?

Answer: As discussed in earlier chapters, due to the number of international copyright conventions and organizations to which the U.S. belongs, it is best to treat foreign works as you would something created and published in the United States. See Flowchart 11.8 (p. 196) for more information. Also remember that having the ability and equipment/materials to copy something does not automatically make such copying legal.

Flowchart 11.7. Using Videos in Multimedia Projects

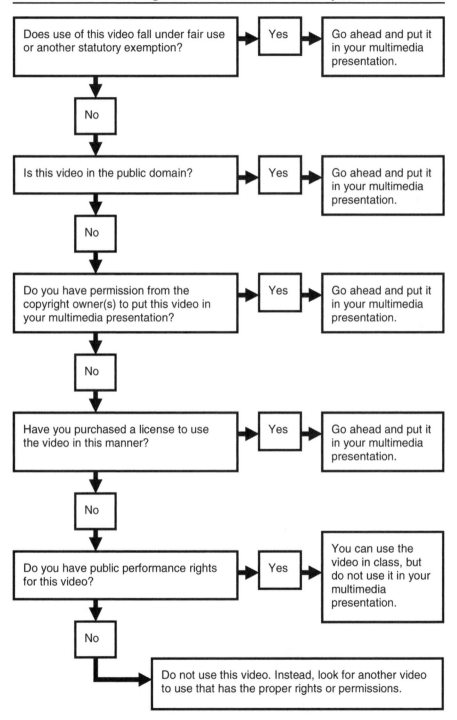

Flowchart 11.8. Copying Media to a Server for Curricular Use

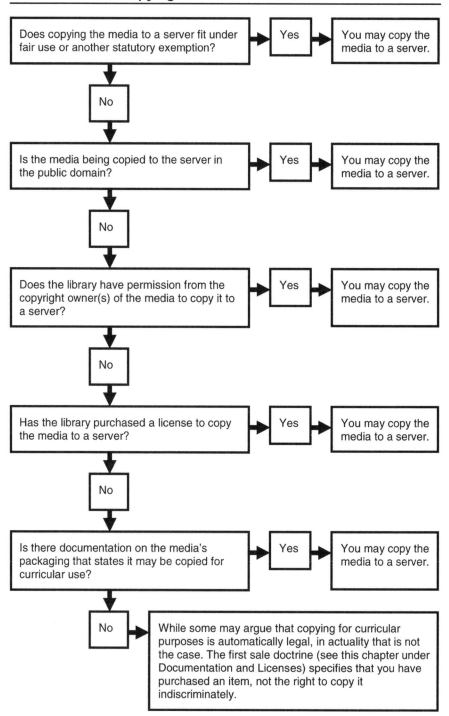

AVOIDING COPYRIGHT PROBLEMS

Question: One of my sixth-graders wants to obtain copyright registration for the multimedia project he did in art class. Can he do so, since he is underage?

Answer: Sure he can. The U.S. Copyright Office "issues registrations to minors" as well as adults for copyright purposes (U.S. Copyright Office, 2010a).

Question: We are working on a parody unit in English class. I would like to collect a bunch of film and music parodies from the web and from popular media, and string them together into one cohesive whole that I can then use with my class. Is this okay to do?

Answer: By borrowing parodies from a number of websites and popular media and stringing them together, you are creating a derivative work. However, there is a way that you can use these parodies in class, as part of the classroom exemption: just link to each parody separately while you are teaching.

Question: The middle school variety show is coming up next week. We have several parents who record the whole show—songs, poetry readings, short skits, dances, etc. I think that they are creating a multimedia derivative work, which could be a copyright infringement. Should I warn them?

Answer: You have three different things going on here. First of all, is it legal for parents to record the variety show? As with most things copyright, that depends. One might be able to argue that this is a type of personal fair use, i.e., the parent is recording the performance in order to watch it in the home at a later time. (See Flowchart 11.9, p. 198, for information.) Second, have the parents, by recording the acts that are performed one after another, created a derivative work? One could argue that a derivative work has been created. That said, one could follow Flowchart 11.9 (p. 198) because there are some instances in which creating a derivative work would be fine, for example, if the items in question were in the public domain or if the right permissions, licenses, or documentation had been obtained. Last, should you warn them? This may put you in the uncomfortable position of becoming the "copyright police." We discuss this in more depth in Chapter 14. However, you might choose to inform the parents, in a nonconfrontational manner, that such a public taping may well be a copyright infringement.

Question: I teach fifth-grade science. As part of a unit on the planets, I plan to collect images, music, video—any media I can find that has been named after a planet. The final product will be a multimedia production that I will show to the class. One of my students has created an array of amazing sketches of Saturn. I would like to include several of these in my production. Since he drew them for my class, can I just take them and add them to the multimedia unit?

Answer: Original work—no matter the age of the individual creating it—is automatically copyright-protected. This means that your student's sketches

Flowchart 11.9. Parents Recording a School Variety Show

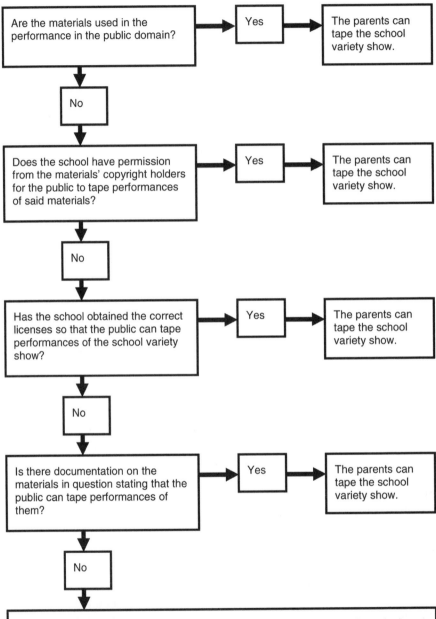

Are the materials used in the performance in the public domain? → **Yes** → The parents can tape the school variety show.

No

Does the school have permission from the materials' copyright holders for the public to tape performances of said materials? → **Yes** → The parents can tape the school variety show.

No

Has the school obtained the correct licenses so that the public can tape performances of the school variety show? → **Yes** → The parents can tape the school variety show.

No

Is there documentation on the materials in question stating that the public can tape performances of them? → **Yes** → The parents can tape the school variety show.

No

In all probability, there will be some things that can be taped by the public and other things for which there are no permissions, licenses, or documentation for public taping. If the parent keeps the school variety show tape in the home, for personal use only, one might be able to argue that such use is acceptable. Otherwise, it is best not to tape the school variety show.

are copyrighted, and you need to ask permission from him to use these drawings in your multimedia production. In addition, since he is a minor, it would be prudent to also check with his parents or guardian before using his work. Finally, obtain the permission in writing, including the date and the signatures of the borrower (yourself) and those who are granting permission for use (in this case, the student and his parents/guardian).

CONCLUSION

It is important to remember that the more you borrow without obtaining permission from the owner/creator of a work, the greater the likelihood that you might be in infringement of copyright law. Sometimes all that the owner/creator wants is recognition for his or her work. Therefore, on all your educational multimedia creations (and other creations as well) remember to include a reference section at the beginning, end, or in the body of your work where you cite those from whom you have obtained material. However, because a multimedia product may contain a number and variety of formats as part of its whole, obtaining the needed rights for use can, at times, be complicated and/or time-consuming.

REFERENCES

The Center for Internet and Society. 2010. "A Fair(y) Use Tail." Stanford Law School. Accessed November 13. http://cyberlaw.stanford.edu/documentary-film-program/film/a-fair-y-use-tale.

Donaldson, Michael C. 2008. *Clearance & Copyright: Everything You Need to Know for Film and Television.* 3rd ed. Los Angeles: Silman-James Press.

"Fair Use Guidelines for Educational Multimedia." 2003. University of Washington, Classroom Support Services. Modified March 12. http://www.washington.edu/classroom/emc/fairuse.html.

Harper, Georgia K. 2007. "Copyright Crash Course: Building on Others' Creative Expression: Fair Use Guidelines for Educational Multimedia." University of Texas Libraries. http://copyright.lib.utexas.edu/ccmcguid.html.

U.S. Copyright Law. 1976. Public Law 94-553, sec. 107.

U.S. Copyright Office, Library of Congress. 2006. "Copyright: FAQ: Assignment/Transfer of Copyright Ownership." U.S. Copyright Office. Revised July 12. http://www.copyright.gov/help/faq/faq-assignment.html.

———. 2010a. "Copyright: FAQ: Who Can Register?" U.S. Copyright Office. Accessed November 11. http://www.copyright.gov/help/faq/faq-who.html.

———. 2010b. Copyright Law of the United States of America. Section 109(a). U.S. Copyright Office. Accessed December 5. http://www.copyright.gov/title17/92chap1.html#109.

United States Patent and Trademark Office. 2010. "Trademark, Copyright, or Patent?" Department of Commerce, United States Patent and Trademark Office. Modified January 11. http://www.uspto.gov/trademarks/basics/trade_defin.jsp.

Utah Education Network. 2010. "Ed Technology Glossary of Terms." Utah Education Network. Accessed November 9. http://www.uen.org/core/edtech/glossary.shtml#M.

CHAPTER 12

Print Works and Copyright Law: Is it Legal to Copy Print Works for Class at the Last Minute?

INTRODUCTION

Print, as a medium of communication, has been around for literally thousands of years. In the past, print forms included tomb encryptions, illuminated manuscripts, and codices. Today, common print items consist of books, newspapers, magazines, poetry, play scripts, cartoons, recipes, and more. In addition, the invention of computers, iPads, and handheld digital devices like Kindles and Nooks, and even cell phones with text message functions, have brought print into the digital world. Are issues of copyright a part of this new level of print? Although these new media may make copyright seem even more confusing than before, the answer to that question is a definite yes. So let's begin this chapter by taking a look at print and fair use (law and guidelines), both of which are very important for K–12 educators.

When copying or borrowing from print sources, it is important to be aware not only of the fair use factors discussed in Chapter 2's coverage of U.S. law but also of the brevity, spontaneity, and cumulative effect tests. These three "tests" are guidelines, endorsed by U.S. Congress, for purposes of educational and classroom copying (printing), and interpreted from the 1976 U.S. Copyright Act. Basically, what they do is help decipher application of the fair use factors. *Brevity* means the least amount possible is to be copied. This amounts to a whole poem if the poem is less than 250 words or an excerpt from a poem of no more than 250 words; 2,500 words or less for an essay or article, or no more than 10 percent or 1,000 words for an excerpt; or one illustration per book or periodical. *Spontaneity* means that the copying is a last-minute request for class, usually instigated by an individual instructor. *Cumulative effect* means the amount of work that is copied over a class term. For print material, this means the following:

(i) The copying of the material is for only one course in the school in which the copies are made. (ii) Not more than one short poem, article, story, essay or two excerpts may be copied from the same author, nor more than three from the same collective work or periodical volume during one class term. (iii) There shall not be more than nine instances of such multiple copying for one course during one class term. (U.S. Copyright Office, 2009: 7)

Be aware that it is possible for print copying to fall under one or more of the fair use factors of the law but not under these guidelines (Crews, 2001). Therefore, while both are addressed in this chapter, if your use of a work is legitimate under the law, then you don't need to worry about guidelines.

This chapter's questions cover print, educators, and copyright. Questions with more than one answer are presented in flowchart form. Remember that when you use the flowcharts in this chapter, you are trying to find any criterion under which you may borrow a work. Therefore, you need only follow each flowchart until you come to that point where you satisfy one of the criteria. Once you reach that point, there is no need to go any further. For more information on each area discussed, please refer to the chapter (in Part I) in which that particular subject is covered.

FAIR USE

Question: I teach biology. I have a textbook that I would like my students to read. However, it is very expensive, and the school budget directors have decided that they will not purchase it for my class. Can I photocopy parts of the book for each member of class?

Answer: Use Flowchart 12.1 to determine if you are allowed to make these copies.

Question: One of my students has visual problems and can read large print only. Can I copy the social studies textbook for my student using the enlarging feature on the copy machine?

Answer: In the 21st century, there are several possible answers to this question (see Flowchart 12.2, p. 204). If the book is not available in large print in a book format or on a device such as a Kindle, Nook, iPad, Playaway, or other handheld appliance that can enlarge text, or in some other form that makes it usable by the visually impaired student, such as an audio book, then copying it for your student may come under fair use. In addition, Section 121 of the U.S. Copyright Law is another statutory exemption important to educators when working with blind and other students with disabilities. This section sets forth limits on the exclusive rights of copyright holders when reproducing works for people who are visually impaired and people with other disabilities. (See Appendix 1E.) This section of the copyright law may allow the book format to be changed for the visually impaired student. In addition, a number of companies make large-print copies of textbooks, and any number of books are now accessible via handheld devices, as already mentioned.

Flowchart 12.1. Photocopying Parts of a Book

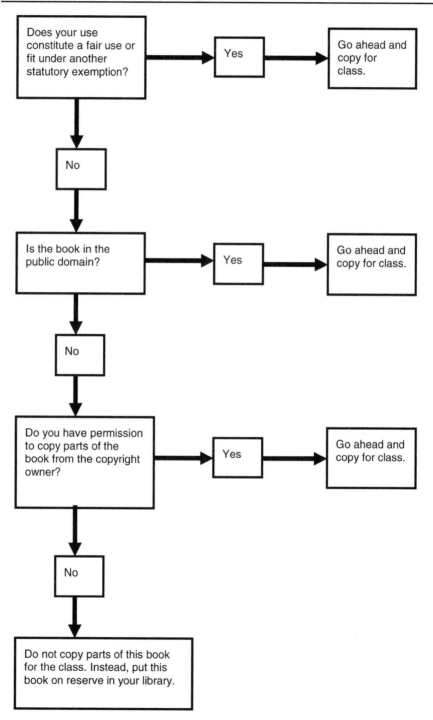

Flowchart 12.2. Copying Textbooks for Visually Impaired Students

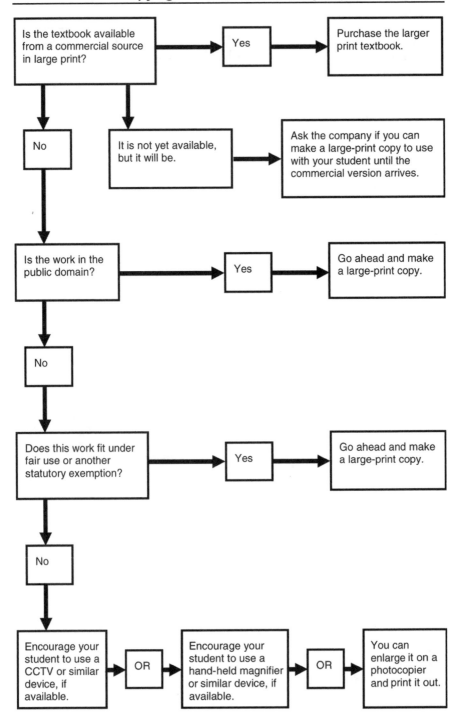

There are also machines, such as closed-circuit television (CCTV) and small handheld magnifiers, which enlarge print. Pursue all of these options before enlarging a textbook for your student. Also, if you have purchased a large-print textbook and it is not yet available, check with the publishers to see if they will let you make an enlarged copy to use until the commercial one arrives.

Question: Does copying one illustration from a picture book fall under fair use?

Answer: Because it is a picture book, i.e., there are many illustrations in the book, one copy of one illustration would fall under the fair use factors, unless each illustration is registered for copyright separately. In that case, copying one illustration from a picture book could be an infringement. Check on the back of the title page. Information on the illustrations' copyrights should be there. Remember that if the information you are looking for is not on this page or elsewhere in the book, you need to go through the basic steps we discuss in this book, including checking to see if the item is in the public domain and, if not, searching for permission to use it. In such a case, a clearinghouse for print materials (see Chapter 4) could come in handy. Also, be sure to check to see if any of the statutory exemptions for classrooms, libraries, or archives apply.

PUBLIC DOMAIN

Question: There is a chapter in a book that I would really like to use in my class. I have tried contacting the publisher, but the company doesn't seem to exist anymore. Does that mean that this book is now in the public domain?

Answer: Use Flowchart 12.3 (p. 206) to determine if the book is in the public domain.

Question: If a magazine is out of print, is it now in the public domain? And is it therefore legal for me to make copies of one of the articles for my class?

Answer: It is important to recognize here that magazine articles can be (1) independently protected by their own copyright registrations or (2) part of the magazine's general copyright registration. How the article is copyright-protected depends on the agreement between the owner of the article and the magazine publisher at the time of publication. Thus, you must check copyright registration for the article; in other words, there is no simple answer to this question. See also Flowchart 12.4 (pp. 208–209) for guidance.

Question: Can the high school theater group put on a Shakespeare play as a public performance without paying royalties to a clearinghouse or theater service? After all, Shakespeare's plays *must* be in the public domain!

Answer: If the group uses an original Shakespeare play with no added directives, illustrations, or updates, then yes, these students may hold a public performance. If the script they use has any added components, however,

Flowchart 12.3. Books in the Public Domain

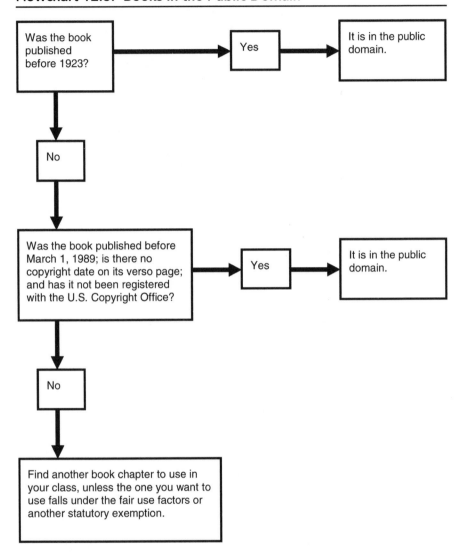

then it may be back under copyright. In such a case, the theater club would need to get permission from the owner of the revisions or go through a theater clearinghouse to perform the play in public. See also Flowchart 12.5 (p. 210).

DOCUMENTATION AND LICENSES

Question: As the school librarian, do I need public performance rights to read a storybook to an elementary class? I know that librarians do this all the time. Are we all copyright infringers?

Answer: Well, the book is being used in a public performance, in a school setting. Assuming that the school is nonprofit, that the performance is occurring in the library or another place dedicated to instruction, and that the storybook was legally obtained, then, yes, you can read the book and not be infringing on someone's copyright (U.S. Copyright Law, 1976). It is also possible that such a reading fits under the four fair use factors. Furthermore, "there are general practices that we have come to accept as OK. These practices have become so normalized that they actually affect the development and interpretation of the copyright law" (Russell, 2003). Therefore, yes, you can read a storybook to a class without public performance rights.

Question: I found a teacher's guide at an education store that says its worksheets may be photocopied for student use. One of the worksheets is two pages long, with five activities listed. I need only activities one, two, and four. Can I photocopy the whole worksheet, cut and paste together the parts that I need, and photocopy the amended version for my students?

Answer: In all likelihood, the action you are describing is an infringement. In this instance, it appears you are creating a derivative work. See Flowchart 12.6 (p. 211) for more guidance.

Question: We do not have enough scripts for our senior class play. Would it be a problem to copy a couple more for the student directors?

Answer: Yes, it's a problem! The theater teacher or the play's producer usually signs a contract with a licensing agency as to which rights have been purchased and which have not. The school then pays royalties to the agency for those rights purchased. Purchased rights can include the number of times the play may be put on in public, the dates between which the play may be put on, the amount and type of advertising that may be done, whether you can make changes to the script (most licenses exclude the making of script changes), or even the copying of scripts (Dramatists Play Service, Inc., 2010). First, check the terms of the license you have signed. Your question may be answered there. If it is not, it is best to ask the licensing agency for permission to copy the scripts, if more are needed.

Question: We are in the process of putting on a musical. How many times can we give public performances of it?

Answer: The contract the school signs with the licensing agency will determine how many times the musical may be performed in public.

Question: I want to copy a magazine article 30 times for a class reading assignment. Can I do this under copyright law?

Answer: Use Flowchart 12.7 (p. 212) to determine if copyright law allows copying this article.

Flowchart 12.4. Magazine Articles in the Public Domain

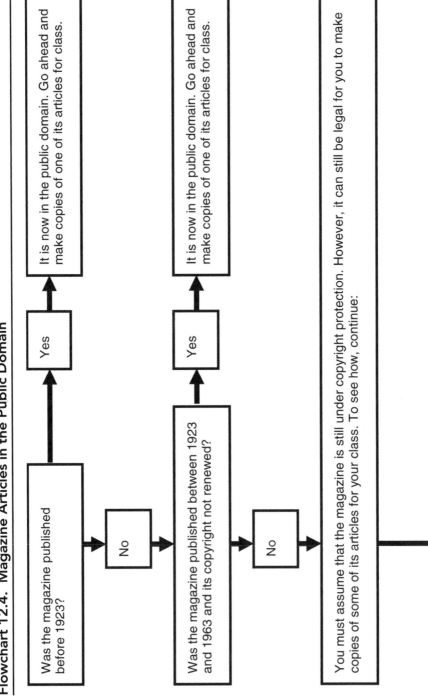

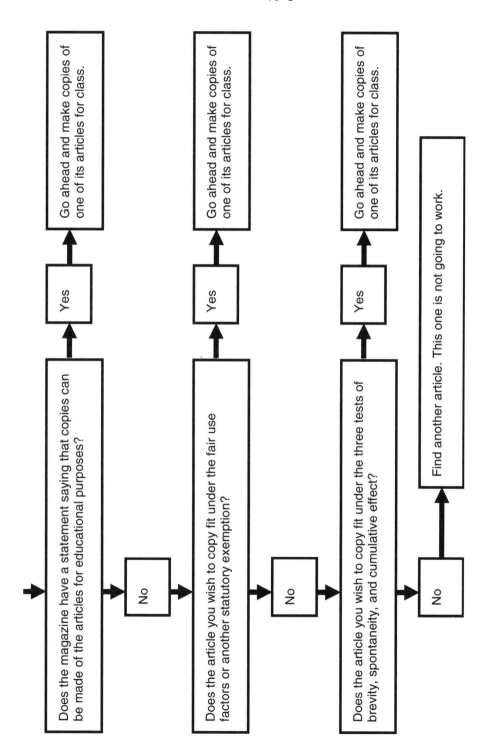

Flowchart 12.5. Performing a Shakespeare Play in Public

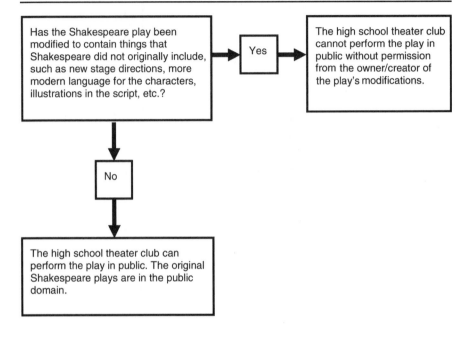

PERMISSIONS

Question: The principal just brought a new student to my class. I don't have another workbook for him to use. Am I allowed to copy pages from another student's workbook for my new student to use?

Answer: Use Flowchart 12.8 (p. 213) to determine if you are allowed to copy from the workbook.

Question: I'd like to start my class computer-based presentation by digitizing a current political cartoon from the local newspaper and inserting it onto the first slide. Is doing this okay?

Answer: Flowchart 12.9 (p. 215) will help you decide if you are allowed to use the cartoon this way. In addition, the following information may be useful:

- The copyright owner of a newspaper cartoon is usually a syndicate, such as United Media, which acts as a vendor for the cartoonist, contacting newspapers, handling royalties, and working with contracts and licenses. However, a few cartoonists may own their own cartoons, or the cartoons could be owned by the newspapers or magazines employing the cartoonist (Stim, 2007).

Flowchart 12.6. Cutting, Pasting, and Photocopying a Teacher's Guide Page

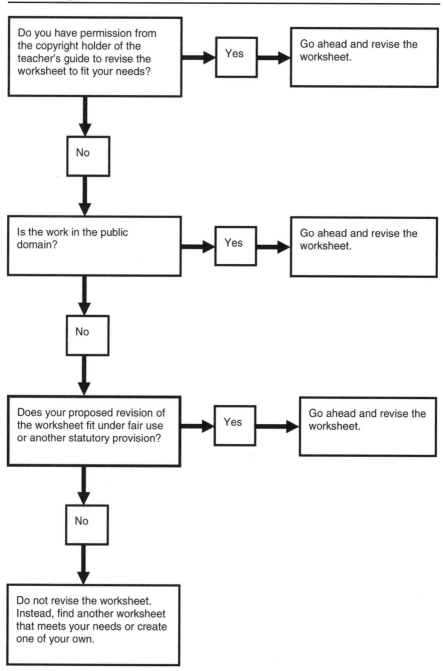

Flowchart 12.7. Making Multiple Copies of Articles

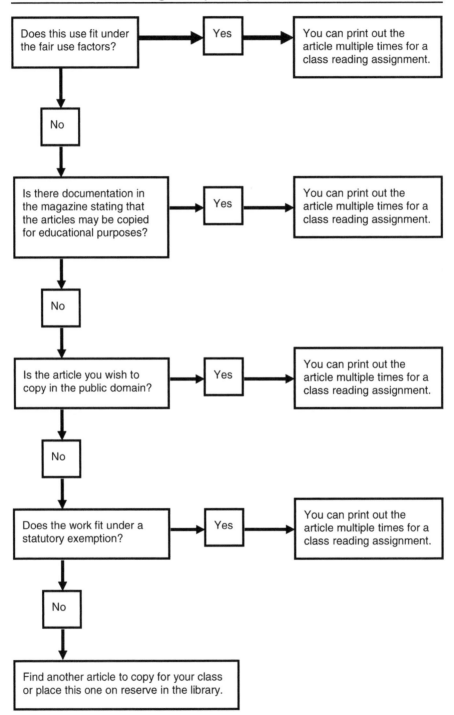

Flowchart 12.8. Copying Workbook Pages

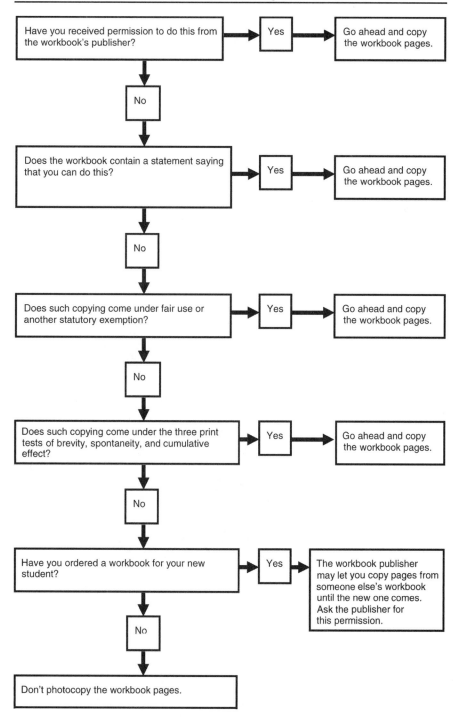

- Section 110(1) of the copyright law says that it is not an infringement for a teacher to display a work in a nonprofit education setting (classroom) if the copy was lawfully made. Section 110(2) adds the following, which may affect the display if you are transmitting it: If the display is a regular part of the instructional activities; if the display is directly related/or material is of assistance to the teaching content of the transmission; and if the transmission of the work is made for classroom reception or for people with disabilities or other circumstances that prevent their attendance in the classroom, then it is not an infringement to use it (U.S. Copyright Law, 1976).
- While it may be impractical to purchase a copy of the cartoon for every student in class, that is a legal option in this case.
- In addition to following Flowchart 12.9, you may want to consider the first sale doctrine. This doctrine gives those who obtain individual copies of a work the privilege of deciding how to use or dispose of said copies in any manner they wish ("First Sale Doctrine," 2010; Lipinski, 2006). It does not give the individual copy owners the right to reproduce the work indiscriminately, however.
- This means that if you purchased the political cartoon legally, then you have the right to display it, keep it, resell it, give it away, or toss it. However, you do not have the right to make copies of your one copy, prepare derivative works, permit other borrowing of the work, or place the original in the public domain. Because in this instance your wish is to make a digital copy of the cartoon, the first sale doctrine here is iffy at best.

Question: Every year the honors teacher hands out a summer reading packet to his students. He includes magazine articles, book chapters, poems, and other readings that he feels his students need. While all the items have been obtained from other sources, he has been very diligent in remembering copyright law, and has received permission from all owners to photocopy their works for inclusion in the packet. Our dilemma is this: He wants to go digital and post these on the school website, instead of handing out print versions. Is this okay?

Answer: Unless the honors teacher received permission to also digitize the readings when he contacted each copyright owner, scanning of the works represents creating derivatives. Thus, all owners again need to be contacted for their permissions.

YOU CREATE IT, YOU OWN IT

Question: Our parent-teacher organization (PTO) wants to do a cookbook as a fundraiser. Students, faculty, and parents will bring in their favorite recipes, and these will be compiled into a school cookbook. Are recipes copyright-protected?

Flowchart 12.9. Digitizing Newspaper Cartoons

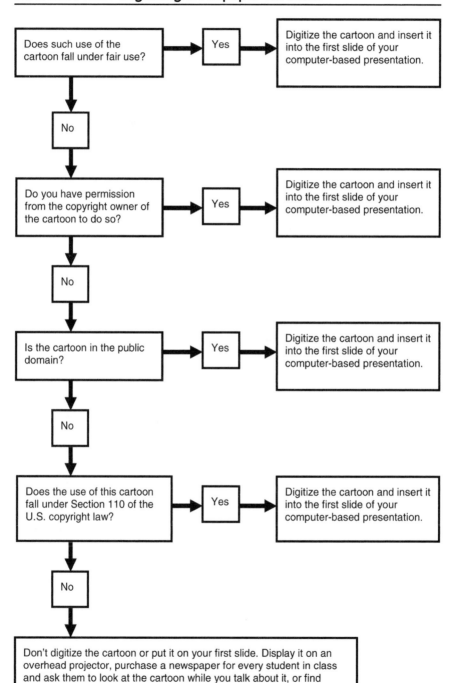

Answer: According to the U.S. Copyright Office, "listings of ingredients as in recipes . . . are not subject to copyright protection. However, where a recipe is accompanied by substantial literary expression in the form of an explanation or directions, or when there is a combination of recipes, as in a cookbook, there may be a basis for copyright protection" (U.S. Copyright Office, 2010). To translate, this means that a compilation or collection of recipes, each recipe individually generic enough to be nonprotected under copyright law, can be copyrighted. This is similar to the discussion in Chapter 6 in which there is a conversation of how links can be in the public domain, but lists of links can be protected under copyright law. What all this means for the school PTO is that recipes out of other cookbooks should not be used. Therefore, the recipes for the school cookbook either need to be original to the students, faculty, and parents donating them or they need to be generic; i.e., lists of ingredients and basic steps to putting them together, without any additional creativity or originality. Moreover, the PTO can officially register the cookbook with the U.S. Copyright Office. (Remember that under U.S. copyright law the cookbook is copyright-protected even if it is not registered with the U.S. Copyright Office.)

Question: The eighth-grade science teachers want to put together their own curriculum. Can they use flowcharts and simple Venn diagrams obtained from a commercial science manual?

Answer: Similar to recipes, flowcharts and diagrams can only be protected by copyright law when they have a considerable amount of originality to them. Basically, the form—unless unusual enough to be considered a work of art—cannot be protected. In addition, the content must convey original information in order for it to be copyright-protected. Flowcharts and Venn diagrams that basically illustrate procedures or processes cannot be copyrighted (personal communication, U.S. Copyright Office, 2003). Since it is highly likely that the flowcharts and diagrams in the science manual are simple procedural works, the science teachers can use them. However, the bottom line is that the science teachers themselves will have to study the flowcharts and Venn diagrams and make their own interpretations. If they determine that the flowcharts and Venn diagrams are original enough to be copyright-protected, then they need to contact the copyright owners of the commercial science manual and ask for permission to use these works.

Question: I am the middle school art teacher. One of my students is amazingly talented. She won a state award for one of her paintings, which she then sold to a local business. The local business has created postcards of her painting, which they plan to sell. The business says that since they bought her painting, they own the copyright to it. I say that the student owns the copyright and that the business must pay royalties if they print up postcards of that painting. Who is right?

Answer: You are. Unless the student consciously transferred the copyright to the painting to the local business, she still owns said copyright. Remember that transfer of the copyright requires a written document/contract. Thus, the local business owns the specific painting; it does not own the right to make derivatives of it or to make copies of it. In all likelihood, they have already infringed on her exclusive rights (copyright) by creating the postcards.

INFRINGEMENTS AND PENALTIES

Question: Is it a copyright infringement if my class uses clip art from the Internet to design book covers for a class unit?

Answer: If this is a class assignment and part of the students' learning, then the answer is no. It is best, however, to direct the class to use clip art from reputable Internet sites, such as sites for which the school has purchased a license. Also, instruct your students to follow the documentation found on the sites they use.

Question: Help! Class starts in ten minutes, and I need a poem! There is a poem that will work in one of my teacher's manuals. Can I copy it for all members of my class? After all, it is a last-minute thing.

Answer: Flowchart 12.10 (p. 218) will help you determine if you can make the copies. Please note that reading the poem to the class or passing the single copy around for everyone to see is allowable under Section 110 of the U.S. Copyright Law.

Question: I am the school librarian in a middle school. Last month, I purchased several kits dealing with the environment for the library collection. Each kit is composed of a DVD, a teacher's manual, several manipulatives, and a collection of activity sheets. The teachers want me to laminate the activity sheets, so they can be used time after time. I am concerned that these are considered consumables and as such laminating them would be a copyright infringement. What should I do?

Answer: Section 109 of the U.S. Copyright Act addresses a concept often called the first sale doctrine. This doctrine "says that a copyright owner gets to control the first transfer of a particular physical copy of the copyrighted work. After that first transfer, the recipient gets to control that physical copy. The copyright owner still owns the copyright, but the recipient owns the copy" (Bhat, 2010). In your situation, this means that—unless there is a statement in the documentation of the kits that the activity sheets may not be laminated or in some other way preserved—you may preserve these materials in your kits by laminating them, since you own these specific activity sheets.

Flowchart 12.10. Last-Minute Copying

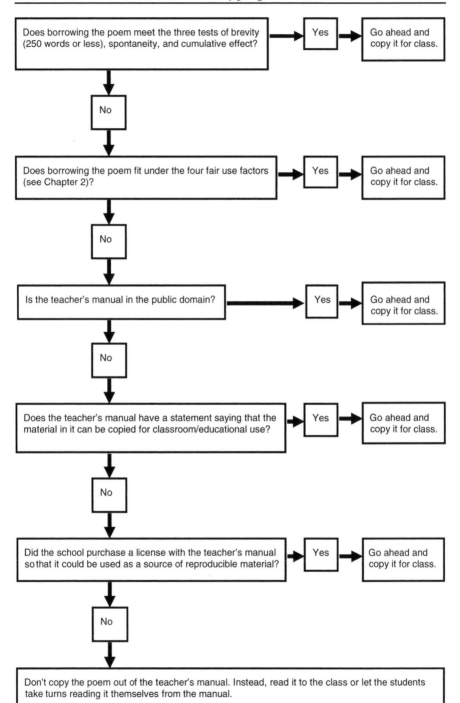

Does borrowing the poem meet the three tests of brevity (250 words or less), spontaneity, and cumulative effect? → Yes → Go ahead and copy it for class.

No

Does borrowing the poem fit under the four fair use factors (see Chapter 2)? → Yes → Go ahead and copy it for class.

No

Is the teacher's manual in the public domain? → Yes → Go ahead and copy it for class.

No

Does the teacher's manual have a statement saying that the material in it can be copied for classroom/educational use? → Yes → Go ahead and copy it for class.

No

Did the school purchase a license with the teacher's manual so that it could be used as a source of reproducible material? → Yes → Go ahead and copy it for class.

No

Don't copy the poem out of the teacher's manual. Instead, read it to the class or let the students take turns reading it themselves from the manual.

INTERNATIONAL COPYRIGHT LAW

Question: One of the high school English classes is studying *Beowolf.* Mr. Smith, the English teacher, has found an excellent article on this subject, published in a British journal, that he would like to share with his fellow English teachers, districtwide. How can he easily—and legally—provide his colleagues with a copy?

Answer: This answer can get complicated. Here are several possible solutions to consider.

1. If use of the article falls under fair use, the article is in the public domain, Mr. Smith has permission or a license from the copyright owner to copy the article, or there is a disclaimer in the magazine saying something to the effect that the articles in it can be copied "for educational purposes" (and his use fits the disclaimer), it will be easy for him to share the *Beowolf* article districtwide. (Remember that since the U.S. belongs to several copyright treaty organizations, it is simplest to treat the work as you would under U.S. law.)

2. If none of these conditions is true, he could ask one of the school libraries to put his copy of the article on reserve for other teachers to use.

3. In addition, the "Guidelines Conforming to Fair Use for Educational Purposes Agreement on Guidelines for Classroom Copying" (made part of the *Congressional Record* in 1976) say that a teacher may make or have made a single copy of an article, chapter, short story, poem, essay (or a diagram or picture in any of these works) (U.S. Copyright Office, 2009). Thus, if following these guidelines, Mr. Smith could make one copy of the article for his use (or request that one copy of the article be made for him).

4. Moreover, under section 108(a) of the 1976 Copyright Act, a library may make one copy of a work if (a) there is no commercial advantage (direct or indirect) to making another copy; (b) the library collection is open to the public, especially researchers; and (c) the copy of the original work includes on it either a copyright notice or a statement saying the work may be under copyright protection. Thus, each of the other English teachers could also either copy the article himself or herself or ask the library to make a copy for him or her. Are you getting confused yet? Well, all of these conditions may apply, depending on your situation.

5. However, the easiest way for Mr. Smith to get this information to his fellow English teachers districtwide is to route it (send it from teacher to teacher through the interdistrict mail)!

Question: I would like to obtain an e-book on Antarctica to place on a library computer. A statement on the webpage that has a copy of this e-book says the book is out of print in the country of origin and that users need to check with their own countries' copyright laws before downloading it. What does this mean for me?

Answer: Since there is no one international copyright law (most countries have their own, and a few do not address copyright law), and the site directions tell you to check with your country's law, the easiest thing to do is to treat the book as if it were published in the United States. Could you legally obtain a digitized copy of it here? Flowchart 12.11 will help you make this decision.

Flowchart 12.11. Placing an E-book on a Library Computer

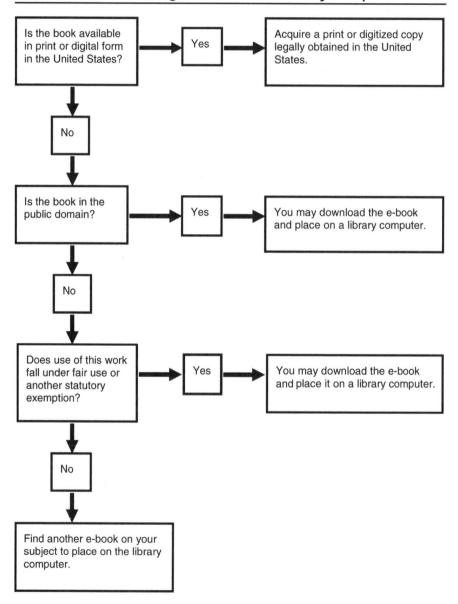

AVOIDING COPYRIGHT PROBLEMS

Question: Can school librarians use copied or scanned images of book covers on bulletin boards and in displays? After all, by doing so we're providing free advertising for the books.

Answer: This question has both a conservative and a liberal interpretation of copyright answer, and you, as the user, will need to decide which approach works best in your situation.

Conservative: According to the basic interpretation of copyright law, this is an infringement because you may be copying works in an unauthorized manner. In other words, you need to obtain the proper permissions. As an alternative, you can put the actual book covers on your bulletin boards and in your displays.

Liberal: The copying or scanning of book covers fits under the fair use factors. You may copy or scan them for use on bulletin boards and in displays. According to Carrie Russell (2002), the American Library Association's copyright specialist, this is another case in which, because the action is so commonplace, it changes how copyright law is understood. As long as the library media specialists are not charging entrance to the media center or in some other way obtaining proceeds from the copied book cover displays, such displays become exceptions to the law; i.e., they promote reading and have only a positive influence on the marketplace. Thus, such displays fit under the four fair use factors.

CONCLUSION

While print has been around longer than many other formats, the same sorts of copyright questions keep popping up. How much copying or borrowing of another's work is too much? What is legal and what isn't? How can we copy and not be liable? Confusing? You bet! This chapter tries very hard to give you a definitive answer. However, in some cases, a cut-and-dry solution simply does not exist. Indeed, I hope that this chapter provides you with usable responses to some of your copyright questions.

REFERENCES

Bhat, Anjali. 2010. "Protecting the First Sale Doctrine: PK Files Amicus Brief in Costco v. Omega." July 9. Washington, DC: Public Knowledge. http://www.publicknowledge .org/blog/protecting-first-sale-doctrine-pk-files-amicu.

Crews, Kenneth D. 2001. "The Law of Fair Use and the Illusion of Fair-Use Guidelines." *Ohio State Law Journal* 62, no. 2. http://moritzlaw.osu.edu/lawjournal/issues/ volume62/number2/crews.pdf.

Dramatists Play Service, Inc. 2010. "Application for Nonprofessional Stage Performance Rights." Dramatists Play Service, Inc. http://www.dramatists.com/cgi-bin/db/secure/ autonpa.asp.

"First Sale Doctrine." 2010. Tabber's Temptations. Updated February 10. http://www.tabberone.com/Trademarks/CopyrightLaw/FirstSaleDoctrine/FirstSale.shtml.

Lipinski, Tomas A. 2006. *The Complete Copyright Liability Handbook for Librarians and Educators.* New York: Neal-Schuman.

Russell, Carrie. 2002. "Is It a Crime to Copy?" *School Library Journal* 48, no. 1 (January): 41.

———. 2003. "A Get-Rich-Quick Scheme? Your School's Fund-Raiser May Not Qualify for a Copyright Exemption." *School Library Journal* 49, no. 2 (February): 43.

Stim, Richard. 2007. *Getting Permission: How to License & Clear Copyrighted Materials Online and Off.* 3rd ed. Berkeley, CA: Nolo. U.S. Copyright Law. 1976. Washington, DC. Public Law 94-553, sec. 110, 121.

U.S. Copyright Law. 1976. Public Law 94-553, sec. 107.

U.S. Copyright Office, Library of Congress. 2009. "Circular 21: Reproduction of Copyrighted Works by Educators and Librarians." November. U.S. Copyright Office. http://www.copyright.gov/circs/circ21.pdf.

U.S. Copyright Office, Library of Congress. 2010. "Copyright: Recipes." U.S. Copyright Office. Revised December 22. http://www.copyright.gov/fls/fl122.html.

CHAPTER 13

Distance Education and Copyright Law: How Is This Different from Applying Copyright Law in a Face-to-Face Classroom?

INTRODUCTION

What is distance education? According to Wherry (2008: 59), distance education describes "classes that are delivered to a location distant from the originating... by any medium." While distance education in K–12 schools is not as common as it is in institutions of higher learning (Secker, 2010; Wherry, 2008), we are finding, as distance-education technologies evolve, that more and more K–12 institutions are adapting some form of it for their use. Even as, at present, there appear to be more online private high schools than there are public high schools or online public or private elementary and middle schools, we are also finding online homeschooling curriculums, elementary through senior high ("Best Online High Schools," 2010; Global Student Network, 2010; K12 Inc., 2010). However, for all groups, when it comes to copyright law and learning in a non-traditional environment, there is confusion and dissension. Today's distance education comprises digitized web-based delivery, asynchronous and synchronous communications, television transmissions, and other forms of delivery. Distance education must either rely on the fair use factors (discussed in Chapter 2) or abide by Section 110(2), for which the Technology, Education, and Copyright Harmonization Act (TEACH Act) is the current version (North Carolina State University, 2010). Unhappily for us as users, federal copyright legislation is often confusing. Therefore, the TEACH Act is subsequently briefly summarized, in terms of distance education, with focus on the K–12 environment.

TECHNOLOGY, EDUCATION, AND COPYRIGHT HARMONIZATION ACT (TEACH ACT)

Educators who follow the TEACH Act support a much more liberal interpretation of copyright use and access of lawfully obtained materials than old Section

110(2) of the Copyright Act. Old Section 110(2) of the Copyright Act, Instructional Broadcasting, explains copyright coverage under the 1976 law. Covering classroom exemptions in light of face-to-face teaching, it was replaced by the TEACH Act. The old section is much more conservative than the TEACH Act, and much of it means little in light of digital transmissions (Gasaway, 2002), which were not a consideration when this part of the copyright law was written.

The TEACH Act was written to update "the existing distance learning exception to the Copyright Act to accommodate the growth of digital age distance learning" (American Association of Community Colleges et al., 2002) or as Nelson states, to address "an imbalance between traditional and distance education classrooms" (2009: 83). The TEACH Act is actually a new Section 110(2), as of November 2002. This act expanded existing "face-to-face" teaching exemptions in the copyright law to allow teachers at accredited, nonprofit educational institutions throughout the United States to use copyright-protected materials in distance education—including on websites and by other digital means—without prior permission from the copyright owner and without payment of royalties (American Libraries Online, 2002). In order to use the TEACH Act, your educational organization needs to follow a long list of requirements, which are noted here in the sidebar. All of these criteria must be met.

To explain the instructor responsibilities listed previously more clearly: Some copyright owners have been concerned with the idea that their analog materials could be converted to a digital format, thus making downloading and dissemination of their materials much easier. The concern is that owners' control over their materials would become much more difficult. Therefore, the TEACH Act includes a statement that prohibits digital conversion of analog materials, with some exceptions. The first exception is that "the amount that may be converted is limited to the amount of appropriate works that may be performed or displayed, pursuant to the revised section 110(2)" (American Library Association, 2010). What this means is that the distance-education instructor needs to make sure that the material converted to digital format falls within the materials' scope and portion margins allowable under the TEACH Act. The second exception is that teachers and other distance educators should check to make sure there is not already a copy of the work they want to utilize in a digitized format (American Library Association, 2010). If such a copy is available for use, then users should obtain that copy.

In addition to the responsibilities of the administration, technology coordinators, support people, and the class instructors, school librarians also find that they need to meet the TEACH Act requirements. School librarians are poised, because of their training, to develop and interpret copyright and other access policies; store distance-education course transmissions; find other sources of materials for nontraditional class use; and so on. However, school librarians are not specifically listed in the TEACH Act.

Abiding by the numerous terms of new Section 110(2) (the TEACH Act) can be difficult. Because of this, many institutions elect to simply follow the fair use factors instead. Either set of rules can be followed, just not both.

Requirements of the TEACH Act to Be Met by All Institutions Using It

INSTITUTIONAL RESPONSIBILITIES

The institution must:

- be an accredited nonprofit institution;
- have a copyright policy;
- provide copyright information to its faculty, students, and staff;
- provide notice to students that all distance education materials may be copyright protected; and
- limit class access to students enrolled in it.

INFORMATION TECHNOLOGY RESPONSIBILITIES

Those who work with the information technologies that support distance education in your organization must:

- limit access to students enrolled in a specific class;
- apply technological controls on storage and dissemination to prevent course students from retaining the material for longer than a class session;
- assure that the distance education delivery systems used don't defeat technological measures used by copyright owners to keep their works under control;
- limit short-term retention of copies; and
- limit long-term copies' preservation.

INSTRUCTOR RESPONSIBILITIES

The distance education course instructors must:

- use only works exclusively permitted;
- not use works clearly disqualified;
- supervise all course materials' access;
- mediate all instructional activities;
- ensure that no digital versions of a work are available;
- corroborate the specific material and amount of said material to be digitized; and
- evaluate access control implications. (American Library Association, 2010)

Working with distance-education copyright issues is extremely complicated and beyond the scope of this book. In fact, it could be a whole book in its own right. However, Flowchart 13.1 (p. 226) will give distance educators an idea of which set of rules they should abide by: new Section 110(2) (the TEACH Act) or the fair use factors.

CONCLUSION

As more and more elementary and secondary schools use distance-delivery systems to support curriculum and student needs, copyright rules will be challenged and new limits set. The fact that "digital copyright law is built upon analogue copyright law" (Stokes, 2009: 20) can make copyright law's intersection

Flowchart 13.1. Distance Educator's Flowchart

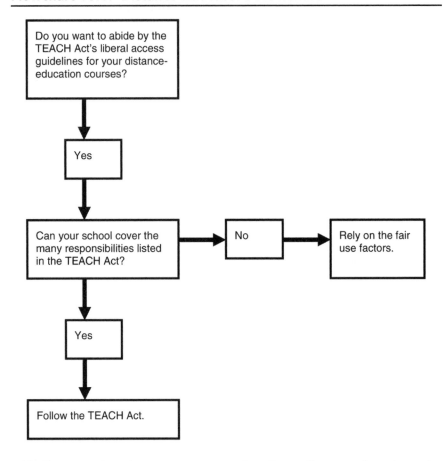

with distance education seem very complex. Some distance education rules of thumb that can be helpful, especially when addressing online education components, include the following:

- Make sure all material used is lawfully obtained.
- Take digital content off the web after the class is over.
- Include copyright notices.
- Limit access to the class website:
  - students registered for a course,
  - closed, secure system,
  - password or pin number, and
  - students advised that they are not permitted to make copies of or distribute class materials to others.
- Terminate access at the end of the class term.
- Use as little of a copyrighted work as is needed.
- Apply the law.

With all of these things swirling around your head, a thought to consider is that "the intent of copyright law... is that creators deserve the right to be compensated for their work and have some control over how it is used" (Harris, 2011: 110). In addition, access the U.S. Copyright Office (2010) at http://www.copyright.gov/disted/ for more information on distance education.

REFERENCES

American Association of Community Colleges et al. 2002. Letter to the Honorable Dennis J. Hastert, Speaker of the U.S. House of Representatives and the Honorable Richard A. Gephardt, Minority Leader, U.S. House of Representatives [signed by 38 groups and 4 individuals]. August 5. http://www.educause.edu/ir/library/pdf/NET0319.pdf.

American Libraries Online. 2002. "President Bush Signs Distance-Ed Copyright Bill" [News Archive]. American Library Association. November 11. http://www.ala.org/ala/alonline/currentnews/newsarchive/2002/november2002/presidentbush.cfm.

American Library Association. 2010. "Distance Education and the TEACH Act." American Library Association. http://www.ala.org/Template.cfm?Section=Distance_Education_and_the_TEACH_Act&Template=/ContentManagement/ContentDisplay.cfm&ContentID=25939.

"Best Online High Schools." 2010. DegreePress. http://www.bestonlinehighschools.com/.

Gasaway, Laura N. 2002. "TEACH Act—Amended Section 110(2)." University of North Carolina. November. http://www.unc.edu/~unclng/TEACH.htm.

Global Student Network. 2010. "Online Homeschool Curriculum." Global Student Network, LLC. http://www.globalstudentnetwork.com/homeschool/index.php.

Harris, Frances Jacobson. 2011. *I Found It on the Internet: Coming of Age Online*. 2nd ed. Chicago, IL: American Library Association.

K12 Inc. 2010. "Online Public Schools." K12 Inc. http://www.k12.com/schools-programs/online-public-schools/.

Nelson, Erik. 2009. "Copyright and Distance Education: The Impact of the Technology, Education, and Copyright Harmonization Act." *AACEJ* 17, no. 2: 83–101.

North Carolina State University. 2010. "The TEACH Act: Section 110(2) of the Copyright Act." North Carolina State University. http://www.provost.ncsu.edu/copyright/toolkit/.

Secker, Jane. 2010. *Copyright and E-Learning: A Guide for Practitioners*. London: Facet Publishing.

Stokes, Simon. 2009. *Digital Copyright: Law and Practice*. Portland, OR: Hart Publishing.

U.S. Copyright Office. 2010. "Copyright and Digital Distance Education." U.S. Copyright Office. Accessed September 9. http://www.copyright.gov/disted/.

Wherry, Timothy Lee. 2008. *Intellectual Property: Everything the Digital-Age Librarian Needs to Know*. Chicago: American Library Association.

CHAPTER 14

Conclusion: What Does All of This Mean for K–12 Teachers and Librarians?

INTRODUCTION

The first five chapters of this book focus on defining the most important issues within copyright for the K–12 teacher or librarian. Chapters 6 through 13 reflect on how teachers, school librarians, technology coordinators, technology specialists, administrators, and others in the schools can best apply copyright law in elementary, middle, and secondary school environments. This, the final chapter, covers options for avoiding copyright problems as well as how we can best work with those who would have us infringe on others' copyrights.

I'LL NEVER GET CAUGHT

Should you violate copyright law, it is possible that you will not be discovered. It is also possible that a software company, video company, or an organization representing whatever work you are copying will recognize that you are using their work illegally and decide that it is not worth the time or money to prosecute. However, be aware that "in some cases, software producers and distributors, as well as the organizations to which they belong, provide ways for consumers and concerned citizens to report cases of . . . piracy. Usually this can be done through the Internet or by phone, with the information kept confidential. In some cases, finders' fees may be available" (Butler, 2002: 42). An example of a report template and FAQ (frequently asked questions) for reporting alleged software piracy is available from the Business Software Alliance (2010). Similar reporting models hold true for movie piracy, and examples can be viewed at the Motion Picture Association of America (MPAA) (2010) website and, depending on the organization, may also be applicable for other types of media. So, while you might not get caught, then again, you also might. Copyright infringement is enforced by the Federal Bureau of Investigation (FBI) and can be a felony. However, whether the infringement is judged to be criminal or civil, it is punishable by law. Penalties can include sizeable fines, payment of attorneys' fees, and even prison (Scott, 2010). You must decide for yourself: Is it worth the risk?

WAYS TO AVOID COPYRIGHT PROBLEMS

How can we avoid copyright problems? The best ways are to understand copyright law and remain current as technology and the law evolve. However, in real life, copyright is just one small part of our teaching responsibilities. Therefore, practicing these guidelines can be very difficult. Nevertheless, here are a few pointers to help you on your way to copyright compliance:

- Follow fair use and other statutory exemptions (i.e., the law); or follow copyright guidelines.
- Obtain permissions and licenses when necessary.
- Read documentation and other copyright information for each work you use or from which you borrow, and encourage others to do the same. This way you and other users will know what rights for a work are available.
- Pay royalties as required.
- Consult your school district copyright policy or ethics code. If your district does not have one, encourage your administration to develop one and follow its policies and procedures.
- Consult your school district attorney when questions and problems occur.
- Put the purpose and intended use on all purchase orders. This way, the publisher/vendor will know what you want the material for and can make sure that you obtain the permissions/licenses you need.
- Follow books, such as this one, that can help you answer copyright questions. In addition, find and use materials that can support you and your school/district as you pursue copyright compliance (Butler, 2008, 2009a, 2009b).
- Consult copyright articles in print journals and on the web to be as up-to-date as you possibly can.
- Do not attempt to profit from your copying.
- Cite what you quote. (Remember that citing is no substitute for permissions, licenses, etc. However, most copyright owners want credit for their works, and some—believe it or not—do not care as much about the monetary rewards. Thus, you can at least be careful not to plagiarize.)
- Participate in workshops, conferences, and in-service events that inform you about copyright law.
- Use material that you have created yourself.
- Observe and model responsible copyright practices.
- When in doubt, don't copy!

HOW TO DEAL WITH THOSE WHO WOULD HAVE YOU BREAK THE LAW

Unfortunately, there will always be some who believe that they are above the law. They may be your administrators, fellow teachers, technology specialists, students, or parents—almost anyone. How do you deal with someone—especially a person who is technically your supervisor—who asks you to infringe on another individual's or group's copyrights?

Well, especially if you are new and untenured, you might choose to (1) do what your colleague/supervisor asks. Chances are that no one will be the wiser. You could also (2) choose to confront the individual on this issue and say no, although this option might jeopardize your relationship with him or her. A better idea would be to (3) give this person a brief rundown on copyright law and why it is important to not be in violation. You might also be able to (4) persuade him or her of a better option, should you be aware of one. However, assume that your supervisor is the requestor, and he or she says that you are to do as you are told—no questions asked or answered. Now you are in a very sticky situation. You are being asked to do something that you know is illegal, but you are afraid not to do it. If you do what your supervisor asks, (5) document the occurrence, so that should some sort of retaliation transpire involving the copyright owners, you would have a record of your stance and actions; (6) place such documentation in your personnel files; (7) contact your teachers' union advocate, explain the situation, and ask for help and advice; (8) contact your school district attorney, inform him or her of the situation and request guidance; and/or (9) contact your professional organization(s) for support on what actions to take.

Other ways to deal with someone who asks you to violate copyright law include (10) encourage correct action; (11) provide examples of infringements and the actions taken against the infringers; (12) supply a copy of those parts of the law of importance in your specific instance; (13) remain composed and empathetic; (14) point out those parts of the work's documentation that list what the copyright owners consider infringement; (15) encourage records' keeping of all licenses, permissions, etc.; and (16) remind others that they will be held accountable for what they do (Butler, 2003). It is possible that some educators are simply not aware of how important copyright law is in their world. For example, many educators believe that in a nonprofit educational setting the borrowing of another's works is allowed indiscriminately. This is simply not true, as has been discussed at length in this book. (An interesting point to note here is that some administrators and faculty become so concerned about copyright issues that they choose to enforce a "no copy" rule and/or establish directives, such as one that allows for little or no use of videos in the classroom. Obviously, this is the "other" side of copyright in education—when the fear of disobeying the law becomes so paramount that nothing can be borrowed or copied.) Therefore, keeping copyright information at the forefront of educators' minds is imperative. Perhaps the best way to achieve compliance with copyright law is to educate—something that teachers and librarians have been trained to do.

HOW AND WHY TO TEACH/TRAIN STUDENTS, COLLEAGUES, ADMINISTRATION, AND OTHERS ABOUT COPYRIGHT LAW

In our society, copyright and other intellectual property issues are not often taught in the schools. For some reason, once you become an adult, it is assumed that you will—by osmosis?—know when you are infringing on an owner's copyright and when you are not, as well as how to tell the difference. Obviously, this isn't true. Everyone needs to learn about copyright law, and this involves being educated as to its various components, concepts, and issues. A number of universities across the nation offer classes which deal, all or partially, with copyright law, educators, and media. (For example, this book's author teaches classes on copyright and technology at Northern Illinois University, DeKalb.) Assuming that a teacher, school librarian, technology specialist, or administrator takes such a course, that person could return to his or her school or school district and offer in-services or teacher workshops on copyright law in K–12 education. Such workshops should ideally occur at the beginning of the school year and involve the administration. The workshop instructor should be prepared to (1) present copyright in terms of both law and ethics; (2) help others work through copyright problems; (3) use as many local examples of violations as possible; (4) have answers ready to promote copyright compliance versus noncompliance; and (5) explain fair use—the copyright concept that most teachers and librarians believe they understand. Be aware that the web contains any number of sites that can be used with and by teachers and librarians for copyright information (Brewer, 2007; "Copyright and Plagiarism Resources," 2008; Copyright Advisory Network, 2010; Indian Prairie School District 204, 2004; Jassin, 2010; Movie Licensing USA, 2010; Open Source Initiative, 2010; Soundzabound, 2010; Center for Learning Enhancement, 2008). Now, what about the students?

Students, elementary through secondary, can also be taught everything from the rudiments of copyright à la the parts of the book (lower elementary) to the extensive copyright information needed to create a viable multimedia presentation (high school). When teaching the parts of a book, the location of the copyright date on the verso (back) of the title page should be pointed out, as well as the symbol for a copyright notice (©). In the case of students, teachers can take it upon themselves to provide a copyright unit in their classes or ask the school librarian or technology coordinator to do so. In addition, outside resources, such as the school district's copyright attorney, might be brought in for a presentation to both students and faculty. As the author of this as well as two other books on copyright for teachers and librarians, I recommend that students be given copyright instruction starting in elementary school and that such lessons expand in complexity as students go through the grades up to, and including, their senior year.

Where can teachers find lessons and curricular support with which to teach their students about copyright and related issues, including plagiarism? Units and activities often exist in library instructional manuals and books. In addition, the Internet is a treasure trove of copyright information (ranging from fairly conservative to quite liberal interpretations), including lesson plans and activities aimed at or that can be used with students, grades K–12. Activities on such websites range from making copyright web pages to quizzes and tests to copyright worksheets to a webquest to a copyright comic book (Aoki, Boyle, and Jenkins, 2006; BrainPOP, 2010; Center for Social Media, 2010; Common Sense Media, 2010; Copyright Alliance, 2009; The Copyright Society of the U.S.A., 2007; DeForest, 2007; Independent Lens, 2010; Love, 2010; Joseph, 2008; "Kids Copyright Laws," 2010; Library of Congress, 2010; Electronic Frontier Foundation, 2010; and Web Site Design Lesson Plans, 2010). It is important to remember that as you access books and websites on copyright, because copyright is a gray area, not all authors agree. In addition, copyright law may change as new works or formats for works are developed and new ways of using works are created. Because of this, it is also important to be aware of the date of the material you consult; i.e., what you seek advice from, ideally, should be as current as is possible. In addition, always look for reputable Internet sites, print sources, and other informational media.

CONCLUSION

Fair use, public domain, permissions, licenses, documentation—these copyright terms are found throughout this book; without them, copyright and media usage in K–12 schools would be a moot point. As can be seen, such terms overlap—sometimes one will work while another will not—sometimes two or more will help you as you copy or borrow others' work to support your curriculum and instruct your students. It varies exponentially. As Hobbs states, "copyright confusion affects the spread of innovative instructional practices, limits access to high-quality teaching materials, and perpetuates misinformation" (2010: 21). I hope that this book helps to clarify copyright in education and points you, the K–12 teacher and librarian, in the right direction when working with your students, fellow faculty, administrators, and others, as you instruct the next generation of copyright-compliant individuals.

REFERENCES

Aoki, Keith, James Boyle, and Jennifer Jenkins. 2006. "Bound by Law?" Center for the Study of the Public Domain, Duke University. http://www.law.duke.edu/cspd/comics/zoomcomic.html.

BrainPOP. 2010. "Copyright." FWD Media, Inc. http://www.brainpop.com/english/writing/copyright/preview.weml.

Brewer, Michael. 2007. "Is It Protected by Copyright?" American Library Association, Office for Information Technology Policy. http://librarycopyright.net/digitalslider/.

Business Software Alliance. 2010. "Report Piracy Now!" Business Software Alliance. https://reporting.bsa.org/usa/report/add.aspx?pr=1&intcmp=irphp000043b.

Butler, Rebecca P. 2002. "Software Piracy: Don't Let It Byte You." *Knowledge Quest* 31, no. 2 (November/December): 41–42.

———. 2003. "Copyright Law and Organizing the Internet." *Library Trends* 52, no. 2 (Fall): 307–317.

———. 2008. "Join the Copyright Compliance Team." *Knowledge Quest* 36, no. 3: 66–68.

———. 2009a. "Proactive Copyright: Workplace Compliance." *TechTrends* 53, no. 3: 9–10.

———. 2009b. *Smart Copyright Compliance for Schools: A How-To-Do-It Manual.* New York: Neal-Schuman.

Center for Learning Enhancement. 2008. "Copyright Resources." University of North Texas. http://copyright.unt.edu/content/copyright-resources.

Center for Social Media. 2010. "Fair Use." School of Communications, American University. http://www.centerforsocialmedia.org/fair-use.

Common Sense Media. 2010. "Considering Copying." Common Sense Media, Inc. http://cybersmartcurriculum.org/mannersbullyingethics/lessons/6-8/considering_copying/.

Copyright Advisory Network. 2010. "Section 1201 Rulemaking Updated." Copyright Advisory Network. http://librarycopyright.net/wordpress/.

Copyright Alliance. 2009. "Copyright and the Classroom." Copyright Alliance Education Foundation. http://www.copyrightfoundation.org/.

"Copyright and Plagiarism Resources." 2008. Kent School District, Kent, Washington. http://www1.kent.k12.wa.us/KSD/it/inst_tech/StudentParentResources/copyright_plagiarism.html.

The Copyright Society of the U.S.A. 2007. "Welcome to Copyright Kids!" The Copyright Society of the U.S.A. http://www.copyrightkids.org.

DeForest, Carrie. 2007. "Copyright WebQuest." Roselle (IL) Middle School, Media Center. Updated January 25. http://www.sd12.k12.il.us/education/components/docmgr/default.php?sectiondetailid=85631&linkid=nav-menu-container-4-481.

Electronic Frontier Foundation. 2010. "Teaching Copyright." Electronic Frontier Foundation. Accessed November 16. http://www.teachingcopyright.org.

Hobbs, Renee. 2010. *Copyright Clarity: How Fair Use Supports Digital Learning.* Thousand Oaks, CA: Corwin.

Independent Lens. 2010. "Copyright Criminals." Public Broadcasting System/Independent Television Service. http://www.pbs.org/independentlens/copyright-criminals/classroom.html.

Indian Prairie School District 204. 2004. "Indian Prairie Community Unit School District 204: Administrative Procedures." May 3. Indian Prairie Community Unit School District 204. http://clow.ipsd.org/documents/lmc_manual_revisions/Board_Policy_602_R.pdf.

Jassin, Lloyd J. 2010. "Locating Copyright Holders." CopyLaw.com. http://www.copylaw.com/new_articles/permission.html.

Joseph, Linda C. 2008. "Copyright with CyberBee." Adventures of CyberBee. Updated May 4. http://www.cyberbee.com/copyrt.html.

"Kids Copyright Laws." 2010. Queen Anne's County Public Schools. Schoolwires, Inc. Accessed November 16. http://www.qacps.k12.md.us/comtek/k-5_lessons/Book_4/KidsCoprightLaws/KidsCopyrightLawsLessonPlan.htm.

Library of Congress. 2010. "Taking the Mystery Out of Copyright." Library of Congress. Accessed November 16. http://www.loc.gov/teachers/copyrightmystery/.

Love, Cassandra. 2010. "ReadWriteThink: Students as Creators: Exploring Copyright." International Reading Association/National Council of Teachers of English. http://www.readwritethink.org/classroom-resources/lesson-plans/students-creators-exploring-copyright-1085.html.

Motion Picture Association of America (MPAA). 2010. "Report Piracy." Motion Picture Association of America. http://www.mpaa.org/contentprotection/report-piracy.

Movie Licensing USA. 2010. "Show Copyrighted Movies in Your School or Library—Legally." Swank Motion Pictures, Inc. Accessed November 16. http://www.movlic.com/.

Open Source Initiative. 2010. "The Open Source Definition (Annotated)." Version 1.9. OpenSource.org. Accessed November 16. http://www.opensource.org/docs/definition.php.

Scott, Brian. 2010. "The Penalties for Copyright Violation or Infringement." Research Copyright.com. November. http://www.researchcopyright.com/article-penalties-for-copyright-infringement.php.

Soundzabound. 2010. "Royalty Free Music for Schools." Soundzabound Music Library. http://www.soundzabound.com.

Web Site Design Lesson Plans. 2010. "Lesson Plans for High School Web Site Design Course." HighSchoolWebDesign.com. http://highschoolwebdesign.com/lessons/copyright-law/lesson-plan.

Appendixes

Selected Sections of
the U.S. Copyright Law

The following sections (A through H) contain selected sections of the U.S. Copyright Law, 1976: Public Law 94-553 (Title 17 of the U.S. Code). These sections include important parts of the law for K–12 educators: the rights of the copyright owner; the fair use provisions; statutory exemptions for libraries, educators, and people with disabilities; copyright ownership provisions; copyright duration; and damages for infringement. For the complete law, see http://www.copyright.gov/title17.

A. EXCLUSIVE RIGHTS IN COPYRIGHTED WORKS

§ 106. Exclusive rights in copyrighted works

Subject to sections 107 through 122, the owner of copyright has the exclusive rights to do and to authorize any of the following:

(1) to reproduce the copyrighted work in copies or phonorecords;

(2) to prepare derivative works based upon the copyrighted work;

(3) to distribute copies or phonorecords of the copyrighted work to the public by sale or other transfer of ownership, or by rental, lease, or lending;

(4) in the case of literary, musical, dramatic, and choreographic works, pantomimes, and motion pictures and other audiovisual works, to perform the copyrighted work publicly;

(5) in the case of literary, musical, dramatic, and choreographic works, pantomimes, and pictorial, graphic, or sculptural works, including the individual images of a motion picture or other audiovisual work, to display the copyrighted work publicly; and

(6) in the case of sound recordings, to perform the copyrighted work publicly by means of a digital audio transmission.

B. LIMITATIONS ON EXCLUSIVE RIGHTS: FAIR USE

§ 107. Limitations on exclusive rights: Fair use

Notwithstanding the provisions of sections 106 and 106A, the fair use of a copyrighted work, including such use by reproduction in copies or phonorecords or by any other means specified by that section, for purposes such as criticism, comment, news reporting, teaching (including multiple copies for classroom use), scholarship, or research, is not an infringement of copyright. In determining whether the use made of a work in any particular case is a fair use the factors to be considered shall include—

(1) the purpose and character of the use, including whether such use is of a commercial nature or is for nonprofit educational purposes;

(2) the nature of the copyrighted work;

(3) the amount and substantiality of the portion used in relation to the copyrighted work as a whole; and

(4) the effect of the use upon the potential market for or value of the copyrighted work.

The fact that a work is unpublished shall not itself bar a finding of fair use if such finding is made upon consideration of all the above factors.

C. LIMITATIONS ON EXCLUSIVE RIGHTS: REPRODUCTION BY LIBRARIES AND ARCHIVES

§ 108. Limitations on exclusive rights: Reproduction by libraries and archives

(a) Except as otherwise provided in this title and notwithstanding the provisions of section 106, it is not an infringement of copyright for a library or archives, or any of its employees acting within the scope of their employment, to reproduce no more than one copy or phonorecord of a work, except as provided in subsections (b) and (c), or to distribute such copy or phonorecord, under the conditions specified by this section, if—

(1) the reproduction or distribution is made without any purpose of direct or indirect commercial advantage;

(2) the collections of the library or archives are (i) open to the public, or (ii) available not only to researchers affiliated with the library or archives or with the institution of which it is a part, but also to other persons doing research in a specialized field; and

(3) the reproduction or distribution of the work includes a notice of copyright that appears on the copy or phonorecord that is reproduced under the provisions of this section, or includes a legend stating that the work may be protected by copyright if no such notice can be found on the copy or phonorecord that is reproduced under the provisions of this section.

(b) The rights of reproduction and distribution under this section apply to three copies or phonorecords of an unpublished work duplicated solely for purposes of preservation and security or for deposit for research use in another library or archives of the type described by clause (2) of subsection (a), if—

(1) the copy or phonorecord reproduced is currently in the collections of the library or archives; and

(2) any such copy or phonorecord that is reproduced in digital format is not otherwise distributed in that format and is not made available to the public in that format outside the premises of the library or archives.

(c) The right of reproduction under this section applies to three copies or phonorecords of a published work duplicated solely for the purpose of replacement of a copy or phonorecord that is damaged, deteriorating, lost, or stolen, or if the existing format in which the work is stored has become obsolete, if—

(1) the library or archives has, after a reasonable effort, determined that an unused replacement cannot be obtained at a fair price; and

(2) any such copy or phonorecord that is reproduced in digital format is not made available to the public in that format outside the premises of the library or archives in lawful possession of such copy. For purposes of this subsection, a format shall be considered obsolete if the machine or device necessary to render perceptible a work stored in that format is no longer manufactured or is no longer reasonably available in the commercial marketplace.

(d) The rights of reproduction and distribution under this section apply to a copy, made from the collection of a library or archives where the user makes his or her request or from that of another library or archives, of no more than one article or other contribution to a copyrighted collection or periodical issue, or to a copy or phonorecord of a small part of any other copyrighted work, if—

(1) the copy or phonorecord becomes the property of the user, and the library or archives has had no notice that the copy or phonorecord would be used for any purpose other than private study, scholarship, or research; and

(2) the library or archives displays prominently, at the place where orders are accepted, and includes on its order form, a warning of copyright in accordance with requirements that the Register of Copyrights shall prescribe by regulation.

(e) The rights of reproduction and distribution under this section apply to the entire work, or to a substantial part of it, made from the collection of a library or archives where the user makes his or her request or from that of another library or archives, if the library or archives has first determined, on the basis of a reasonable investigation, that a copy or phonorecord of the copyrighted work cannot be obtained at a fair price, if—

(1) the copy or phonorecord becomes the property of the user, and the library or archives has had no notice that the copy or phonorecord would be used for any purpose other than private study, scholarship, or research; and

(2) the library or archives displays prominently, at the place where orders are accepted, and includes on its order form, a warning of copyright in accordance with requirements that the Register of Copyrights shall prescribe by regulation.

(f) Nothing in this section—

(1) shall be construed to impose liability for copyright infringement upon a library or archives or its employees for the unsupervised use of reproducing equipment located on its premises: Provided, That such equipment displays a notice that the making of a copy may be subject to the copyright law;

(2) excuses a person who uses such reproducing equipment or who requests a copy or phonorecord under subsection (d) from liability for copyright infringement for any such act, or for any later use of such copy or phonorecord, if it exceeds fair use as provided by section 107;

(3) shall be construed to limit the reproduction and distribution by lending of a limited number of copies and excerpts by a library or archives of an audiovisual news program, subject to clauses (1), (2), and (3) of subsection (a); or

(4) in any way affects the right of fair use as provided by section 107, or any contractual obligations assumed at any time by the library or archives when it obtained a copy or phonorecord of a work in its collections.

(g) The rights of reproduction and distribution under this section extend to the isolated and unrelated reproduction or distribution of a single copy or phonorecord of the same material on separate occasions, but do not extend to cases where the library or archives, or its employee—

(1) is aware or has substantial reason to believe that it is engaging in the related or concerted reproduction or distribution of multiple copies or phonorecords of the same material, whether made on one occasion or over a period of time, and whether intended for aggregate use by one or more individuals or for separate use by the individual members of a group; or

(2) engages in the systematic reproduction or distribution of single or multiple copies or phonorecords of material described in subsection

(d): Provided, That nothing in this clause prevents a library or archives from participating in interlibrary arrangements that do not have, as their purpose or effect, that the library or archives receiving such copies or phonorecords for distribution does so in such aggregate quantities as to substitute for a subscription to or purchase of such work.

(h)

(1) For purposes of this section, during the last 20 years of any term of copyright of a published work, a library or archives, including a nonprofit educational institution that functions as such, may reproduce, distribute, display, or perform in facsimile or digital form a copy or phonorecord of such work, or portions thereof, for purposes of preservation, scholarship, or research, if such library or archives has first determined, on the basis of a reasonable investigation, that none of the conditions set forth in subparagraphs (A), (B), and (C) of paragraph (2) apply.

> (2) No reproduction, distribution, display, or performance is authorized under this subsection if—
> (A) the work is subject to normal commercial exploitation;
> (B) a copy or phonorecord of the work can be obtained at a reasonable price; or
> (C) the copyright owner or its agent provides notice pursuant to regulations promulgated by the Register of Copyrights that either of the conditions set forth in subparagraphs (A) and (B) applies.

> (3) The exemption provided in this subsection does not apply to any subsequent uses by users other than such library or archives.

(i) The rights of reproduction and distribution under this section do not apply to a musical work, a pictorial, graphic or sculptural work, or a motion picture or other audiovisual work other than an audiovisual work dealing with news, except that no such limitation shall apply with respect to rights granted by subsections (b) and (c), or with respect to pictorial or graphic works published as illustrations, diagrams, or similar adjuncts to works of which copies are reproduced or distributed in accordance with subsections (d) and (e).

D. LIMITATIONS ON EXCLUSIVE RIGHTS: EXEMPTION OF CERTAIN PERFORMANCES AND DISPLAYS

§ 110. Limitations on exclusive rights: Exemption of certain performances and displays

Notwithstanding the provisions of section 106, the following are not infringements of copyright:

> (1) performance or display of a work by instructors or pupils in the course of face-to-face teaching activities of a nonprofit educational institution, in a classroom or similar place devoted to instruction, unless, in the case of a motion picture or other audiovisual work, the performance, or the display of individual images, is given by means of a copy that was not lawfully made under this title, and that the person responsible for the performance knew or had reason to believe was not lawfully made;

(2) except with respect to a work produced or marketed primarily for performance or display as part of mediated instructional activities transmitted via digital networks, or a performance or display that is given by means of a copy or phonorecord that is not lawfully made and acquired under this title, and the transmitting government body or accredited nonprofit educational institution knew or had reason to believe was not lawfully made and acquired, the performance of a nondramatic literary or musical work or reasonable and limited portions of any other work, or display of a work in an amount comparable to that which is typically displayed in the course of a live classroom session, by or in the course of a transmission, if—

   (A) the performance or display is made by, at the direction of, or under the actual supervision of an instructor as an integral part of a class session offered as a regular part of the systematic mediated instructional activities of a governmental body or an accredited nonprofit educational institution;

   (B) the performance or display is directly related and of material assistance to the teaching content of the transmission;

   (C) the transmission is made solely for, and, to the extent technologically feasible, the reception of such transmission is limited to—

      (i) students officially enrolled in the course for which the transmission is made; or

      (ii) officers or employees of governmental bodies as a part of their official duties or employment; and

   (D) the transmitting body or institution—

      (i) institutes policies regarding copyright, provides informational materials to faculty, students, and relevant staff members that accurately describe, and promote compliance with, the laws of the United States relating to copyright, and provides notice to students that materials used in connection with the course may be subject to copyright protection; and

      (ii) in the case of digital transmissions—

         (I) applies technological measures that reasonably prevent—

            (aa) retention of the work in accessible form by recipients of the transmission from the transmitting body or institution for longer than the class session; and

            (bb) unauthorized further dissemination of the work in accessible form by such recipients to others; and

         (II) does not engage in conduct that could reasonably be expected to interfere with technological measures used by copyright owners to prevent such retention or unauthorized further dissemination;

(3) performance of a nondramatic literary or musical work or of a dramatico-musical work of a religious nature, or display of a work, in the course of services at a place of worship or other religious assembly;

(4) performance of a nondramatic literary or musical work otherwise than in a transmission to the public, without any purpose of direct or indirect commercial advantage and without payment of any fee or other compensation for the performance to any of its performers, promoters, or organizers, if—

(A) there is no direct or indirect admission charge; or

(B) the proceeds, after deducting the reasonable costs of producing the performance, are used exclusively for educational, religious, or charitable purposes and not for private financial gain, except where the copyright owner has served notice of objection to the performance under the following conditions:

(i) the notice shall be in writing and signed by the copyright owner or such owner's duly authorized agent; and

(ii) the notice shall be served on the person responsible for the performance at least seven days before the date of the performance, and shall state the reasons for the objection; and

(iii) the notice shall comply, in form, content, and manner of service, with requirements that the Register of Copyrights shall prescribe by regulation;

(5)

(A) except as provided in subparagraph (B), communication of a transmission embodying a performance or display of a work by the public reception of the transmission on a single receiving apparatus of a kind commonly used in private homes, unless—

(i) a direct charge is made to see or hear the transmission; or

(ii) the transmission thus received is further transmitted to the public;

(B) communication by an establishment of a transmission or retransmission embodying a performance or display of a nondramatic musical work intended to be received by the general public, originated by a radio or television broadcast station licensed as such by the Federal Communications Commission, or, if an audiovisual transmission, by a cable system or satellite carrier, if—

(i) in the case of an establishment other than a food service or drinking establishment, either the establishment in which the communication occurs has less than 2,000 gross square feet of space (excluding space used for customer parking and for no other purpose), or the establishment in which the communication occurs has 2,000 or more gross square feet of space (excluding space used for customer parking and for no other purpose) and—

(I) if the performance is by audio means only, the performance is communicated by means of a total of not more than 6 loudspeakers, of which not more than 4 loudspeakers are located in any 1 room or adjoining outdoor space; or

(II) if the performance or display is by audiovisual means, any visual portion of the performance or display is communicated by means of a total of not more than 4 audiovisual devices, of which not more than 1 audiovisual device is located in any 1 room, and no such audiovisual device has a diagonal screen size greater than 55 inches, and any audio portion of the performance or display is communicated by means of a total of not more than 6 loudspeakers, of which not more than 4 loudspeakers are located in any 1 room or adjoining outdoor space;

(ii) in the case of a food service or drinking establishment, either the establishment in which the communication occurs has less than 3,750 gross square feet of space (excluding space used for customer parking and for no other purpose), or the establishment in which the communication occurs has 3,750 gross square feet of space or more (excluding space used for customer parking and for no other purpose) and—

(I) if the performance is by audio means only, the performance is communicated by means of a total of not more than 6 loudspeakers, of which not more than 4 loudspeakers are located in any 1 room or adjoining outdoor space; or

(II) if the performance or display is by audiovisual means, any visual portion of the performance or display is communicated by means of a total of not more than 4 audiovisual devices, of which not more than 1 audiovisual device is located in any 1 room, and no such audiovisual device has a diagonal screen size greater than 55 inches, and any audio portion of the performance or display is communicated by means of a total of not more than 6 loudspeakers, of which not more than 4 loudspeakers are located in any 1 room or adjoining outdoor space;

(iii) no direct charge is made to see or hear the transmission or retransmission;

(iv) the transmission or retransmission is not further transmitted beyond the establishment where it is received; and

(v) the transmission or retransmission is licensed by the copyright owner of the work so publicly performed or displayed;

(6) performance of a nondramatic musical work by a governmental body or a nonprofit agricultural or horticultural organization, in the course of an annual agricultural or horticultural fair or exhibition conducted by such body or organization; the exemption provided by this clause shall extend to any liability for copyright infringement that would otherwise be imposed on such body or organization, under doctrines of vicarious liability or related infringement, for a performance by a concessionnaire,

business establishment, or other person at such fair or exhibition, but shall not excuse any such person from liability for the performance;

(7) performance of a nondramatic musical work by a vending establishment open to the public at large without any direct or indirect admission charge, where the sole purpose of the performance is to promote the retail sale of copies or phonorecords of the work, or of the audiovisual or other devices utilized in such performance, and the performance is not transmitted beyond the place where the establishment is located and is within the immediate area where the sale is occurring;

(8) performance of a nondramatic literary work, by or in the course of a transmission specifically designed for and primarily directed to blind or other handicapped persons who are unable to read normal printed material as a result of their handicap, or deaf or other handicapped persons who are unable to hear the aural signals accompanying a transmission of visual signals, if the performance is made without any purpose of direct or indirect commercial advantage and its transmission is made through the facilities of: (i) a governmental body; or (ii) a noncommercial educational broadcast station (as defined in section 397 of title 47); or (iii) a radio subcarrier authorization (as defined in 47 CFR 73.293–73.295 and 73.593–73.595); or (iv) a cable system (as defined in section 111 (f));

(9) performance on a single occasion of a dramatic literary work published at least ten years before the date of the performance, by or in the course of a transmission specifically designed for and primarily directed to blind or other handicapped persons who are unable to read normal printed material as a result of their handicap, if the performance is made without any purpose of direct or indirect commercial advantage and its transmission is made through the facilities of a radio subcarrier authorization referred to in clause (8) (iii), provided that the provisions of this clause shall not be applicable to more than one performance of the same work by the same performers or under the auspices of the same organization; and

(10) notwithstanding paragraph (4), the following is not an infringement of copyright: performance of a nondramatic literary or musical work in the course of a social function which is organized and promoted by a nonprofit veterans' organization or a nonprofit fraternal organization to which the general public is not invited, but not including the invitees of the organizations, if the proceeds from the performance, after deducting the reasonable costs of producing the performance, are used exclusively for charitable purposes and not for financial gain. For purposes of this section the social functions of any college or university fraternity or sorority shall not be included unless the social function is held solely to raise funds for a specific charitable purpose.

The exemptions provided under paragraph (5) shall not be taken into account in any administrative, judicial, or other governmental proceeding to set or adjust the royalties payable to copyright owners for the public performance or display of their works. Royalties payable to copyright owners for any public performance or display of their works other than such performances or displays as are exempted under paragraph (5) shall not be diminished in any respect as a result of such exemption.

In paragraph (2), the term "mediated instructional activities" with respect to the performance or display of a work by digital transmission under this section refers to activities that use such work as an integral part of the class experience, controlled by or under the actual supervision of the instructor and analogous to the type of performance or display that would take place in a live classroom setting. The term does not refer to activities that use, in 1 or more class sessions of a single course, such works as textbooks, course packs, or other material in any media, copies or phonorecords of which are typically purchased or acquired by the students in higher education for their independent use and retention or are typically purchased or acquired for elementary and secondary students for their possession and independent use.

For purposes of paragraph (2), accreditation—

(A) with respect to an institution providing post-secondary education, shall be as determined by a regional or national accrediting agency recognized by the Council on Higher Education Accreditation or the United States Department of Education; and

(B) with respect to an institution providing elementary or secondary education, shall be as recognized by the applicable state certification or licensing procedures. For purposes of paragraph (2), no governmental body or accredited nonprofit educational institution shall be liable for infringement by reason of the transient or temporary storage of material carried out through the automatic technical process of a digital transmission of the performance or display of that material as authorized under paragraph (2). No such material stored on the system or network controlled or operated by the transmitting body or institution under this paragraph shall be maintained on such system or network in a manner ordinarily accessible to anyone other than anticipated recipients. No such copy shall be maintained on the system or network in a manner ordinarily accessible to such anticipated recipients for a longer period than is reasonably necessary to facilitate the transmissions for which it was made.

E. LIMITATIONS ON EXCLUSIVE RIGHTS: REPRODUCTION FOR BLIND OR OTHER PEOPLE WITH DISABILITIES

§ 121. Limitations on exclusive rights: Reproduction for blind or other people with disabilities

(a) Notwithstanding the provisions of section 106, it is not an infringement of copyright for an authorized entity to reproduce or to distribute copies or phonorecords of a previously published, nondramatic literary work if such copies or phonorecords are reproduced or distributed in specialized formats exclusively for use by blind or other persons with disabilities.

(b)

    (1) Copies or phonorecords to which this section applies shall—

        (A) not be reproduced or distributed in a format other than a specialized format exclusively for use by blind or other persons with disabilities;

        (B) bear a notice that any further reproduction or distribution in a format other than a specialized format is an infringement; and

        (C) include a copyright notice identifying the copyright owner and the date of the original publication.

    (2) The provisions of this subsection shall not apply to standardized, secure, or norm-referenced tests and related testing material, or to computer programs, except the portions thereof that are in conventional human language (including descriptions of pictorial works) and displayed to users in the ordinary course of using the computer programs.

(c) For purposes of this section, the term—

    (1) "authorized entity" means a nonprofit organization or a governmental agency that has a primary mission to provide specialized services relating to training, education, or adaptive reading or information access needs of blind or other persons with disabilities;

    (2) "blind or other persons with disabilities" means individuals who are eligible or who may qualify in accordance with the Act entitled "An Act to provide books for the adult blind", approved March 3, 1931 (2 U.S.C. 135a; 46 Stat. 1487) to receive books and other publications produced in specialized formats; and

    (3) "specialized formats" means braille, audio, or digital text which is exclusively for use by blind or other persons with disabilities.

F. OWNERSHIP OF COPYRIGHT

§ 201. Ownership of copyright

(a) Initial Ownership.—Copyright in a work protected under this title vests initially in the author or authors of the work. The authors of a joint work are co-owner of copyright in the work.

(b) Works Made for Hire.—In the case of a work made for hire, the employer or other person for whom the work was prepared is considered the author for purposes of this title, and, unless the parties have expressly agreed otherwise in a written instrument signed by them, owns all of the rights comprised in the copyright.

(c) Contributions to Collective Works.—Copyright in each separate contribution to a collective work is distinct from copyright in the collective work as a whole, and vests initially in the author of the contribution. In the absence of an express transfer of the copyright or of any rights under it, the owner of copyright in the collective work is presumed to have acquired only the privilege of reproducing and distributing the contribution as part of that particular collective work, any revision of that collective work, and any later collective work in the same series.

(d) Transfer of Ownership.—

(1) The ownership of a copyright may be transferred in whole or in part by any means of conveyance or by operation of law, and may be bequeathed by will or pass as personal property by the applicable laws of intestate succession.

(2) Any of the exclusive rights comprised in a copyright, including any subdivision of any of the rights specified by section 106, may be transferred as provided by clause (1) and owned separately. The owner of any particular exclusive right is entitled, to the extent of that right, to all of the protection and remedies accorded to the copyright owner by this title.

(e) Involuntary Transfer.—When an individual author's ownership of a copyright, or of any of the exclusive rights under a copyright, has not previously been transferred voluntarily by that individual author, no action by any governmental body or other official or organization purporting to seize, expropriate, transfer, or exercise rights of ownership with respect to the copyright, or any of the exclusive rights under a copyright, shall be given effect under this title, except as provided under title 11.

G. DURATION OF COPYRIGHT: WORKS CREATED ON OR AFTER JANUARY 1, 1978

§ 302. Duration of copyright: Works created on or after January 1, 1978

(a) In General.—Copyright in a work created on or after January 1, 1978, subsists from its creation and, except as provided by the following subsections, endures for a term consisting of the life of the author and 70 years after the author's death.

(b) Joint Works.—In the case of a joint work prepared by two or more authors who did not work for hire, the copyright endures for a term consisting of the life of the last surviving author and 70 years after such last surviving author's death.

(c) Anonymous Works, Pseudonymous Works, and Works Made for Hire.—In the case of an anonymous work, a pseudonymous work, or a work made for hire, the copyright endures for a term of 95 years from the year of its first publication, or a term of 120 years from the year of its creation, whichever expires first. If, before the end of such term, the identity of one or more of the authors of an anonymous or pseudonymous work is revealed in the records of a registration made for that work under subsections (a) or (d) of section 408, or in the records provided by this subsection, the copyright in the work endures for the term specified by subsection (a) or (b), based on the life of the author or authors whose identity has been revealed. Any person having an interest in the copyright in an anonymous or pseudonymous work may at any time record, in records to be maintained by the Copyright Office for that purpose, a statement identifying one or more authors of the work; the statement shall also identify the person filing it, the nature of that person's interest, the source of the information recorded, and the particular work affected, and shall comply in form and content with requirements that the Register of Copyrights shall prescribe by regulation.

(d) Records Relating to Death of Authors.—Any person having an interest in a copyright may at any time record in the Copyright Office a statement of the date of death of the author of the copyrighted work, or a statement that the author is still living on a particular date. The statement shall identify the person filing it, the nature of that person's interest, and the source of the information recorded, and shall comply in form and content with requirements that the Register of Copyrights shall prescribe by regulation. The Register shall maintain current records of information relating to the death of authors of copyrighted works, based on such recorded statements and, to the extent the Register considers practicable, on data contained in any of the records of the Copyright Office or in other reference sources.

(e) Presumption as to Author's Death.—After a period of 95 years from the year of first publication of a work, or a period of 120 years from the year of its creation, whichever expires first, any person who obtains from the Copyright Office a certified report that the records provided by subsection (d) disclose nothing to indicate that the author of the work is living, or died less than 70 years before, is entitled to the benefit of a presumption that the author has been dead for at least 70 years. Reliance in good faith upon this presumption shall be a complete defense to any action for infringement under this title.

H. REMEDIES FOR INFRINGEMENT: DAMAGES AND PROFITS

§ 504. Remedies for infringement: Damages and profits

(a) In General.—Except as otherwise provided by this title, an infringer of copyright is liable for either—

  (1) the copyright owner's actual damages and any additional profits of the infringer, as provided by subsection (b); or

  (2) statutory damages, as provided by subsection (c).

(b) Actual Damages and Profits.—The copyright owner is entitled to recover the actual damages suffered by him or her as a result of the infringement, and any profits of the infringer that are attributable to the infringement and are not taken into account in computing the actual damages. In establishing the infringer's profits, the copyright owner is required to present proof only of the infringer's gross revenue, and the infringer is required to prove his or her deductible expenses and the elements of profit attributable to factors other than the copyrighted work.

(c) Statutory Damages.—

(1) Except as provided by clause (2) of this subsection, the copyright owner may elect, at any time before final judgment is rendered, to recover, instead of actual damages and profits, an award of statutory damages for all infringements involved in the action, with respect to any one work, for which any one infringer is liable individually, or for which any two or more infringers are liable jointly and severally, in a sum of not less than $750 or more than $30,000 as the court considers just. For the purposes of this subsection, all the parts of a compilation or derivative work constitute one work.

(2) In a case where the copyright owner sustains the burden of proving, and the court finds, that infringement was committed willfully, the court in its discretion may increase the award of statutory damages to a sum of not more than $150,000. In a case where the infringer sustains the burden of proving, and the court finds, that such infringer was not aware and had no reason to believe that his or her acts constituted an infringement of copyright, the court in its discretion may reduce the award of statutory damages to a sum of not less than $200. The court shall remit statutory damages in any case where an infringer believed and had reasonable grounds for believing that his or her use of the copyrighted work was a fair use under section 107, if the infringer was: (i) an employee or agent of a nonprofit educational institution, library, or archives acting within the scope of his or her employment who, or such institution, library, or archives itself, which infringed by reproducing the work in copies or phonorecords; or (ii) a public broadcasting entity which or a person who, as a regular part of the nonprofit activities of a public broadcasting entity (as defined in subsection (g) of section 118) infringed by performing a published nondramatic literary work or by reproducing a transmission program embodying a performance of such a work.

(d) Additional Damages in Certain Cases.—In any case in which the court finds that a defendant proprietor of an establishment who claims as a defense that its activities were exempt under section 110(5) did not have reasonable grounds to believe that its use of a copyrighted work was exempt under such section, the plaintiff shall be entitled to, in addition to any award of damages under this section, an additional award of two times the amount of the license fee that the proprietor of the establishment concerned should have paid the plaintiff for such use during the preceding period of up to 3 years.

Definitions for Web Terms in Chapter 6

Adobe Connect: Adobe Connect is Internet conferencing software (Adobe, 2010).

Animoto: "Animoto is a web application that, with the click of a button, produces videos using images and music that a user selects" (Animoto, 2006).

Blackboard: "The *Blackboard Learning System* is a comprehensive and flexible e-Learning software platform that delivers a complete course management system" (Blackboard Inc., 2004).

blog: "A blog is a type of website, usually maintained by an individual with regular entries of commentary, descriptions of events, or other material such as graphics or video. Entries are commonly displayed in reverse-chronological order.... Many blogs provide commentary or news on a particular subject; others function as more personal online diaries. A typical blog combines text, images, and links to other blogs, Web pages, and other media related to its topic. The ability for readers to leave comments in an interactive format is an important part of many blogs" (Rhode, 2010).

Box.net: "Box.net provides virtual storage space on the Internet. The company allows individuals and small businesses to store, share, and access files from anywhere" (Business Wire, 2006).

BrainPOP: BrainPOP is an animated educational Internet site that "engages students, supports educators, and bolsters achievement. [It also features] ... free lesson plans, video tutorials, professional development tools, graphic organizers, [and] best practices" (BrainPOP, 2010).

Chatroulette: A "social Web site [that] drops you into an unnerving world where you are connected through webcams to a random, fathomless succession of strangers from across the globe" (Bilton, 2010).

cloud computing: "Cloud computing is a general term for delivering hosted services over the Internet... These services can include blogs, YouTube videos, still-image slide shows, and a range of other applications" (Northern Illinois University, 2010).

computational knowledge engines: Relatively new in the cloud-computing realm, these engines can complement traditional search engines, such as Google, by providing computable answers to questions posed by users. At present, computational knowledge engines, such as Wolfram Alpha, are in the development stage (May, 2009).

concept-mapping tools: Digital media used in the production of concept maps. Concept maps are schema that demonstrate the relationships between and among concepts (Dictionary.com, 2010). Inspiration (http://www.inspiration.com/Inspiration) may be considered a concept-mapping software tool.

content aggregators: "A content aggregator is an individual or organization that gathers Web content (and/or sometimes applications) from different online sources for reuse or resale. There are two kinds of content aggregators: (1) those who simply gather material from various sources for their Web sites, and (2) those who gather and distribute content to suit their customer's needs" (SearchSOA, 2010). Aggregators, like Google Reader, bring desired information to one spot.

Delicious: "Delicious is a social bookmarking system, that... allows users to qualify content" (Housley, 2010). When using Delicious, the more often a website is bookmarked or identified with a tag, the more prominent it becomes.

Digital Rights Management (DRM): "DRM refers to a collection of systems used to protect the copyrights of electronic media. These include digital music and movies... [and] can be accomplished by using digital watermarks or proprietary file encryption" (Tech Terms Dictionary, 2010).

Electronic Toolbox: "Electronic Toolbox combines electronic reference material with calculation and conversion tools" (Roskosch, 2010).

e-readers: "E-readers are a growing technology that allow users to read their favorite books, magazines, pdf and word files straight from a simple handheld mobile device" (Wishpot Inc., 2010).

Excite MIX: "Excite MIX works like your very own personal web, where you can add all the latest content from your favourite sites via their RSS feed... gets updated automatically" (Webtwitcher, 2006).

Facebook: "The world's largest social network... [with] 500 million users around the world" (Wyld, 2010).

file sharing: "File sharing is the practice of making files available for other individuals to download. It can be as simple as sharing a file for general consumption via My WebSpace or enabling file sharing on your computer's operating system so that you can access your home computer files at work" (CIO and Vice Provost for Information Technology, 2010).

Flickr: "An online photo management and sharing application" (Turnbull, 2005).

Goodreads: "Goodreads is the largest social network for readers in the world. . . . Goodreads members recommend books, compare what they are reading, keep track of what they've read and would like to read, form book clubs" (Goodreads, 2010).

Google Wave: One of many online Google tools, Google Wave was intended to encourage collaboration in the cloud (on the web). However, because it has not been a popular product, Google planned to maintain Google Wave only through 2010. Its technology will be used in other Google products (The Official Google Blog, 2010).

hyperlink: "A hyperlink is a graphic or a piece of text in an Internet document that can connect readers to another webpage, or another portion of a document" (wiseGEEK, 2010).

Hulu: Hulu is a "free and legal" online video service that provides popular television shows, current movies, and more to its viewers "through an advertising supported model" (Hulu, 2010).

Kindle: "A portable e-book device from Amazon.com that provides wireless connectivity to Amazon for e-book downloads as well as Wikipedia and search engines" (Computer Desktop Encyclopedia, 2010).

iPad: A technological "gadget" whose function comes from the way the consumer uses it. Sometimes described as a "big iPhone," the iPad can operate as an e-book reader; a provider of information, from recipes to star charts, via the Internet and a myriad of free and purchasable applications ("apps"); a video game player; a word processor; an iPod; and more (Phelan, 2010).

iPod: The original iPod was a portable music player. Newer versions (Nano, Shuffle, and Touch) add such features as high-definition (HD) video recording, shopping, access to television and movies, and game centers (Apple Inc., 2010a).

iTunes: "iTunes is a free application for your Mac or PC. It organizes and plays your digital music and video on your computer. It keeps all your content in sync. And it's a store on your computer, iPod touch, iPhone, iPad" (Apple Inc., 2010b).

LimeWire: LimeWire is an example of a peer-to-peer (P2P) software that is used to obtain "free" music and videos by downloading files from the computers of others who have joined the network. Much file sharing using P2P software violates copyright law, because it involves the replication of copyrighted works (CIO and Vice Provost for Information Technology , 2010).

LinkedIn: LinkedIn is an online networking tool for business professionals (LinkedIn, 2008).

Moodle: "Moodle is a Course Management System (CMS), also known as a Learning Management System (LMS) or a Virtual Learning Environment (VLE). It is a Free web application that educators can use to create effective online learning sites" (Moodle, 2010).

Mousebreaker: This is an example of an online website with free online games (Mousebreaker, 2005).

MP3 player: An MP3 player is a portable digital audio device popular for playing music (Logan, 2009).

MySpace: MySpace is a social networking website.

myYearbook: Started in 2005 by a high school sister and brother team, myYearbook is a social networking site where users play games and meet new people (myYearbook, 2010).

Netvibes: "Founded in 2005, Netvibes pioneered the first personalized dashboard publishing platform for the Web" (Netvibes, 2010). With Netvibes, users can pull onto one access point all of their digital communications.

Ning: "Based in Palo Alto, Calif., Ning offers an easy-to-use service that enables people to create custom branded social networks" (Ning, 2010).

Nook: The Nook is an e-book reader available from Barnes and Noble (Barnes and Noble, 2010).

Pageflakes: "Pageflakes allows you to put all your web favorites, including news, email and search engines, onto one personalized page using 'flakes', or widgets" (CrunchBase, 2010).

Playaway: "They come fully loaded with your favorite book titles... [a] portable...audio book option" (Pemberton Library, 2007).

podcast and **vodcast:** "The term podcast is derived from the words iPod and broadcasting. Podcasting enables audio files to be made available via the internet in compact format (for example MP3).... The term vodcast derives from 'Video on Demand' and 'broadcasting'. Vodcasting works in much the same way as podcasts, but uses video files instead of audio files" (TU Delft, 2009).

Plurk: Plurk is a social network which defines itself as "a social journal for your life" (Plurk, 2010).

Prezi: Somewhat similar to PowerPoint (PPT), Prezi uses a canvas concept instead of the slides of PPT. Items such as text, audio, video, etc., can be dragged, tilted, zoomed in or out, and connected to create an animation effect (Northern Illinois University, 2010).

Protopage: This is a web application that can be used to combine personal RSS feeds, sticky notes, and Internet bookmarks into one package (Pash, 2005).

RSS feed: "Short for Really Simple Syndication or Rich Site Summary... They're basically simple text files that, once submitted to feed directories, will allow subscribers to see content within a very short time after it's updated" (Boswell, 2010). With an RSS feed, the user can access only that information in which he or she is interested, i.e., one can choose to receive only news about sports.

ScreenToaster: "ScreenToaster is a free web-based screen recorder designed to capture your screen activity, audio and webcam images in real-time then publish and share your video in blogs and websites. . . . ScreenToaster works in all browsers and doesn't require any download so that you can use it anywhere, anytime" (ScreenToaster, 2009).

Scribd: "On Scribd, you can easily turn any file-such as PDF, Word and Power-Point-into a web document and immediately connect with passionate readers and information-seekers . . . through connected sites such as Facebook or Twitter and search engines such as Google" (Scribd, 2010).

Second Life: Second Life is an example of a 3-D virtual world, where participants create avatars in order to go to school and libraries, attend conferences, shop, visit, etc.

Shelfari: "A gathering place for authors, aspiring authors, publishers, and readers . . . has many tools and features to help these groups connect with each other in a fun and engaging way" (Le Penske, 2006).

Skype: "Skype is an IP telephony service provider that offers free calling between subscribers and low-cost calling to people who don't use the service. In addition to standard telephone calls, Skype enables file transfers, texting, video chat and videoconferencing. The service is available for desktop computers, notebook and tablet computers and other mobile devices, including mobile phones" (Glushakow-Smith, 2009).

SlideShare: "SlideShare is a business media site for sharing presentations, documents and pdfs." On SlideShare, you can "embed slideshows into your own blog or website . . . share slideshows publicly or privately . . . synch audio to your slides . . . market your own event . . . join groups to connect with SlideShare members who share your interests . . . download the original file" (SlideShare, 2010).

social gaming networks: "The category has its roots in casual gaming, where users played alone and titles cost a fee to download. Social games . . . are built to be enjoyed and shared with friends through existing social networks and platforms like the iPhone. The games don't necessarily involve real-time competition or interaction. Many are asynchronous, meaning players can play on their own time while checking in at various points in the day. But because they tap into existing connections in one form or another, they heighten the sense of camaraderie, competition and pride found in gaming" (Kim, 2009).

social media: "A website that doesn't just give you information, but interacts with you while giving you that information" (Nations, 2010a). It can allow users to communicate or interact with others also involved in a particular social media.

TeacherTube: TeacherTube is "an online community for sharing instructional videos . . . professional development with teachers teaching teachers . . . [and] a site where teachers can post videos designed for students to view in order to learn a concept or skill" (TeacherTube, 2010).

Twitter: Twitter is an example of a microblog (Rhode, 2010).

video game: "An electronic game played by means of images on a video screen and often emphasizing fast action" (Merriam-Webster, 2010).

video streaming: "Streaming video is a sequence of 'moving images' that are sent in compressed form over the Internet and displayed by the viewer as they arrive. Streaming media is streaming video with sound. With streaming video or streaming media, a Web user does not have to wait to download a large file before seeing the video or hearing the sound. Instead, the media is sent in a continuous stream and is played as it arrives. The user needs a player, which is a special program that uncompresses and sends video data to the display and audio data to speakers. A player can be either an integral part of a browser or downloaded from the software maker's Web site" (Arndt, 2005).

Web 2.0: Web 2.0 technologies include blogs, wikis, social media, mobile learning, and cloud computing (Secker, 2010: 125). Essentially Web 2.0 "is participatory as users are encouraged to create and upload content often in a collaborative manner" (Stokes, 2009: 172).

web feed: A web feed or RSS feed "is a content delivery vehicle. It is the format used when you want to syndicate news and other web content. When it distributes the content it is called a feed. You could think of RSS as your own personal wire service" (PRESSfeed Co., 2010).

web syndication: "A syndicate is a group that forms an association for the sake of a common interest. Starting in print journalism, syndication was an approach to widening the market for a comic strip or a columnist by allowing simultaneous publication in multiple venues. Web syndication can refer to either this strategy adapted to the Internet or to a format that allows readers to gather updates from their favorite websites into one place" (Elizabeth, 2010).

wikis: Wikis are webpages that can be modified by anyone who has access to a computer and the Internet; they provide collaboration among users and are asynchronous (Educause Learning Initiative, 2005).

Wordle: Wordle is a website that creates "word clouds" that are generated "from text that you provide. The clouds give greater prominence to words that appear more frequently in the source text. You can tweak your clouds with different fonts, layouts, and color schemes. The images you create with Wordle are yours to use however you like" (Feinberg, 2009).

Xanga: "Xanga is a social blogging website . . . a combination of a social network and a blog host" (Nations, 2010b).

YouTube: YouTube is a popular website for sharing videos.

REFERENCES

Adobe. 2010. "Adobe Connect: The Next Best Thing to Meeting in Person." Adobe Systems Incorporated. Accessed September 10. http://www.adobe.com/products/acrobatconnectpro/.

Animoto. 2006. "Animoto's Channel." Animoto Productions, Inc., YouTube. April. http://www.youtube.com/user/Animoto.

Apple Inc. 2010a. "Introducing the New iPod Touch." Apple Inc. Accessed September 10. http://www.apple.com.

———. 2010b. "What Is iTunes?" Apple Inc. Accessed September 10. http://www.apple.com/itunes/what-is/.

Arndt, Ole. 2005. "Streaming Video on Your Website_Convert Visitors into Customers." June. http://ezinearticles.com/?Streaming-Video-on-Your-Website—-Convert-Visitors-into-Customers&id=40805.

Barnes and Noble. 2010. "Nook." Barnesandnoble.com LLC. Accessed September 28. http://www.barnesandnoble.com/nook/index.asp?r=1&cds2Pid=30919.

Bilton, Nick. 2010. "The Surreal World of Chatroulette." *New York Times*, February 20. http://www.nytimes.com/2010/02/21/weekinreview/21bilton.html.

Blackboard Inc. 2004. "About the Blackboard Academic Suite (Release 6.1) Instructor Manual." http://library.blackboard.com/docs/r6/6_1/instructor/bbls_r6_1_instructor/.

Boswell, Wendy. 2010. "RSS Feeds." About.com. Accessed September 7. http://websearch.about.com/od/rsssocialbookmarks/f/rss.htm.

BrainPOP. 2010. "About Us: Who We Are." FWD Media, Inc. Accessed September 10. http://www.brainpop.com/about/.

Business Wire. 2006. "Box.net Lands Funding, Expands Offering." October 23. Business Wire. http://www.businesswire.com/news/home/20061023006139/en/Box.net-Lands-Funding-Expands-Offering.

CIO and Vice Provost for Information Technology. 2010. "Understanding File Sharing." University of Wisconsin-Madison. Accessed September 7. http://www.cio.wisc.edu/security/filesharing.aspx.

Computer Desktop Encyclopedia. 2010. "Kindle." YourDictionary.com. Accessed September 21. http://computer.yourdictionary.com/kindle.

CrunchBase. 2010. "Pageflakes." Edited October 14. http://www.crunchbase.com/company/pageflakes.

Dictionary.com. 2010. "Concept Map." Dictionary.com, LLC. Accessed September 26. http://dictionary.reference.com/browse/conceptmap.

Educause Learning Initiative. 2005. "7 Things You Should Know About Wikis." EDUCAUSE. July. http://www.educause.edu/ELI/7ThingsYouShouldKnowAboutWikis/156807.

Elizabeth, Mary. 2010. "What Is Web Syndication?" September. WiseGEEK. http://www.wisegeek.com/what-is-web-syndication.htm.

Feinberg, Jonathan. 2009. "Wordle_Beautiful Word Clouds." Wordle. http://www.wordle.net.

Glushakow-Smith, Steve. 2009. "What Is Skype? Definition." September. http://search unifiedcommunications.techtarget.com/sDefinition/0,,sid186_gci1050583,00.html.

Goodreads. 2010. "About Us: What Is Goodreads?" Goodreads Inc. Accessed September 28. http://www.goodreads.com/about/us.

Housley, S. 2010. "What Is Delicious? Understanding Social Bookmarking." Small Business Software, NotePage, Inc. Accessed September 28. http://www.small-business-software.net/using-delicious.htm.

Hulu. 2010. "Media Info." Hulu. June. http://www.hulu.com/about.

Kim, Ryan. 2009. "Social Networking Is Next Big Thing for Gaming." August. http://articles.sfgate.com/2009-08-03/business/17178226_1_casual-gaming-mafia-wars-social-gaming.

Le Penske, Cherie. 2006. "Press Release: Shelfari Launches World's First Social Media Site for Books." Shelfari. October. http://www.shelfari.com/Shelfari/Press/10-11-06.aspx.

LinkedIn. 2008. "About Us." LinkedIn Corporation. Accessed September 28, 2010. http://press.linkedin.com/about.

Logan, Gail. 2009. "Define MP3 Players." eHow, Inc. http://www.ehow.com/facts_5447652_define-mp-players.html.

May, Simon Mackie. 2009. "Wolfram Alpha: Impressive, But Not the Future of Search, Yet." GigaOM. May. http://gigaom.com/collaboration/wolfram-alpha-impressive-but-not-the-future-of-search-yet/.

Merriam-Webster. 2010. "Video Game." Merriam-Webster. Accessed September 26. http://www.merriam-webster.com/dictionary/video+game.

Moodle. 2010. "Welcome to the Moodle Community!" Moodle Trust. Accessed September 28. http://moodle.org.

Mousebreaker. 2005. "Welcome to Mousebreaker." Mousebreaker. http://www.mousebreaker.co.uk/.

myYearbook. 2010. "Our Story." myYearbook. Accessed September 28. http://www.myyearbook.com/our_story.php.

Nations, Daniel. 2010a. "What Is Social Media?" About.com, Web Trends. Accessed September 21. http://webtrends.about.com/od/web20/a/social-media.htm.

___. 2010b. "What Is Xanga?" About.com, Web Trends. Accessed September 10. http://webtrends.about.com/od/pro5/fr/what-is-xanga.htm.

Netvibes. 2010. "About Netvibes." Netvibes. Accessed September 28.: http://about.netvibes.com/.

Ning. 2010. "About Ning." Ning. Accessed September 28. http://about.ning.com/.

Northern Illinois University. 2010. "Teaching with Technology Institute." DeKalb, IL: Northern Illinois University.

The Official Google Blog. 2010. "Update on Google Wave." Google, Inc. August. http://googleblog.blogspot.com/2010/08/update-on-google-wave.html.

Pash, Adam. 2005. "Create a Personalized Homepage with Protopage." LifeHacker.com. December. http://lifehacker.com/141588/create-a-personalized-homepage-with-protopage.

Pemberton Library. 2007. "What Are Playaways?" Pemberton Library. May. http://pembertonplayaway.blogspot.com/2007/05/playaways-are-newest-addition-to-world_17.html.

Phelan, David. 2010. "The iPad: What Is It Good For?" *The Independent*, May. Accessed September 10. http://www.independent.co.uk/life-style/gadgets-and-tech/features/the-ipad-what-is-it-good-for-1982635.html.

Plurk. 2010. "Plurk Is a Social journal for Your Life." Plurk.com. Accessed September 7. http://www.plurk.com.

PRESSfeed. 2010. "RSS Feeds, A Tutorial." PRESSfeed Co. Accessed September 21. http://www.press-feed.com/howitworks/rss_tutorial.php#whatarewebfeeds.

Rhode, Jason. 2010. "Writing in the Cloud: What are Blogs?" Northern Illinois University. June. http://writinginthecloud.blogspot.com/.

Roskosch, Marcus. 2010. "Electronic Toolbox, iPhone Application." Marcus Roskosch. Accessed September 21. http://www.iphone.roskosch.de/electronictoolbox.php?engl=1.

ScreenToaster. 2009. "About Us: Company." ScreenToaster. http://about.screentoaster.com/about.

Scribd. 2010. "About Scribd." Scribd. Accessed September 21. http://www.scribd.com/about.

SearchSOA. 2010. "Look Up Tech Terms: Content Aggregator." TechTarget. April. http://searchsoa.techtarget.com/sDefinition/0,,sid26_gci815047,00.html.

Secker, Jane. 2010. *Copyright and E-Learning: A Guide for Practitioners*. London: Facet Publishing.

SlideShare. 2010. "What Is SlideShare?" SlideShare. Accessed September 10. http://www.slideshare.net/about.

Stokes, Simon. 2009. *Digital Copyright: Law and Practice*. 3rd ed. Portland, OR: Hart Publishing.

TeacherTube. 2010. "About Us." TeacherTube. Accessed September 26. http://www.teachertube.com/staticPage.php?pg=about.

Tech Terms Dictionary. 2010. "DRM: Digital Rights Management." TechTerms.com. Accessed September 21. http://www.techterms.com/definition/drm.

TU Delft. 2009. "What Is Pod/Vodcasting?" Delft University of Technology, Netherlands. http://www.icto.tudelft.nl/en/ict-in-education/podvodcasting/.

Turnbull, Giles. 2005. "What Is Flickr (and Hot Tips for Using It)." O'Reilly Media, Inc. August. http://oreilly.com/pub/a/mac/2005/08/02/flickr.html.

Webtwitcher. 2006. "What's This MIX Page You Keep Going on About?" Excite.com. November. http://webtwitcher.excite.co.uk/news/234/Whats-this-MIX-page-you-keep-going-on-about.

wiseGEEK. 2010. "What Is a Hyperlink?" Conjecture Corporation. Accessed September 28. http://www.wisegeek.com/what-is-a-hyperlink.htm.

Wishpot Inc. 2010. "E-Readers." Wishpot Inc. and Epik Inc. Accessed September 21. http://www.ereaders.net/.

Wyld, Adrian. 2010. "Facebook." *The New York Times*. September 23. http://topics.nytimes.com/top/news/business/companies/facebook_inc/index.html.

Index

Page numbers for flowchart titles are bolded.

A

Adding Commercial Film Excerpts to
Class-Created DVDs and Videos, **105**
Adding Popular Music to Webpages, **155**
Adobe Connect, 67, 255
Advertisements, 5, 14, 117
American Library Association (ALA), 16,
21, 30, 53, 74, 143, 221, 224–225
American Psychological Association
(APA), 58–59. *See also* Citing
American Society of Composers, Authors,
and Publishers (ASCAP), 31, 35–36,
162, 165
Analog, 37, 224–225, 248
Animation, 189, 193, 258
Animoto, 67, 255
Archival copies, 149
Articles, 5, 8, 15, 17, 26, 36, 38, 43, 46, 58,
73, 86, 147, 205, 212, 214, 219, 230
Asynchronous, 183, 223, 260–261
Attaching an Online Chart to a Wiki, **82**
Audio-Recording Picture Books, **168**
Audio recordings, 5, 57
Author/authors, 4–5, 7–8, 10, 22, 31, 33,
35–37, 75, 80, 152, 165, 184, 233,
249–251, 259
   authoring, 59
   author's death, 250–251
   authorship, 5, 10, 80
Automatic copyright, 5, 22

B

Bill of Rights, 23
Blind. *See* Handicaps and disabilities

Blogs xvi, xvii, 5, 58, 67, 255, 259, 260
Books, 3–5, 7, 8, 11, 17, 21, 23, 26, 36, 49,
54, 56, 58–59, 67–68, 83–84, 86, 106,
133, 137, 154, 162, 165, 168–169,
201–202, 204, 206, 213, 216, 221, 230,
232, 239, 248–249, 256–257
   bookseller, 7, 68
   bookstore, 4, 59
   e-books, 67, 133, 137
   textbooks, 54, 202, 204, 248
   workbooks, 8, 11 54, 56, 210, 213
Books in the Public Domain, **206**
Borrowing All or Parts of Webpages, **77**
Borrowing from Software, **136**
Borrowing Movie Clips, **100**
Borrowing Music from One Website for
Another, **171**
Borrowing a Variety of Works for a
Multimedia Production, **185**
Borrowing works, 3, 16–17, 19, 26, 45,
53–54, 58, 67–68, 77, 80, 84, 86,
99–100, 134, 136, 151, 171, 185, 187,
197, 201, 214, 221, 231
Box.net, 67, 255
BrainPOP, 67, 233, 255
Brevity, spontaneity, and cumulative
effect, 201–202. *See also* Guidelines
Broadcast Music, Inc. (BMI), 36, 162, 165
Burning Videos to DVDs, **91**
Business Software Alliance, 228

C

Cable. *See* Television
Cartoons, 9, 34, 201, 210, 215
Catalog of Copyright Entries, 22

CD-ROMs/CDs, xvi, 5, 11, 29, 34, 36, 56,
    89, 91, 93, 95, 97, 99, 101, 103, 105,
    107, 109–111, 113–115, 152–154, 162,
    173, 194
Cease and desist letter, 74
Cell phones. See Handheld devices
Chatroulette 67, 255
Chicago Manual of Style, 44, 58–59
    See also Citing
Christian Copyright Licensing
    International (CCLI), 37
Circumvention of technological
    measures, 52
Citing, 31, 58–59, 60, 187, 189
Classroom copying, 49, 56, 60, 134, 201, 219
Classroom exemptions, 47, 90, 96, 104,
    111, 127
    See also Statutory exemptions
Clearinghouses, xvi, 30–31, 33–37, 95–96,
    152, 164–165, 180, 205–206
    cartoons, 34
    images, 34–35
    music, 35, 164–165, 180
    other, 37
    print, 36
    religious, 36–37
    theatrical performances, 37
    video and motion picture, 34
Clip art, 23, 26, 143, 193, 217
Closed-circuit system, 99, 101
Closed-Circuit Systems and DVDs, 101
Cloud, 67, 84–85, 255–257, 260–261
Codes, 4–5, 31, 43, 46, 48–52, 56–57,
    133–134, 149, 230, 239
Commercials, 119, 127, 129
Computational knowledge engines, 67,
    256
Computer-based technologies, 133, 149
    See also CD-ROMs/CDs; Computer
        software; DVDs; E-books; Internet;
        Multimedia; Networks; Policies
        and codes
Computer software, 5, 11, 41–42, 117,
    133–135, 137, 139, 141, 143, 145–147,
    149, 193
    downloading, 144
    educational, 6, 143
    illegal, 145, 146

personal, 137–138, 149
    servers, 175, 194, 196
Concept-mapping, 67, 256
CONFU (Conference on Fair Use), 16–17
Content aggregators, 67, 256
Contracts, 34, 42–43, 74, 143, 147, 210
Converters, 106
Cookbooks, 214–216
Copying, 3, 13–15, 36, 42, 44–46, 48–49, 52,
    55–56, 58–59, 60, 67, 76, 80–81, 92, 98,
    110, 118–119, 133–134, 138, 140–141,
    144–145, 153, 156–159, 194, 196,
    201–221, 229, 230
    last minute, 3, 201–221
    for preservation purposes, 48
    for private study, 48
Copying a DVD, 98
Copying from the Internet, 81
Copying Lists, 76
Copying Media to a Server for Curricular
    Use, 196
Copying Movie Clips, 92
Copying Personal Software to a Classroom
    Computer, 138
Copying Popular Music for Class Use, 156
Copying Sheet Music, 159
Copying Software to Another Format, 141
Copying Textbooks for Visually Impaired
    Students, 204
Copying Workbook Pages, 213
Copyleft, 44
Copyright, definition of, 4
Copyright Act. See U.S. Copyright Act
Copyright clearance, 15, 34, 37, 46, 189
Copyright Clearance Center (CCC), 38
Copyright Law. See U.S. Copyright Law
Copyright Office. See U.S. Copyright Office
Copyright police, 3, 197
Copyright policies, 73–74, 99, 149, 225, 230
Copyright Renewal Database, 22
Copyright Term Extension Act, 20, 52
    See also Sonny Bono Copyright Term
        Extension Act
Creative Commons, xvi, xvii, 22–23, 30,
    44–45, 90, 111, 137, 187
Creator, 6, 8, 15–16, 20, 22–23, 36, 41, 43,
    56, 79–80, 84, 95, 134, 143–144, 151,
    186–187, 193, 199, 227

Critical Commons, 89
C-SPAN, 120
Cutting, Pasting, and Photocopying a
    Teacher's Guide Page, **211**

D

Databases, 21, 42–43, 46, 50, 52–53, 73–74,
    133, 147
    See also International copyright
Declaration of Independence, 23
Deep Linking, **75**
Delicious. *See* Social bookmarking
Derivative works, 6–8, 26, 43, 45, 106,
    119–120, 127, 143, 154, 158, 161, 170,
    187, 194, 197, 207, 239, 252
Digital Copyright Slider, 21, 26, 30
Digital images. *See* Images
Digital Millennium Copyright Act
    (DMCA), xvi, 50–54, 83, 90, 140
    See also International copyright
Digital rights management, 133, 140, 256
Digital transmissions, 224, 244, 248
Digitizing Newspaper Cartoons, **215**
Digitizing a Television Program, **128**
Distance education, xvi, 37, 47, 52, 183,
    189–190, 223–227
    analog, 37, 224–225
    asynchronous, 183, 223
    student examples, 190
    synchronous, 183, 223
    television transmissions, 47, 223
    See also TEACH Act
Distance Educator's Flowchart, **226**
Documentation, xvi, 11, 26, 41–43, 55, 60,
    72–74, 86, 119–120, 132, 134–137,
    143–144, 147, 149, 158, 162, 170, 180,
    187–189, 206–207, 217, 230–231, 233
    domain names, 51, 191–192
    dupliChecker, 58 (*see also* Plagiarism)
DVDs, xvi, 5, 8, 29, 34, 42, 57, 89–115,
    117, 131, 173, 194
    personal, 112–113
    purchased, 114
    See also Movies; Videos
DVDs, xvi, 4–5, 8, 11, 29, 31–34, 42, 51,
    54–57, 98–114, 117, 119, 127, 131,
    133–135, 140, 173, 194, 217

E

Easybib.com, 59. *See also* Citing
E-books, 67, 133, 137
Educational software, 6, 143
    See also Computer software
Educators, xvi, 3–4, 6, 9, 15, 17, 19, 23, 25,
    27, 46–48, 50, 53–54, 56, 60, 86,
    117–118, 120, 127, 133, 140, 143, 151,
    153, 161, 183–184, 201–202, 223–226,
    231–232, 239, 255, 258
    administrators, xvi, 3, 13, 26, 49, 73, 106,
        117, 145, 149, 229–233
    school librarians, 3, 6, 23, 28, 37, 47, 52,
        54, 56, 74, 83, 96, 120, 123, 140, 170,
        206, 217, 221, 224, 229, 232
    technology coordinators, vi, 3, 6, 50–51,
        55, 73, 144, 224, 229, 232
    technology specialists, 230
Electronic toolbox, 67, 84, 86–87, 256
E-mail, 5–6, 10, 25, 32–33, 41, 68, 77, 80
E-readers, 256
Ethics, xvi, 49, 144, 149, 230, 232
Excite MIX, 67, 256
Exclusive rights, 7, 13, 42, 47–48, 56, 110,
    202, 217, 239–250
Exemptions. *See* Statutory exemptions
Expired copyrights, 23

F

Facebook. *See* Social networking
Face-to-face teaching, xvi, 47, 95, 183, 190,
    223–224, 243
Fair use, 13–17, 68, 89–90, 117–119,
    133–134, 153–154, 183–184, 202–204
Fairy tales, 19, 103, 104
File conversion, 147–148
File sharing, 154, 256–257
File swapping, 80
Filters, 110, 147
First sale doctrine, 143, 173, 187, 214,
    217
Flickr, 67, 257
Flowcharts, xvii, xix, 60, 68, 88, 96, 114,
    117, 133, 153, 183, 202, 216
    See also individual flowchart titles
Folk tales, 103–104

For-Profit Recording of School Concerts for Home Distribution, **177**
Free material, xvi, 19
Free Software Foundation, 44–45, 90
Freedom of Information Act, 93
Free-of-Charge Recording of School Concerts for Home Distribution, **176**
Freeware, 143

G

Games, xvii, 5–7, 9, 29, 67, 80, 144, 162, 175, 257–260
GNU, 44–45
Goodreads. *See* Social networking
Google, 58, 67, 99, 256–257, 259
Google Wave, 67, 257
Government documents, xvi, 23–25, 93
federal, 23–24
local, 24–25
state, 24–25
Graphics, 5, 7, 24, 48, 183, 239, 243, 255, 257
Guidelines, xvi, 15–17, 21, 25, 46, 48–49, 56, 60, 90, 118, 120, 123, 134, 158, 161, 184, 201–202, 220, 230

H

Handheld devices, xvii, 35, 67, 80, 84, 137, 147, 151, 157, 162, 165, 167, 175, 201–202, 205, 256–258
cell phones, xvii, 67, 151, 201
iPads, 67, 80, 84, 137, 151, 167, 201–202, 257
iPods, xvi, 35, 67, 157, 162, 175, 257–258
Kindles, 67, 84, 162, 201–202, 257
MP3 players, 35, 67, 147, 162, 258
Nooks, 67, 84, 162, 201–202, 258
Playaways, xvii, 67, 162, 202, 258
Handicap exemption, xvi, 47
See also Statutory exemptions
Handicaps and disabilities, xvi, 47, 154, 202, 204, 214, 239, 247–249
blind, 154, 202, 247–248
deaf, 247

other, 247–249
visually impaired, 202, 204
Harry Fox Agency (HFA), 36, 165
Heart of the work, 14, 68, 162
See also Fair use
History of copyright, xvi, 7–8
Home distribution, 176–177
Homeschooling, 223
How to Decide Whether an Image Is in the Public Domain, **72**
Hyperlinks, 44, 67, 194, 257

I

Images, 2, 7, 16, 34–35, 68–69, 71–72, 74, 99, 103, 147, 183, 193–194, 197, 221, 239, 243, 255–256, 259–261
Infringements, 12, 41, 54–57, 60, 80, 108, 121, 143–145, 170–173, 180, 192–194, 217, 231, 243, 246, 252
contributory, 56–57, 144
direct, 56, 144
vicarious, 57, 144, 246
Instruction, 22, 29, 47, 49–50, 95, 106, 112, 114, 118, 123–124, 187, 194, 207, 214, 224–225, 232–233, 243–244, 248, 260
Intellectual property, 4, 7–8, 46, 50–52, 147, 231
Interlibrary loan, 41, 45–46, 48, 60, 140, 242
International copyright, xvi, 20, 25, 37, 41, 50–53, 60, 83–84, 110–111, 130–131, 145–147, 173–175, 194–195, 219–220
Berne Convention for the Protection of Literary and Artistic Works, 50–52, 83, 147
database protection, 52, 54, 147
Digital Millennium Copyright Act (DMCA), xvi, 53, 83,
European Union Database Directive, 52
General Agreement on Tariffs and Trade (GATT Treaty), 25, 50
Sonny Bono Copyright Term Extension Act, 20–21, 25, 50, 52–53
Trade-Related Aspects of Intellectual Property Rights (TRIPS), 50, 51, 147
Universal Copyright Convention (UCC), 51

Uruguay Round Agreements Act of 1994, 25

World Intellectual Property Organization (WIPO), 51–52, 147

Internet, xvi, xvii, 3–6, 8–9, 19, 23, 26, 30, 36, 41, 43, 45, 50–51, 54, 56, 58–59, 67–87, 99, 110, 112, 120, 130, 133–134, 137, 140, 144–145, 147, 152, 165, 167, 170, 175, 183, 187, 189, 192, 194, 217, 229, 232–233, 255, 257, 259–261

Intranet, 84

IPads. *See* Handheld devices

IPods. *See* Handheld devices

Is an Electronic Toolbox Legal?, **87**

iTunes, 67, 99, 137, 151, 162, 257

K

Kindles. *See* Handheld devices

L

Last-Minute Copying, **218**

Law. *See* U.S. Code; U.S. Copyright Act; U.S. Copyright Law

Legislation and court cases, xv, xvi, 4, 8, 15, 24, 41, 48, 53–54, 120, 223

American Geophysical Union et al. v. Texaco, Inc., 15

federal court, 24

future copyright, 53

House, 4, 8, 24, 53, 120

Senate, 8, 24, 53, 120

Libraries and archives exemptions, xvi, 47–48

Library, xvi, 9, 16, 21, 23, 30, 41, 43–48, 53–54, 56, 60, 68, 74, 80, 89–90, 106, 110, 112, 120, 137, 140, 143, 147, 149, 158, 160–161, 165, 170, 173, 175, 189, 194, 206–207, 217, 224, 219–221, 232, 239–243, 252, 259

Library exemption, xvi, 47–48

See also Statutory exemptions

Library media center, 23, 137

Library of Congress, 9, 22, 25, 29, 37, 48, 50, 52–53, 79, 151, 157, 187, 233

Library reserve, 189

Licenses and licensing, xvi, 7, 15, 31, 32, 34–37, 41–44, 46, 54–56, 61, 72–74, 90, 93–97, 100, 104, 110, 119–120, 122, 134–140, 144, 147, 149, 153, 158–162, 166, 180, 183, 187–189, 191, 197, 206–209, 230–233, 248

browse-wrap, 42

click-wrap, 41

compulsory, 152

mechanical rights, 35, 153

performance, 176

print, 206–207

shrink-wrap, 42, 144

synchronization, 35

LimeWire, 67, 257

LinkedIn. *See* Social networking

Links and linking, 41–42, 59, 67, 73–75, 84, 194, 197, 216, 255, 257–258

Lip dub videos, 177, 179

Lyrics, 9, 17, 35–36, 151–152, 163, 166–167

M

Magazine Articles in the Public Domain, **208**

Making Multiple Copies of Articles, **212**

Making School Software Available for Students, **142**

Marketability of the work. *See* Fair use

McLeod, Kembrew, 31

Mechanical rights. *See* Rights

Modern Language Association, 58–59

See also Citing

Moodle, xvii, 67, 258

Motion Picture Association of America (MPAA), 229

Motion Picture Licensing Corporation (MPLC), 31, 36

Mousebreaker, 67, 258

Movie Licensing USA, 34, 96, 232

Movies, xvi, 3, 5, 9, 29–30, 32, 80, 89–90, 92, 94, 95–97, 99–100, 104–105, 110–111, 154, 187, 191, 256–257

clips, 90, 92, 99–100, 111, 183, 187, 191

commercial film excerpts, 105

movie night, 95

public performance rights, 95–96, 206–207

MP3 players. *See* Handheld devices
Multimedia, xvi, 5, 9, 15–16, 25, 32, 34, 49,
 54, 133, 165, 183–199, 232
 defined, 183
 student-created, 183–184, 186–187,
  190–191, 194–197
 teacher-created, 185, 187–199
Multiple copies, 175, 212, 242
Music and audio, xvi, 5, 8, 9, 15, 35–36, 42,
 51, 56–58, 110, 151–180, 246, 239,
 257–259
 audio, xvi, 5, 8, 36, 56, 58, 110, 151–180,
  246, 258–259
 cassette tapes, 35, 150
 downloading, 151, 257
 for-profit, 177
 lyrics, 9, 17, 35–36, 151–152, 163,
  166–167
 musical compositions, 151–153
 musical sound, 35
 performing, 31, 57, 162, 166
 phonorecords, 36, 151, 175, 239–244,
  247–249, 252
 popular, 29, 154–157, 162, 165–166, 175,
  178
 public domain, 154–158
 public events, 158, 162, 166
 recorded, 158, 160–161
 royalty-free, 164, 165, 180
 sampling, 162
 sheet music, 5, 15, 35, 42, 151–153,
  158–159, 170, 180
 sound recordings, 5, 9, 35, 51, 151–153,
  175, 239
Musical Theatre International (MTI), 37
MySpace. *See* Social networking
MyYearbook. *See* Social networking

N

Names, 10, 23, 51, 75, 165, 191
National Education Association (NEA), 16
Nature of work. *See* Fair use
Netiquette, 74, 194
Netvibes, 67, 258
Networks, xvi, xvii, 4–5, 67, 71, 73, 119,
 130, 244, 248, 256–259, 261
Nings, 67, 258

NoodleTools, 59. *See also* Citing
Nooks. *See* Handheld devices

O

Off-air recording, 49, 118–119, 123
Online video games. *See* Games
Open source, 44, 143, 232
Original rights, 20
Orphan works, 197
Owner of copyright, 239, 249–250
 See also Author/authors; Creator;
  Publishers

P

Pageflakes, 67, 258
Paine, Thomas, 7
Paintings, 216
Parents Recording a School Variety Show,
 198
Parodies, 14, 170, 197
Patents, 7, 191
Penalties, xvi, 41, 43, 52, 54, 57, 60, 80, 106,
 127, 143–145, 147, 170–173, 192–194,
 217–218, 229
Performance rights. *See* Rights
Performing a Shakespeare Play in Public,
 210
Performing Popular Music at Public
 Events, **166**
Permission letter, xvi, 32–33
Permissions, xvi, 7, 11, 16, 33–35, 38, 41,
 55–56, 73–77, 96–99, 110, 112, 119,
 123–126, 140–143, 152–153, 158,
 162–169, 180, 183, 189–191, 197,
 210–214, 221, 230–231, 233
Photocopying, 36, 158, 203, 211
 See also Photographs; Print
Photocopying Parts of a Book, **203**
Photographs, 6, 9, 16, 34–35, 50, 68, 71, 75,
 78, 110, 184, 186
Photographs on the Web, **71**
Piracy, 111, 133, 145–146, 229
 pirated software, 145, 146
 See also Computer software; DVDs;
  Movies; Videos
Pirated Software, **146**

Placing an E-book on a Library Computer, **220**

Placing Lip Dub Videos That Feature Popular Songs on a Website, **179**

Placing Software on Multiple Computers, **139**

Plagiarism, xvi, 41, 57–60, 84, 233

Playaways. *See* Handheld devices

Playing an E-book Aloud for a Class, **172**

Playing Popular Music at School Sporting Events, **178**

Playing Recorded Music in the Library, **160**

Plays and musicals, 5, 9, 37, 47, 205, 221, 241–243, 248, 257

Plurk, 62, 258

Podcasts, xvi, xvii, 3, 5, 9, 67, 258

Poems/poetry, 5, 16, 58, 165, 183, 197, 201, 214, 217, 220

Policies and codes, xvi, 49–51, 73, 79, 99, 133, 147, 224, 230, 244

acceptable use, 4

ethics codes, 149, 230

Poor man's copyright, 170

Posting a Song on a Video-Sharing Website, **163**

Presentations. *See* Multimedia

Preservation copies, 48, 140, 143, 225, 241, 243

Prezi, 67, 258

Print, xvi, xvii, xix, 3–5, 7, 8, 11, 14–17, 20, 21–24, 26, 32, 33, 36–38, 41, 43, 45–46, 48–49, 54, 56–59, 60, 67–68, 73, 83–84, 86, 89, 96, 106, 114, 117, 133, 137, 140, 147, 153–154, 162, 165, 168–169, 183, 189, 191, 201–221, 230, 232, 233, 239, 247–249, 256–257, 260

articles, 5, 15, 17, 26, 36, 38, 43, 46, 58, 73, 86, 147, 205, 212, 214, 219, 230

book covers, 68, 217, 221

books, 3–5, 7, 11, 17, 21, 23, 26, 36, 49, 54, 58–59, 67–68, 83–84, 86, 106, 133, 137, 154, 162, 165, 168–169, 201–202, 204, 206, 216, 221, 230, 232, 239, 248–249, 256–257

brevity, spontaneity, and cumulative effect test, 201

columns, 34

cookbooks, 214–216

editorial features, 34

flowcharts, xvii, xix, 60, 68, 89, 96, 114, 117, 133, 154, 183, 202, 217

illustrations, 16, 32, 48, 202, 205, 243

magazines, 4, 14, 33, 36, 45–46, 86, 201, 205, 207, 210, 214, 219, 256

newsletters, 5, 22

newspapers, 5, 140, 147, 183, 189, 201, 211, 215

picture books, 83, 165, 168–169, 205

rights (*see* Rights)

textbooks, 54, 202, 204, 248

storybooks, 207

Venn diagrams, 216

workbooks, 8, 11, 54, 56, 210, 213

Printing from a DVD or CD-ROM, **135**

Printing Lyrics from the Internet, **167**

Printing Webpages, **70**

Privacy, 94, 145, 184

Private schools, 90

Protopage, 67, 259

Public domain, xvi, 19–27, 44, 51–53, 55–56, 59, 71–72, 74, 84, 86, 93–94, 104, 110, 120, 134, 137, 144, 147, 152, 154, 157–158, 161, 164, 175, 180, 183–187, 189, 193, 197, 205–206, 214, 216, 219, 233

Public Domain Movies, **94**

Public performance rights, 95–96, 206–207

Public performances, 31, 34, 36, 55, 84, 90, 95–96, 161, 164–165, 174–175, 177, 180, 206–207, 248

Publishers, 15–16, 31–33, 35–37, 41, 43, 53, 72, 93, 104, 135, 165, 205, 230, 259

Purpose and character of use. *See* Fair use

Q

Quantity of work. *See* Fair use

R

Reading a Book in the Cloud, **85**

Recipes, 9–10, 201, 214, 216, 257

Recording, 5, 9, 26, 35, 47, 49, 51–52, 57, 110, 117–127, 131, 151–153, 158, 162, 165, 168–169, 173–177, 180, 197, 239
devices, 110
school variety show, 176–177, 197–198
Recording Foreign Television, **131**
Recording from a Major Network, **121**
Recording Off-Air from Satellite or Cable Transmissions, **125**
Recording Television Programs for Instructional Use, **124**
Registering your work, 5–6, 8–10, 26, 79, 154, 157, 170, 191, 197, 216
Rewards, 97, 230
Right of publicity. *See* Rights
Rights, 4, 6–8, 13, 15, 20–24, 29–31, 35–36, 42–44, 47–51, 56–57, 60, 74, 79, 83, 90, 93, 95–96, 110–111, 118–120, 126, 133, 137, 140, 143–144, 147, 152–153, 158, 187–188, 199, 202, 206–207, 217, 229–230, 239–253, 256
mechanical, 35, 153
performance 35, 95–96, 206–207
print, 35
of publicity, 167
synchronization, 35, 153
Royalty/royalties, 15, 24, 33, 36–37, 43, 152–154, 164, 165, 180, 189, 207, 310, 216, 224, 230, 247–248
RSS feeds, xvii, 67, 256, 259, 260

S

Safeassign, 58. *See also* Plagiarism
Sample Flowchart, **61**
Sampling, 162
Satires. *See* Parodies
School concerts, 176–177
SchoolTube, 161
Screen savers, 75, 78
ScreenToaster, 67, 259
Scribd, 67, 259
Scripts, 9, 11, 14, 37, 42, 103, 201, 205–206, 207
Sculptures, 48, 99, 103
Second Life, xvii, 67, 82, 83, 259
Servers, 175, 194, 196
SESAC, Inc., 36

Sheet music, 5, 15, 42, 151–153, 158–159, 170, 180
Shelfari. *See* Social networking
Showing Student-Owned Works during Recess, **109**
Skype, xvii, 67, 259
Slideshare, 67, 259
Social bookmarking, xvii, 67, 256
Social networking, xvi, xvii, 4, 67, 73, 119, 256–260
Goodreads, xvii, 67, 257
Facebook, xvii, 67, 73, 256, 259
LinkedIn, xvii, 67, 73, 258
MySpace, xvii, 67, 258
MyYearbook, 67, 258
Shelfari, xvii, 4, 67, 73, 259
Twitter, xvii, 67, 73, 259–260
Software. *See* Computer software
Software & Information Industry Association, 16
Sonny Bono Copyright Term Extension Act, 20–21, 25, 50, 52–53
See also International copyright
Sound recordings, 5, 9, 35, 51, 150, 152–153, 175, 239
Source code, 43
State copyright laws, xvi, 7, 24–25
Statues, 5, 104
Statues, Filming, and Copyright, **104**
Statutory exemptions, 46–48, 60, 90, 202, 205, 230, 239
Streaming Video and Copyright, **115**
Stringing Commercials Together to Use in Class, **129**
Student-owned works, 109
Students, best examples, 4, 126
Synchronization rights. *See* Rights
Synchronous, 183, 223, 261

T

TEACH Act, xvi, 47, 223–225
TeacherTube, 11, 67, 147, 260
Teaching and training others about copyright, 231–232
Television, xvi, 4–5, 8, 14, 32, 35–36, 56, 99, 101, 110, 117–131, 191, 205, 223, 245, 257

cable networks, 117–118, 120, 122–126, 245

closed-circuit systems, 99, 101, 205

commercials, 119, 127, 129

digitizing, 128

foreign, 131

instructional, 123–124

off-air taping, 117–118, 121–125

real-time, 191

satellite, 99, 117–118, 123–125, 245

Textbooks, 54, 202, 204, 248

Text-to-speech, 162

TiVo, xvii, 120, 123

Trademarks, 7, 191

Transferring Videos to DVDs, **107**

Turnitin, 58, 59–60. *See also* Plagiarism

Twitter. *See* Social networking

U

United Media, 34, 210

University of Pennsylvania's "Online Books Page," 21

U.S. Code, 4–5, 46–47, 52, 56–57, 239

U.S. Constitution, 7–8, 23

U.S. Copyright Act, 4, 13, 20, 49, 68, 90, 118, 147, 217, 220, 224

U.S. Copyright Law, 4, 11, 13–14, 20, 34, 44, 46–47, 50–52, 55, 68, 74, 79–80, 95–96, 110–111, 133, 140, 147, 151–152, 170, 173, 175, 184, 202, 207, 214, 239–253

U.S. Copyright Office, 6, 8–11, 21, 29, 37, 54, 79, 93, 118, 151, 153–154, 158, 165, 170, 175, 184, 191, 197, 216, 227

Using a Foreign Recording for a Public Performance, **174**

Using a Photograph from the Web as a Screen Saver, **78**

Using Clip Art in Multimedia Projects, **193**

Using Entertainment DVDs in Class, **95**

Using File Conversion Programs, **148**

Using Locally Purchased DVDs in Class, **114**

Using Movies as Rewards, **97**

Using Personal DVDs on a School Outing, **113**

Using Photographs in Multimedia Projects, **186**

Using Place-Shifting Technologies/Video Streaming in the School, **130**

Using Recorded Cable Programs in the Classroom, **122**

Using Student Examples in Distance Education, **190**

Using Student or Commercial Works in Computer-Based Presentations, **188**

Using Video on Demand, **102**

Using Videos in Multimedia Projects, **195**

V

Venn diagrams, 216

Verso, 21, 231

Video games. *See* Games

Video streaming, xvi, 67, 89, 91, 93–116, 130, 260

Videos, 5, 16, 29, 31, 37, 55, 58, 89–115, 126, 147, 176–177, 179, 195–196, 231, 255–257, 260–261

compressed, 261

on demand, 91, 97, 99, 102–103

lip dub, 176–177, 179

in multimedia projects, 183–184, 189, 195

place-shifting technologies, 129–130

public performance rights, 35, 95–96, 206–207

sharing, 161

streaming, xvii, 67, 89, 91, 112, 114–115, 117, 130, 260

See also DVDs; Movies; Multimedia

Videotaping Volunteers Reading from a Novel, **108**

Violations, xvi, 5, 15, 55–57, 60, 79, 99, 103, 106, 110–111, 127, 154, 165, 173, 189, 194, 231–232

See also Infringements

Visual transcriptions, 35

Vlogs, xvi, xvii, 5, 22

Vodcasts, xvii, 258

VoiceThread, 67, 83–84

W

Warning notices, 57, 149, 241–242

Washington, George, 8, 14

Web 2.0, 67, 260

Web feeds, 67, 260

Web Images, **69**

Web syndication, xvii, 67, 260

Webster, Noah, 7

Who Owns Teacher-Created Multimedia?, **192**

Wikis, xvi, xvii, 3, 5, 9, 19, 58, 67, 80, 82, 257, 260–261

Wordles, 67

Work for hire, 6, 20, 22, 24, 79, 80, 191

Workbooks, 8, 11, 54, 56, 210, 213

Works, commercial, 187, 189

Works, student, 93, 99, 109, 126, 143, 153–154, 162, 165, 170, 176–177, 183–184, 186, 188–190, 194, 197, 205, 216–217

Works in the public domain, xvi, 19–27, 44, 51–53, 55–56, 59, 71–72, 74, 84, 86, 93–94, 104, 110, 120, 134, 137, 144, 147, 152, 154, 157–158, 161, 164, 175, 180, 183–187, 189, 193, 197, 205–206, 214, 216, 219, 233

federal documents, 23

phone books, 23

See also Clip art; Expired copyrights; Freeware

Works that can be copyright-protected, 5

X

Xanga, 67, 261

Y

YouTube, xvii, 67, 73, 93, 147, 255, 260

About the Author

Rebecca P. Butler is a Presidential Teaching Professor in the Department of Educational Technology, Research, and Assessment, College of Education, at Northern Illinois University (NIU) in DeKalb, Illinois. At NIU, she teaches graduate (master's and doctoral) students in school library media and instructional technology. Prior to moving to NIU in 1998, she was an Assistant Professor in the Department of Curriculum and Instruction at East Tennessee State University (ETSU). While a faculty member at NIU and ETSU, she has conducted a variety of workshops, conferences, and graduate classes on the topic of copyright. Although the majority has been geared for K–12 teachers and school librarians, she has also done numerous presentations on the subject for university faculty and staff; public, medical, museum, and other librarians; technology coordinators; and more. Dr. Butler has written numerous articles and columns on copyright, for a number of library and technology professional journals, including *Knowledge Quest,* the journal of the American Association of School Librarians; *TechTrends,* the journal of the Association of Educational Communications and Technology; *School Libraries Worldwide,* the journal of the International Association of School Librarians; and *Library Trends,* a library and information science journal. In addition, she has written two other copyright books, both published by Neal-Schuman: *Copyright for Teachers and Librarians* (2004) and *Smart Copyright Compliance for Schools: A How-To-Do-It Manual* (2009).

Dr. Butler earned a BA in library science from the University of Northern Iowa in 1972; an MSLS from the University of Kentucky in 1978; and a PhD in educational technology/curriculum and instruction from the University of Wisconsin–Madison in 1995. She has worked in a variety of library positions, including several years as a school librarian and library media specialist in public schools (K–12) in Fort Dodge, Dubuque, and Scott County, Iowa, and in a private school in Caracas, Venezuela; as a reference and young adult public librarian in Naperville, Illinois; as a medical librarian in Aurora, Illinois; and as a historian/special librarian in Coshocton, Ohio. During her career as a librarian and educator, Dr. Butler has been an active member, serving on a wide variety of committees, in a number of professional organizations, including the American Library Association, the American Association of School Librarians, the Association for Educational Communications and Technology, the Illinois School Library Media Association, the Tennessee Library Association, the American Educational Research Association, the Freedom to Read Foundation, the International Association of School Librarianship, the Cooperative Children's Book Center, and the Wisconsin Educational Media Association. She currently belongs to three national professional organizations' committees concerned with copyright issues: the American Library Association Washington Office's Committee on Legislation (COL) Subcommittee on Copyright, the Association of Educational Communication's Professional Ethics Committee, and the Association of Educational Communication's Intellectual Property Committee.

In addition to her copyright publications, Dr. Butler has written a number of articles, columns, and chapters on such subjects as the history of intellectual freedom in American school libraries, histories of women and technology, histories of educational technology hardware, the Harry Potter phenomenon, libraries worldwide, and gaming in the school library. In her spare time, Dr. Butler enjoys reading and adventure travel.